TASTELAND

Quindaro Press
Kansas City

TASTELAND

Aaron Barnhart

This book is dedicated
to my longtime contributor and friend
Thomas Allen Heald
1972–2009

*Tasteland: Featuring the 100 Best TV Shows You Can Watch, Rent, or Download,
With an Authoritative Guide to Television's Most Turbulent Era*

Quindaro Press
quindaropress.com
Copyright © 2010 Aaron Barnhart. Reproduction prohibited.
All rights reserved. Published 2010
14 13 12 11 10   1 2 3 4 5

Printed in the United States of America
Book and cover design: Aaron Barnhart

ISBN-13 (paper): 978-0-9764434-3-8

Cover and title page photographs taken at the farm of Ken and Phyllis
Schmidt, Greensburg, Kansas (thanks to Nancy Magliery for permission).

Photo of Conan O'Brien on page 9 courtesy of KSHB-TV.

Introduction

Like everyone else with an unusual job title, I'm asked from time to time how I became a television critic. Well, it's a great story and I'm always happy to share the quick particulars: how, on Valentine's Day 1994, I typed up a newsletter for fans of the *Late Show with David Letterman* called *Late Show News,* posted it online and instantly drew notice, because back then almost nobody posted original "content" to the Net for free; how this quickly led to my own column in the *Village Voice*; and how the gigs just kept coming until two and a half years later, when I was offered a position at a big-city newspaper writing about television. I think it's a great story, at least, because it needs no embellishment to be wholly flattering to me.

There are some details I usually leave out. When I began writing *Late Show News,* I was twenty-eight years old and toiling away at a white-collar job. I did not have a journalism degree, nor any plans to work in journalism. And I had only recently put a TV set in my house. Explaining how I got from there to here probably would require more time than either I or my hearer would be willing to spend. (Also, I suspect it might take some of the shine off my wholly flattering version.) My editor, however, has urged me to tell that backstory in the pages of *Tasteland*, and with some reluctance I have agreed to do so. After all, who knows me better than my wife?

If you had grown up with me in the 1970s, I think you would have found it perfectly plausible that I would one day become a television critic. During those years I was as wrapped up in TV as any kid, perhaps more than most. It was a faithful companion when I needed one. My brother moved out after my parents divorced, and my sister moved out just after my mother met my stepfather. Mom and Bob married when I was nine, and shortly after that we moved, and then we moved again, into a single-wide trailer on the outskirts of Billings, Montana. I was not the most socially adept kid to start with, and making close friends at new schools that were miles away from my old neighborhood proved to be slow going.

Since Mom and Bob both had jobs, that meant that almost every day after school, I let myself in alone and watched TV until they came home. They liked to have their time together, so I would go to my room, where I had my own black-and-white Zenith. I was the only kid I knew with a television in his bedroom. Bruce Helford, who created *The Drew Carey Show*, grew up in a working-class family in Chicago, where the TV sat right on the dining room table. "We didn't need to talk," he said once. "We *knew* we loved each other." In our household, the role of the TV set was to *keep* me from talking. Love had nothing to do with it.

In that pre-videotape era, I recorded hours of TV on Bob's cassette recorder and played it back to amuse myself when nothing better was on. A few years ago, an FM radio station in Kansas City began airing the audio of NASCAR races, and I remember thinking that sounded like the dumbest thing — until I listened to one of the broadcasts and had a flashback to the time when I taped the Rebel 500 off ABC's *Wide World of Sports* and, on a very boring car trip, played it over and over.

That first Christmas in the trailer, Mom and Bob gave me my own recorder, a sturdy black Gambles model. They could not have picked a better gift. The cassette recorder got quite a workout sitting next to the speaker of the Zenith. I made a sixty-minute tape out of nothing but TV theme songs. (Back then, you didn't need that many to fill up an hour.) I recorded *Get Smart* reruns and popular shows of the day. I taped every episode of *Saturday Night Live*. I stayed up and recorded Johnny Carson some nights, not for the monologue but for the guests, especially those Vegas headliners like Rich Little and Don Rickles who acted like old friends around Johnny.

Mom and Bob are both gone now, and long ago I forgave them their inability to help me emotionally through those years. In many other ways, they did a lot for me. But I cannot deny that one reason I stayed on this path — the one that led me to an improbable career writing about television — is that TV shows were there for me in painful times. In fact, I am not sure how you can do a job like this for very long without some abiding emotional attachment to the medium you're writing about. I know where mine was forged, and I am grateful for it.

Fast forward to my junior year of college, when I moved into a house off-campus with two graduate students. There was an old black-and-white set in the front room. By then, real life had become more interesting to me than mediated life, so the TV stayed off most of the time. But every weeknight at 11:30, my roommates and I tried to get back to the house in time to watch *Late Night with David Letterman* together. (It occurs to me now that this was when TV became a social activity of mine, rather than a solitary one.) After college I still watched television only sporadically, on other people's sets — but I still managed to see a lot of Letterman. His show was just better than anything else on TV, by a long shot. I even liked how Dave and his writers expressed their contempt for TV, its banality and phoniness.

By the time I turned twenty-eight, I was trying to figure out what to make of myself. After graduation I had spent a year in Washington, D.C., in an attempt to figure out if the political life was for me. It was not. I then spent the next two years in graduate school trying to find out if the academic life suited me any better. It did not. I then found a succession of office jobs to help pay down my student debt as I pondered my next move.

Instead of television, I was spending much of my recreational time on the Internet. This was about six months after Al Gore invented it, so there was no Web, no blogs, no multimedia. Mostly what you did was converse with people, either through newsgroups (the precursors of today's blogs) or bulletin boards (the closest thing to chat back then). On the Internet people are either lurkers or posters, and I was a poster from the get-go. I posted messages to a whole slew of groups, from rec. radio.broadcasting to alt.culture.african-american to comp. risks. I enjoyed writing for friends and strangers on the Internet. The feedback I was getting, while not uniformly positive, was enough to spur me onward. In 1992 and 1993 I poured a lot of unfocused energy into writing. Then something came along to provide the focus.

On August 30, 1993, David Letterman signed on at CBS. I remember watching the first episode in a hotel room while attending, of all things, the World Parliament of Religions. It was an electrifying debut. Everyone expected Letterman to be competitive against Jay Leno, but instead he came roaring out of the gate. His *Late Show* was not only the biggest thing in late night, it was the biggest thing on TV. It was all anyone could talk about. And I, along with many other longtime Letterman fans, found myself caught up in it. I don't know if we were all reliving our college years or what, but the base was definitely ginned up.

I spent many a late night over at Diane's house, watching Dave. I would make several visits a day to the alt.fan.letterman newsgroup to swap messages with fellow fans. Like most newsgroups, this one had an FAQ, maintained by a volunteer. In November of that year, the person entrusted with the FAQ posted a message asking for someone else to take over. I applied, and a couple of days later was emailed the document. It hadn't been updated much since the CBS show began, so I started adding material, and soon had made it three times longer. I threw in lots of questions that weren't frequently asked at all: "When exactly did Dave start referring to himself as Regis Philbin?" The newsgroup regulars loved it, and they started suggesting trivia of their own, which I continued shoveling into the FAQ. I had no idea where this was leading, and I was having too much fun in the moment to care. Finally, I got my own TV, and I bought my first VCR.

On January 30, 1994, the *New York Times Magazine* published an excerpt of Bill Carter's book *The Late Shift*, with its juicy behind-the-scenes account of the struggle to succeed Johnny Carson as host of the *Tonight Show*. To those of us commiserating online, *The Late Shift* offered irrefutable evidence that Letterman had indeed been screwed out of the job that was given to Leno. We discussed passages from the book on the newsgroup, and people passed along other references to the late-night wars that they had seen in the press. It was clear to me that there had been a surge in media coverage of late night talk shows in the wake of *The Late Shift*. I would hear items on the radio at work, see reports on entertainment shows, find stories almost daily in the two Chicago newspapers. Some of the news went into the FAQ, but that wasn't the right venue for items about a new favorite of mine, Conan O'Brien.

Preparing to interview Conan O'Brien, March 2009.

One day, it occurred to me that if you aggregated all the news about late-night television into a newsletter, there might be a lot of people interested ... and that's when the two fronts collided. The chocolate touched the peanut butter. The frustrated writer and the boy with the tape recorder joined forces. And the result was *Letterman News*. I finished my first edition in a couple of hours, and waited only three days to put out the second, which bore the slightly more generic-sounding name of *Late Show News*. Three weeks later, and still a house on fire, I received email from a writer at the *Village Voice* named Richard Gehr. He had seen the newsletter and wanted to interview me for a story. When we spoke on the phone a few days later, however, Richard said he now had a different idea. Instead of him writing a story *about* a late-night newsletter, what if *I* started writing a version of my newsletter for the *Voice*? Richard said he had already talked to his editor about it. Almost in passing, he mentioned that I would get paid. As we discussed his proposal, I got very excited — but it seemed a little unreal. Was the *Village Voice* offering me a column? I knew it wouldn't be enough to pay the bills, but that was beside the point. Until that moment, *it had not occurred to me* that I was ever going to get paid to write about television.

I began taking my lunch breaks at the Museum of Broadcast Communications, a couple of blocks from work, where I watched old videos of *The Tonight Show, The Tomorrow Show,* Letterman, Steve Allen, *Studio One,* Ed Murrow, the *$64,000 Question,* and so on. I was educating myself. When I felt ready to try the freelance waters a year later, my new wife generously allowed me to quit my day job. I fell out of love with the Letterman show, and to my surprise I found I could write about that as well. *The New York Observer* started assigning me stories, as did *The New York Times,* thanks to another journalist who'd befriended me, Marc Gunther. My bylines found their way into *Entertainment Weekly, CD Review, The Isthmus,* and, unfortunately, *Hamptons.* (More about that later.) And then, late in 1996, the *Kansas City Star* came calling — one last surprise twist that ended my freelance career and began an entirely new adventure for Diane and me.

About this book

At the time I started this project, my aim was to commemorate fifteen years in journalism. That was a year ago. (As Maxwell Smart would say, "Missed it by *that* much.") As my work on *Tasteland* evolved, so did my thinking about what the book should be. I decided that it should not be, primarily, a collection of my writings but instead a guide to this extraordinary decade and a half of American television. I don't know if this is any more of a "golden age" of TV than the 1950s. I'm not even sure that American television in any age could approach British television at its finest. However, I am sure that, just like my morning coffee, the television that is available to me now is much, *much* better than what was available when I was growing up. In these nearly sixteen years there has also been tremendous change in how we consume television. There was an explosion in content, as well as some explosive real-life events that we watched on television. And, not least, there was all that late-night ferment at the beginning — and now end — of this sixteen-year span. So I decided to structure *Tasteland* as a meta-narrative, a story of excellence and turbulence on the television beat, and I unsentimentally chopped up and rewrote my old articles in service of that narrative.

All in all, and I'm guess-timating here, I wrote more than 5,000 newspaper stories, original blog posts, and newsletters over the years. To keep this book reasonable in size and engaging to the reader, I opted to use excerpts instead of whole columns. Even the featured stories (the ones in boxes) are usually much shorter than their published versions.

I wanted this book to have some reference value, like my earlier *Barnhart's Unauthorized* fall preview guides. Thus the back section consists of the 100 finest programs I watched on my beat that can be rented, bought or streamed online — more than a thousand hours of viewing total. "The 100 Best" is my counter-argument to the Newton Minows of the world, who ask how I can fritter away my life watching that "vast wasteland" of television. The book's title is obviously a play on that famous phrase. (You will read later in *Tasteland* how Minow's speech set off a chain reaction that resulted in some rather unintended consequences.)

Acknowledgments

The *Kansas City Star* graciously allowed me to raid my archives for most of the raw materials that were then shaped into this book. I am grateful to Mike Fannin and Doug Weaver as well as my editors who looked at these stories in their earlier form: Mary Lou Nolan, Steve Paul, Carol Powers, David Frese, Georgann Norton, Paula Southerland, Gary Marx, Sharon Hoffmann, Robert Folsom, and Ward Triplett.

The John Bohlinger profile appeared in *Montana Quarterly*, edited by my high school classmate Nick Ehli; I thank him for the assignment. The Conan O'Brien story did *not* appear in a magazine edited by Andy Eddy, who apologized profusely for the publication's quick demise, which he had no part in. I thank him for that assignment as well.

Right after I launched TV Barn, history repeated itself as P.J. Bednarski, then the executive editor of *Electronic Media*, asked if I would be willing to adapt my web columns for *EM*'s print edition. I did that for five years, first with P.J. and then Tom Gilbert and Chuck Ross. I thank them all.

Before it was common for people to start their own blogs, I welcomed contributions to TV Barn from friends of mine who had their own unique insights on television. Several people were generous with their ideas, design help and stories over the past eleven years: Jon Delfin,

John Zipperer, Greg Hall, Andy Ihnatko, Gregg Winsor, Andy Lewis, Julio Garcia, Joe Mallon, and above all, the late Tom Heald, to whom this book is dedicated.

Diane — or as I call her online, Mrs. TV Barn — was patient and supportive as I hoarded my free time to concentrate on this book. She also read the manuscript carefully and offered her usual catalog of very helpful corrections and comments.

Finally, this book would be incomplete without a roll call of those people who gave me encouragement and opportunities as I found my way into this most unexpected life: Sue Trowbridge, Richard Gehr, Jeff Salomon, Marc Gunther, Bill Carter, Roger Ebert, Gene Siskel, Peter Kaplan, Jim Windolf, Joel Brown, Jane Weston, Felicity Barringer, John Higgins, Steve Paul, Art Brisbane, Mark Zieman, ElRene and Robert Dorn (aka Mom and Bob), and Diane Eickhoff.

Aaron Barnhart
Kansas City
February 2010

THE ANNALS OF
TASTELAND

Chicago Profile

Aaron Barnhart

JOHN H. WHITE/SUN-TIMES

Internet Star

He writes "Late Night News," a newsletter about late-night TV shows. He puts it on the Inter-

signments." One is "a monthly column in the Village Voice on late-night television."

His Day Jobs

1994

It was a glimpse of our future. As the white Ford Bronco led authorities on a low-speed chase along the Los Angeles freeways, NBC was carrying the chase *and* Game 5 of the NBA Finals at the same time, using a split screen. At the time it seemed an impractical, not to mention bizarre, notion that millions of TV watchers would want to look at two screens at once. But that was before most of us started bringing our laptops in the living room.

The Nancy Kerrigan Olympics delivered record ratings to CBS and its high-flying *Late Show with David Letterman,* which sent Dave's Mom to Norway to interview Hillary Clinton. In the Nielsens, *60 Minutes* edged out *Home Improvement* and *Seinfeld* as the year's most popular TV show. Luckily for Mike Wallace, the practice of publishing ratings for 18-to-49-year-olds was still a few years off.

I was an apprentice in 1994, and the late shows were my trade.

Jay, squawking

Late Show News, February 17, 1994

Too bad Jay Leno doesn't have his foul-mouthed ex-manager Helen Kushnick around anymore. She could have called up the *Late Night with Conan O'Brien* folks and screamed obscenities at them for booking David Letterman as a guest on February 28. Jay is reportedly peeved at Conan not merely for booking Jay's chief competitor, but for failing to inform the *Tonight Show* and, on top of that, because last year when Conan was named the new *Late Night* host, Jay had him booked immediately on *Tonight* and even went so far as to bump a scheduled guest. Wow ... Jay bumped a guest once. My guess is that a new talk-show war is brewing — who gets the *Tonight Show* when NBC finally dumps Jay's sorry ass! Canny move, Conan. *(Postscript: Even I am amazed at how well the first article I ever published has held up. I did blow the prediction about NBC dumping Leno, but I foretold the drama that would play out 16 years later — Jay versus Conan, with Dave cackling on the sidelines.)*

Visiting the Ed Sullivan

Late Show News, April 5, 1994

On Wednesday — the day before Madonna dropped some F-bombs on the *Late Show with David Letterman* — we had the pleasure of attending a taping at the Ed Sullivan Theatre. The *Late Show* stage is surprisingly tiny. It's larger than the shoebox where Letterman did his NBC show, but director Hal Gurnee has made it seem like it were Chicago Stadium, thanks to some trickery with ceiling cameras and the stage's large footprint. The next time you see old footage of the Sullivan show, notice how Ed looks *up* at the audience. The seats are above the stage, in *two* balconies. Now the upper deck is gone, replaced with wall-to-wall acoustical molding that goes to the ceiling, while most of the seating has moved on to the main floor, where equipment used to be stored. As a result, probably 400 of the 460 audience members each evening see more of the crew than they do of Dave. And so, while he's looking down at them, they're looking up — usually at a monitor, because their view is obstructed. We filed in promptly at 5:15 p.m., shortly before taping was to begin. I was genuinely pleased to see an actual employee of Worldwide Pants up there, standing by the blue doors, dancing to the music, laughing uproariously at the jokes, and generally looking as though for her — as it is for her boss — this was the one hour of the day to live without regrets. The woman, who we found out was Laurie Diamond, Dave's executive assistant, had also enthusiastically greeted the incoming audience in a way that did not, remarkably, trigger my shit detector.

NBC's latest Letterman wannabe

Late Show News, July 12, 1994

The new host of NBC's *Later*, Greg Kinnear, is so transparently emulating the early career of David Letterman it's hard not to admire his cheek, especially since he's doing it so well and since Letterman has made the old Dave we loved *persona non grata* on his CBS show. Like Letterman, Kinnear is already turning out a highly polished product. His "media bites" — smarmy commentary on video clips that he adopted from his last gig as host of E!'s *Talk Soup* — are smart and funny and, as happened with Letterman, made enemies for Kinnear within NBC on the opposite coast. (Some people in New York are upset that he mocked video of a *Dateline* interview with a woman who claimed to be abducted by space aliens.) With guests, Kinnear is learning when it's appropriate to intrude with pretaped diversions, something he should not have done the first week of his show with George Carlin, who should be allowed to talk for an hour without interruption. Kinnear relies much less on that blue index card than he did four months ago, and he eagerly absorbs the show's misfires, making running jokes out of them. With *Later's* ratings up by 25 percent, the next question must be where its host goes from here. Television writers regularly suggest that he should succeed Conan O'Brien as the host of *Late Night*, reflecting the widespread critical disdain of Conan. But one problem still nags. Kinnear still seems more montage than personality — mostly Letterman, but with shades of other performers as well. Perhaps with his own hour-long vehicle, a Greg Kinnear personality can emerge from the shadows. But we're not convinced.

Hello, Tom

Village Voice, August 2, 1994

He's tanned, rested and ready once more for big-time TV. Tom Snyder has completely outgrown his year-and-a-half-old talk show on CNBC and is about to be named the host of the new David Letterman-produced talk show at 12:35 on CBS. Many people's memories of Snyder are influenced by Dan Aykroyd's parody of him during the heyday of the NBC *Tomorrow Show*. Snyder has smoothed some of his bombast since then, but none of his idiosyncrasies: the hearty laugh, the on-camera chats with off-camera intimates, the independently-controlled eyebrows. T.S. has conversations on his show that are as stimulating as any on TV right now, certainly more listenable than the herky-jerky affairs on *Charlie Rose*. But is this what the masses want at 12:35? Yes, according to someone who should know. "When I was growing up there was Jack Paar, who was just a great conversationalist. I thought to bring conversation back would be the original move now." That was Lorne Michaels, as he prepared to launch Conan O'Brien's show last summer on NBC.

Are liberal TV stations stifling Rush?

Late Show News, October 18, 1994

Rush Limbaugh's half-hour syndicated soliloquy is now viewed by upwards of 4 percent of households, a remarkable figure considering the strong lineups he's up against in the first hour of late night. Yet there was his producer, ex-Reagan flack Roger Ailes, complaining in the press last week that Limbaugh's ratings have hit a glass ceiling because "liberal markets" push the show's air time out to the wee wee hours. As it happens, Limbaugh was in contract talks with his syndicator (the program was extended yesterday for two more seasons), so Ailes was just adding some public spin to the negotiations. The truth is that liberal markets want Rush as much as conservative ones do. The *New York Times*, in fact, is now running a TV ad in local markets showing him contentedly leafing through their newspaper. Don't be fooled by last week's call for boycott by the National Organization of Women, which wants the *Times* to dump Limbaugh as spokesman. (N.O.W. boycotting the *Times*: talk about running your own train off the track.) Rush's real enemy is not political, it is commercial: unlike in radio, where he has the middle of the day to himself, here he competes with Koppel, Leno, and Letterman.

Goodbye, Arsenio

Village Voice, May 17, 1994

"Are you really quitting the show? Then let's cut the shit," wheezed comedian Bobcat Goldthwait before he laid waste to the interview area of *The Arsenio Hall Show* on April 29. As the astounded host looked on, Goldthwait spray-painted PARAMOUNT SUCKS on the wall behind the guest couch, upended furniture and equipment, and had to be headlocked by Hall while a delirious studio audience chanted the chorus to "Whoomp! There It Is!" Arsenio said later, "The terrible injustice is that I have to pretend I'm mad at him."

The other injustice is that Hall's viewers had to wait until the show's final month on the air to relive some of the excitement of its first two seasons. When he burst onto the late-show scene in 1987, Hall was a sensation. Show business was more integrated than Carson's and Letterman's shows let on, and *The Arsenio Hall Show* proved it. He gave scores of grateful R&B, rap and gospel artists neon visibility, his unthreatening interview style encouraged big names to sit on his couch, and his on-air activism hit its mark during the L.A. riots and Magic Johnson's HIV announcement. The show wasn't perfect, but it played right in the networks' blind spot and helped Paramount seize a key part of the late-night viewing audience in those early years.

But the show faltered after that great start, and instead of addressing its shortcomings, Hall poured his energies into building a production company. Bobcat may not be happy with the news, but Hall's departure is the right move.

Frenemies: Harvey and Dave

Late Show News, October 11, 1994

When you finish Harvey Pekar and Joyce Brabner's new 224-page comic *Our Cancer Year,* due in bookstores this week, you may find yourself wondering if David Letterman will ever have Harvey back on his show again. Or maybe you will wonder how these two guys ever got connected in the first place.

If you're just joining us, Pekar has for two decades been chronicling his life in the reality comic book series *American Splendor.* Stories such as "Short Changed" (Harvey almost gets charged too much for grapes) and "Lost And Found" (Harvey and Joyce keep forgetting where they left their books) are carefully retold in all their real-life uneventfulness. The enchantment comes in discovering the complexity of ordinary life through Harvey's compulsive, hyperanalytical muse. Some people think that Harvey's brooding is mostly bluster, that he is the Woody Allen of verité funnies. One of those people would clearly be Steve O'Donnell, head writer for the Letterman show at NBC, who picked up the phone in 1986 and called Harvey in Cleveland, offering him a guest spot on *Late Night*. What followed were half a dozen appearances in the span of two years. Harvey and Joyce made off each time with a raft of souvenirs from the Letterman offices which they then sold off. And each time, Harvey came back to Cleveland and wrote about the experience in *American Splendor* in the most unflattering detail possible.

The problem, as Harvey and Joyce tell it, stems from the desire of Letterman's people to control the content of his appearances. Joyce says, "We're not supposed to tell you which casual throwaway lines, lightning-quick put downs, leading questions, canny insights and spontaneous discussions were mapped out ahead of time on those blue index cards Dave holds." Beyond that, Dave's writers wanted to bottle the exuberant hostility of Harvey's first couple of visits and release it again every few months until people got tired of it. Harvey's expectations were quite different, and despite his desire to become a regular on the program, they goaded him into acts of increasing chutzpah. He began to rage against Dave's employer, General Electric, for its work in the defense industry, and was immediately shown the door. The next time, he brought the subject up again, and the shouting match that followed seemingly put an end to his regular visits. But the resilient Letterman crew called back a few months later; a disgusted Pekar turned them down.

Nineteen ninety arrived, and with it Harvey's lymphoma. What followed is the story of *Our Cancer Year,* an unapologetically frank and harrowing account of its treatment. The only mention of Letterman in the book is a frosty telephone exchange between Joyce and Steve O'Donnell toward the end of Harvey's treatment. Steve, who is calling to see about booking Harvey again, gets the news of his illness from Joyce, who adds, "I don't think your audience would find cancer real entertaining." When Steve replies, "Well, you tell Harvey from Dave that he, Steve and Morty are behind him 100 percent," Joyce shoots back, "No they don't ... They don't know Harvey is sick. You only just heard about it. Go back and tell them. Then, if they really feel that way, they can let him know and send a card or something." Just to rub in the point, a caption below reads, "No one did."

1995

The *New York Times* headline said it all: "And the Winner Isn't David Letterman." Dave's worst twelve months began with him bombing as host of the Academy Awards, trying, among other things, to coin a catchphrase in "Uma, Oprah." Later in the year, a Hugh Grant interview commemorated Leno's overtaking Letterman in the late-night ratings.

Westinghouse bought CBS, Walt Disney scooped up ABC, and the UPN and WB networks flickered to life. *Seinfeld* won the Nielsens for the 1994–95 season, followed by rookie sensation *ER*. The year's longest-running reality TV drama ended with a sensational twist, as O.J. Simpson was found not guilty of murder. Another season was ordered after the Goldman family took O.J. to civil court.

Change was everywhere around me in 1995. Diane and I got married, I quit my job, I started pitching story ideas to indifferent editors, and the bloom fell off my affection for Dave (though I did love his defiant performance at the Oscars).

S(omething) N(obody) L(ikes)

Village Voice, March 14, 1995

"The writing sucks this season," *New York* magazine reported *Saturday Night Live* star Adam Sandler as saying. Later, Sandler denied making that statement. He also denied telling the magazine, "It's not fun being recognized on the streets of New York and the first thing people say is 'You should do movies 'cause your show ain't happening,'" though that strikes me as a very Sandleresque thing to say. There's no denying that lousy sketches have made *SNL* arguably as unpleasant for the on-air talent as for the viewers watching them. Yet this is not the root of the show's troubles. If the writing sucks, it's because there is no incentive to improve it. *SNL* was once a lean machine efficiently dispensing new-wave satire — but now it's a welfare state for a privileged elite. The show's original cast moved along after just five seasons. By contrast, the mediocre Kevin Nealon is about to complete his *ninth* season. If I were NBC, I'd tell Lorne Michaels to pare *SNL* back to one hour and emphasize quality over quantity of sketches. I guarantee you many former viewers would be back to check it out. And should Lorne complain he can't get musical acts without promising them two songs, my reply would be, "Who said anything about cutting back on the songs?"

Ted Koppel, having it both ways
Village Voice, April 18, 1995

Following a special panel discussion he had moderated on "The Media and O.J. Simpson," *ABC News Nightline* anchor Ted Koppel turned to the camera to deliver one of his trademark sermonettes. Noting that 60 percent of the American public had told pollsters they were "sick" of the O.J. story and wanted less coverage of it, Koppel pointed out that ratings for Simpson's arraignment had gone through the roof. "Someone," he added dryly, "is not being altogether truthful." He then reminded his audience that "all television sets are equipped with an off button and if enough of you use it when we go overboard, we will get the message." But "overboard" is not a meaningful concept at *Nightline*, which once had the televangelists Jim and Tammy Bakker on sixteen times in a year — not because their pathetic stories were worth hearing, but because *Nightline* had them exclusively. Koppel addresses his viewers as intelligent, sensible citizens, even as he introduces another show devoted to developments in a certain lurid celebrity murder case. The son of a factory owner, Koppel surely is familiar with the concept of loss leaders. So he will give back some high ground by riding the O.J. story to victory in the February sweeps (winning over both Letterman and Leno), but will also moderate a town hall meeting on teen pregnancy and film a week of programs at a North Carolina prison.

Herrrre's Larry!
Late Show News, July 25, 1995

There is nothing in the personal life of Larry Sanders — the talk show host played by Garry Shandling on HBO's *The Larry Sanders Show* — to suggest he is capable of solving anything off the air. Backstage chaos frequently threatens to spill over onto the set; indeed, the show-within-a-show often provides resolution to the plot, as with his guest (and unlikely romantic interest) Roseanne Barr last week. Reviews of *Larry*

Sanders often raise the topic of life imitating art and vice versa. You may know that an episode in which Dave Letterman revealed that his 12:35 man would be Tom Snyder aired several months before Dave made just this announcement at CBS. Likewise, Roseanne agreed to have her real-life marriage to a limo driver woven into the fictional affairs of Larry. In last week's episode, Larry calls his assistant Beverly at 2 a.m. in distress. "What is it, Larry? Did Letterman have Tom Hanks on again?" When Larry says no, she asks, "Did Leno have the Ito Dancers on again?"

Talk Stew is in a soup
Village Voice, October 4, 1995

Paramount is now syndicating *The Jon Stewart Show* as a replacement for *The Arsenio Hall Show.* But with David Letterman on many of the CBS affiliates that used to air *Arsenio,* and NBC affiliates unlikely to drop *Late Night with Conan O'Brien,* Stewart's show has been banished to very late hours in many of the 140 markets where it airs. Despite Paramount's involvement, the new Talk Stew looks as low-budget as the old one did on MTV: no band, no sidekick (unless you count the announcer), not even a cue-card guy. What it does have is a talented host. Stewart is facile and funny without needing to shout, and his interviews are cozy, though oddly not as revealing as Arsenio's were. Jon is a standup comic by training; Conan is a writer, and the contrast is clear. While O'Brien seems to need every moment of *Late Night* to be scripted, Stewart's talker is more in the late-show tradition of "found comedy" — playing off jokes that die, or arranging a theme around the host and riffing off it all night. Last week Stewart staged a "Piña Colada Night" with the guy who invented the drink (and who speaks no English) and Rupert Holmes on the keyboard, whom Stewart persuaded to play the same four bars from his "Piña Colada Song" all night. Handing a drink to each guest didn't hurt.

Jay Leno 2.0

Village Voice, June 20, 1995

Audience members at a recent *Tonight Show* taping got to glimpse a different side of its host when, following the show, he taped a short piece for airing at an NBC affiliates' confab. Introducing himself as "Jay 'One Tenth of a Ratings Point Away' Leno" (a reference to some good weeks his show has been having against top-rated David Letterman), he surprised his hearers by launching into a vicious broadside against his CBS rival. At one point he cackled, "The sharks are in the water and they smell blood!"

It's not always obvious, but there is an Evil Jay lurking inside the person whose ingratiating public persona has led one comedian to joke that Leno is running for Mayor of Late Night. This is the same man, after all, who two years ago eavesdropped on a conference call of NBC executives discussing his fate, then phoned participants the next day to intimidate them by reading back to them, word for word, what they had said about him. This is also the same man who tolerated his agent and his show's first producer, Helen Kushnick, verbally abusing everyone around her on a daily basis until NBC, in desperation, fired her because Leno would not.

Then there are the jokes. Rodney King, picked up for drunk driving last month, has become a nightly staple in an increasingly cruel *Tonight Show* monologue: "Rodney is on his DUI world tour," Jay said the day after King was picked up in Pennsylvania. For a while there, Leno and Howard Stern were the only two broadcasters making fun of O.J. Simpson. Jay later bragged that the jokes gave his show an "edge" over Letterman. Well, there is a word to describe the Dancing Itos, but "edgy" ain't it.

A visit to the Dave Cave

Village Voice, August 29, 1995

On the alt.fan.
letterman newsgroup, the
resident infomaven is Don
Giller — or just Donz5, as
he is known to the regulars.
Donz5 (it's his AOL handle)
can tell you what game
shows David Letterman
appeared on as a celebrity
contestant in the 1970s;
can reconstruct the look and feel of Dave's 1980 morning show on
NBC; can list every date that your favorite entertainer appeared
on *Late Night* or *Late Show*; and can produce detailed CVs for most
every writer and musician who ever worked for the show.

Recently, someone posted a message to the newsgroup asking
who was Dave's worst all-time guest. Besides the usual suggestions
(Cher, Shirley MacLaine), one person nominated "the guy who
invented the graffiti remover stuff that was orange-colored or
-based or something. he had more jewelry than Mr. T." After reading
that, Donz5 dipped into his database and wrote a response: "Don't
recall the jewelry, but that was Rocky Dellutri. Bryant Gumbel
was also a guest on the show, February 26, 1985 (#520) (as were
the immortal Schmenge Brothers, who sang 'Cabbage Rolls and
Coffee'), and since Bryant wasn't wearing socks, Dave spray-painted
them on his ankles."

Donz5 arrived at alt.fan.letterman a little more than a year
ago, when America Online began offering access to newsgroups.
Internet statistics rate it as the second most popular personality
fangroup after Rush Limbaugh's. After Letterman chose Pam Cox,
an Oklahoma City housewife, from his studio audience and made
her cohost-for-a-night of a recent *Late Show* broadcast, she went to
the newsgroup to crow. When others posted messages suggesting
Dave should have picked someone else, she fired back, "This has

been the greatest moment of my life so far and I am not going to let people like you ruin it for me."

Giller has been recording Letterman programs for more than a decade, exchanging rare videotapes (such as broadcasts of Dave's morning show) with other collectors on AOL and CompuServe. He moved to New York in 1978 to earn his masters in historical musicology from Columbia, and works out of his apartment on the Upper West Side as a freelance typesetter for music publishers. His eight-year-old Macintosh sits on a table in the back room. Above it, shelves stretch to the ceiling with software manuals, several years' worth of computer magazines, Beatles albums, bootlegs, and literature. To our left, a stereo sits atop three VCRs; Giller points to the machine on the bottom and jokes, "I use that one as a clock." There is just enough room for the two of us, and none for the videotapes. Those are in the front room — 3,200 tapes and counting, stacked three deep. They share space with hundreds of classical LPs from Giller's musicology days, as well as his bed and his cat.

We get to talking about Rob Burnett, the *Late Show* head writer who is helming Bonnie Hunt's new CBS sitcom. Suddenly, Giller whirls around in his chair and keys "Burnett" into a search field on his computer. Not much happens. "Hold on," he says as he types some new commands, "I know *exactly* what I'm doing." Soon we are looking at a list of every Burnett mention from the Letterman show's closing credits, 1985 to present, an impressive climb from Production Staff 4 to Researchers 2 to Writers 11 and up that totem to the top.

In person, Giller reveals little of the self-assured, sharp-tongued Donz5. He actually seems a bit embarrassed by this trove of Lettermania, at one point saying to me, "There's a fine line between getting information and creeping people out." Later, I'm on the newsgroup and see that someone has challenged Giller's mastery of the permissions guidelines for Dave's on-air phone calls. Sure enough, Donz5 reappears: "Thanks for jumping in; you must be new here. And if you claim it, it must be true: I just make up things around here. Ask around and get back to me."

1996

Whether you knew it or not, 1996 was the year of infrastructure, the ultimate boring-but-important topic. Most metropolitan cable systems got serious about their fiber-optic upgrades, ostensibly because a 500-channel universe was beckoning. (As it happened, all those high-speed lines proved to be ideal for sending Internet packets.) Congress passed the digital TV act to bring high-definition programs and interactive services to our homes within a decade. (The deadline was later extended twice, and most TV channels are still standard def.)

The networks started assigning age ratings like TV-14 to programs based on — well, whatever they wanted to base them on. Meanwhile, the ratings that mattered showed *ER* edging out *Seinfeld* for the top spot, followed by *Friends*. Those three Thursday shows on NBC also dragged *Caroline* and *Boston Common* into the top 10 with them, proving that for every Ronald Reagan there is a Michael Reagan and even a Neil. Rosie O'Donnell was a breath of fresh air in middays and earned the improbable title of "Queen of Nice."

I began 1996 writing for two publications and ended it writing for ten, though getting them to pay me would prove tricky.

Isn't that special

Late Show News, July 30, 1996

What visit to the 818 area code would be complete without attending a taping of *The Tonight Show with Jay Leno*? In my sport coat and khakis, I might've passed for network staff in a line where beach fashion prevailed. Then again, you could hardly blame people for not dressing up, for this was to be a *Tonight Show* "Special Edition" taping, a six-minute sprint through an abbreviated monologue. No music, no guests — no time for that when back in Atlanta, the boys at NBC Sports were itching to get control of the airwaves again, so they could continue showing American athletes winning gold medals for America in events that Americans can easily understand. (Can I just say my life will not be diminished if I never see or hear from Kerri Strug again?) As we were ushered into the studio, Kevin Eubanks and the band were pounding out a 10-minute cover of "Cold Sweat." When we were seated, out stepped Jay. "How 'bout a hand for the Chi-Lites!" he said before posing for photos with members of the studio audience. Try as I might, I could not even manage a smile at most of his monologue. When he told a clever joke about Raymond Chandler, born on that day in 1888, I was literally *the only person* who laughed. Leno immediately turned to head writer Jimmy Brogan, standing offstage, and blamed him for the joke.

Time for Craiggers

Late Show News, August 27, 1996

Doe-eyed and impeccably well-groomed, Craig Kilborn, the former ESPN anchor turned Weekend Update wannabe on Comedy Central's new half-hour topical comedy series *The Daily Show,* knows how to turn on the smarm. Offering his nightly unsolicited promotion for daytime talker *Caryl & Marilyn: Best Friends,* Kilborn never tires of telling us that they really *are* friends, adding, with a glint in his eye, "And that's why it just might work." While legendary fake newsman Dennis Miller reveled in playing the angry outsider, Kilborn takes a decidedly establishmentarian tack. That, and the show's inspired mix of smart-ass material from Lizz Winstead and her staff of writers, help this new half-hour topical comedy series stand apart from its late-night peers. The political humor is surprisingly lame: Colin Powell is a "non-threatening minority" who appears at the Republican Convention because he was "driven out of the house by his wife's vacuuming." But the satires of media and entertainment have teeth, like the feature "This Day in Hasselhoff History," which matches dates in the actor-singer's career with historical events. (Did you know the Hoff's directorial debut coincided with the birthday of Alfred Hitchcock?) In another, the show's "resident videologist" offers a comically nuanced review of a Keith Sweat music video, noting plot twists and character development. A "Peripheral Olympians" segment spotlights Audrey, a dancer at a strip club located "only a few miles from Olympic Stadium," imitating the up-close-and-personal style of NBC's overwrought coverage ("For Audrey, pushing her body beyond its limits is just part of her daily routine"). Despite its shortcomings, *The Daily Show* easily surpasses most of the comedy offerings on broadcast TV this season, which raises the question of why a cable channel that only reaches 40 million homes is carrying it.

It's 4 a.m. — time to polka!

New York Times, September 15, 1996

   What national news program has its own resident polka player
and informs its audience that the weather in Austin, Minnesota, is
"Spammy"? Millions of night owls know that the answer is ABC's
World News Now, the highest-rated and least conventional of the three
overnight network newscasts. With its quirky mix of news, features and
attitude, *WNN* has earned a loyal following — its 0.8 rating equals that
of CNN's *Larry King Live* in prime time — and has invited comparisons
to *NBC News Overnight,* the 1980s late-late newscast with Linda
Ellerbee. *WNN* anchors Thalia Assuras and Mark Mullen do their best to
humor as well as inform their sleepless audience. They allot themselves
"play time," when they can chat or trade good-natured barbs on the air.
The production crew gets in the act as well, choosing eclectic music for
the sports and weather fillers and creating offbeat graphics, like the
montage that makes it appear the Red Sea is parting in the middle of
the newsroom. Long-running staples include the nightly "temperature
index," a mysterious three-digit reading compiled from unspecified
cities — and the weekly rendition of the "World News Polka" by Barry
Mitchell, who began sending his musical parodies to the show in
response to a call for viewer videotapes. Lest anyone confuse *WNN* with
an early-morning zoo, there is a method behind the madness: It gives
the news a distinctive, unhurried feel. After the headlines, sports, and
weather are dispatched, the rest of the half hour contains interviews and
features that can run as long as ten minutes. "That's an extraordinary
opportunity to talk about the issues of the day," Assuras said. Still,
working at *WNN* also means foregoing the opporunity to sleep normally.
Assuras used to do the 5 a.m. newscast in addition to her *WNN* duties,
until she took a nine-month break from overnights last year because "it
just about killed me." Now Mullen works both programs, and tries to be
philosophical about it. "You just try to make peace with it as best you
can," Mullen said. "Personally, I prefer to look at it as late night instead
of early morning."

My so-called freelance life

From July 1995 to December 1996, I was a freelance writer, and looking back, it was an exciting time, a formative time ... but not a very remunerative time. The only steady money I made during that period was as the first "Fraymaster" for *Slate* magazine's reader forums, known collectively as The Fray, for which I received a fat $12 an hour from Jolt (the temp agency that worked closely with Microsoft, then the owner of *Slate)*.

My freelance assignments were almost all for New York publications, thanks to friendly journalists who recommended me to good editors. I'll admit that having those high-profile bylines made the low pay bearable. Writing for the *Times* meant that CEOs returned your calls from the airport. Writing for the *Observer* and *Voice* meant you were read by interesting people. I'm not sure what my endgame was — perhaps leaving Chicago and moving to one of the coasts, a prospect neither I nor my new bride relished — but being hired by the *Kansas City Star* made that a moot question.

The *Times* used to have a television book that was only distributed in the immediate New York City area. This meant that whenever I wrote for it, the editor had to mail me copies because there was literally no other way for me to see my story. It didn't appear in the national edition, and it wasn't included on the *Times'* Internet site. A cover story paid $500 and gave you a thrill — your name on the cover of a magazine read by hundreds of thousands. Other people were thrilled, too. Take the issue whose cover I have reproduced here. Shortly after it was published, I met Brian Williams — then a low-rated cable news anchor — in the green room at *Late Night with Conan O'Brien*. His alert publicist explained that I was the author of the *Times* story. Williams' eyes widened, he grasped my hand and he thanked me profusely. I know he has a well-earned reputation as a ham, but he wasn't overdoing it for laughs (I think).

That wasn't the end of the story. A few weeks later — I was working for the *Star* by this time — Jane Weston, the editor of the *Times* television book, unexpectedly called me up. She was a pleasant, mature, professional woman, but on this phone call she sounded ... *scared,* or at least very nervous. She said she had some questions about the last story I'd written. That would have been my guide to the all-news networks, that story that gave Brian Williams his cover shot. Jane wanted to know how I had decided which networks to include in my story. I found this a strange question. I told her that if it covered news around the clock, and it was on television, I included it. As of the fall of 1996, when my piece appeared, that included CNN, Headline News, MSNBC, C-SPAN, New York 1 and a decidedly non-fire-eating news venture from Fox that had just signed on that fall.

Jane asked if there was a reason why I hadn't included Bloomberg TV. I asked her what she was getting at, and finally she told me that over the weekend, the publisher of the *Times* had been confronted at a party by Mike Bloomberg, who had demanded to know why the *Times* had *slighted* him by omitting *his* channel from a roundup of 24-hour news channels in a story that was read all across the tri-state area.

I explained to Jane — who was undoubtedly hoping for as little turbulence as possible in the remaining years before her retirement — that financial news channels were an entirely different bird, just as the two new competing sports-news channels were a separate genre from all-news or financial-news channels. She wrote down my response, asking me to repeat parts of it until she had committed it all to talking points that, no doubt, she repeated to her boss.

A couple of weeks later, a feature story appeared in the Feb. 17,

1997 edition of the *Times*. "TV Woos Viewers With News of Business," the headline read. Peter Truell's 1,200–word report walked readers through the gauntlet of financial news channels on TV: CNBC, CNNfn, a Dow Jones venture called WBIS and ... Bloomberg Business Television.

Recently, the voters of New York surprised Mayor Bloomberg by re-electing him to a third term of office by a thin margin — much thinner than most experts and pollsters had anticipated. As analysts began asking around for explanations, this pithy one came from the esteemed New York blogger Choire Sicha: "Voting against Mike Bloomberg just felt great," he wrote. I completely understood.

Then there were the thousands of words I slaved over for promised compensation that never came. By far my biggest debtor was *Hamptons Magazine*, founded in 1978 by a twenty-two-year-old party boy named Randy Schindler. *Hamptons* was a slipshod but hugely popular vanity rag full of wet kisses for the nightclubs, clothing stores, and cosmetic surgeons that served the millionaires of Southampton, New York, and advertised in the pages of *Hamptons Magazine*. In the spring of 1996 I received an email from William Monahan, a fiction writer I knew from the Echo bulletin board in New York. Monahan explained that he had been hired as editor of *Hamptons* for the upcoming summer. He told me that he wanted to produce articles of substance and was asking his writer friends, including me, to contribute articles. His timing was perfect, because I had just learned that if I wanted to kick-start my career as a TV critic, I needed to get out to California and attend the critics' press tour. The *Hamptons* imprimatur would help me get a press badge, and my freelance income would cover expenses, which consisted of airfare and $10 a night to stay at the house of a florist, I am not making this up, that I found through a book called *Mennonite Your Way*.

Press tour was as good as I had been told. Even the florist said I was welcome back at his home. Really, the only downside was that I never saw one red cent from *Hamptons*. Apparently Schindler told Monahan (after the fact) that he hadn't authorized freelancers, which raises the question of how he expected a 100–page issue to get written every month. Monahan, who himself was shorted by

Schindler, signed the following statement for me to use if I ever wished to pursue my case against *Hamptons*.

To Whom It May Concern:

Mr. Aaron Barnhart's contractual agreement with Hamptons Magazine for the summer of 1996 was signed in my presence, on the date given, by R.C. Schindler's ordinary and usual signatory, Hamptons accountant Janet Bonawandt, with Mr. Schindler's explicit knowledge and on his direction. Mr. Barnhart fulfilled his contractual obligations, so long as I was his editor, with courtesy, professionalism, and great skill.

Signed,

William Monahan

William Monahan

November 15, 1996

My phone calls and emails to Schindler went unreturned. Diane somehow got him on the phone and the two had a vicious yelling match, to no avail. Two years later, Schindler was sued for $300,000 of unpaid printer's bills and, more importantly, prevented from publishing. A savior named Jason Binn agreed to pay off the debt and become co-publisher. Later, Binn ousted Schindler from the magazine he had founded. As for Monahan, he decided that the real money was in Hollywood, and switched to writing scripts. Martin Scorsese hired him to work on *The Departed*, and that was how I wound up yelling ecstatically at my TV set on Oscars night 2007, as Monahan collected an Academy Award for best adapted screenplay, eleven years after that summer we spent writing for nothing.

Success is the best revenge — doesn't every *Hamptons* divorceé say that?

Harald Schmidt's Lateschau

Village Voice, April 2, 1996

There's an old line
David Letterman used,
back in his days at NBC,
whenever his staff
would come up with
some ludicrous show
enhancement—a robot
arm, for instance, that
would hand him the
evening's Viewer Mail,
one piece at a time. After
trying out one of these

gadgets, he'd turn to the camera grimly and tell the home viewers,
"Someday, ladies and gentlemen, *all* talk shows will be like this."

Punchline or prophecy? I'd always thought the former, but
now that I've seen *Die Harald Schmidt Show,* the new comedy-talk
program airing Tuesdays through Saturdays on Germany's SAT.1
network, I'm not so sure. When it comes to shameless intellectual
larceny, Jay Leno has nothing on this amazingly lifelike *Late Show*
clone, which swipes nearly every on-air element of Letterman's
program, right down to Dave's well-worn hand-chopping motions.
It starts with the show's opening, a familiar montage of city-at-
night copter shots (the city in this case is Köln, not New York)
and floating TV graphics (a rectangular one for the show title,
an oval one for the band, just like on CBS). That's followed by a
smirky intro ("And now, the secret son of the Queen of England . .
. Harallllld Schmidt!") as we segue to the inside of the old theater
restored especially for this show. From the brick-paneled backdrop
to the shiny red floor, this is Letterman's set to a tee.

And heeeeeere's Harald, who slices the air with his arm—the
band's cue to stop, of course—then plunges into his monologue,
with its cavalcade of foreign and domestic celebrities. (References
to British royalty abound.) Schmidt will repeat names like

"Alois Schmidtbauer" over and over, showing the same feigned wonderment with his native tongue that Letterman does.

Die Deutsche Dave also relies on a device practically trademarked by his Yankee counterpart: a stock visual gag dropped into the monologue night after night. A recent favorite features a close-up of a man dressed as Prince Charles's lover Camilla, pounding his hairy arm on the table while demanding that Charles end his sham marriage to Diana. "I want a fucking *Scheidung!*" shrieks Camilla, with only the word for "divorce" in German. Schmidt has also driven the "Knast Kamera" (Jail-Cam) gag into the ground — a set of bars placed across the screen to illustrate what the show looks like from the cell where Steffi Graf's allegedly tax-evading father is being held. (Schmidt told a German newspaper, "*Vater* Graf is to our show what O.J. Simpson is to the Americans.")

One time, a remote camera went to a store adjoining his theater, and Schmidt asked the clerk if he wouldn't mind trading places with an audience member. A few hours later you could have flipped over to RTL2 and watched Dave on tape delay, doing the same shtick with his neighbors. Do Schmidt's writers watch *Late Show* on satellite before going to work?

Late-night entertainment has become a global product in the 1990s, and judging by the email I've gotten from around the world, Letterman is considered the gold standard. If there's an after-hours comedy-talk program in your country, chances are the producer has been recycling some of the same elements from Dave as the Germans. I've heard about a Venezuelan talker from the late 1980s that was based on Dave's NBC show, a Brazilian *Late Show* clone taped in English with Portuguese subtitles, and a show from Norway called *RiksDan*, with a bantering bandleader and nightly Top Six List. ("This is a small country," my source explains.)

Perhaps the best-known of all the Letterman lookalikes over the years is *Tonight Live With Steve Vizard*, which ran on Australia's Channel Seven from 1990 to 1993 and whose host cheerfully confessed to mimicking Dave's NBC show. Vizard, an impresario who serves on national arts councils and organizes his country's version of Lollapalooza, has been an outspoken promoter of Australian television and film. "It's about having a sense of identity," he told a radio interviewer last year, "It goes to people's self-esteem. When people watch an athlete from their own country win a race, it says something about themselves. When people see a performer telling their own story on television, as opposed to a sitcom set in New York, be it however good, it says something about not just my culture, it says something about me. It gives me a sense of worth."

Vizard's suggestion—that a television show is little more than an empty bottle with an affirming cultural message jammed into it—may not completely justify the plunder of programs like Letterman's, but it does help put all the borrowing in some perspective. Let's not forget that Letterman cheerfully confesses to using elements of Jack Paar's and Steve Allen's shows on his own (and truth be told, he's been known to swipe a thing or two from Leno). What can't be borrowed, but must be invented anew each time, is the show's central organizing element. It is the host, through whom all of the raw materials must pass. The host must remain true to his own tastes while affirming those of his viewers (though their tastes are inevitably driven by external cultural forces, not least of which is that program).

In this respect it is useful to compare Schmidt to Conan O'Brien, who in many ways is his mirror opposite. Conan inherited Dave's late-night franchise but chose to remake it completely to reflect his own sensibilities. This decision served him well early on, when it was unclear whether he could broadcast his way out of a wet paper bag. These days, Conan's now-loyal core audience takes pride in the fact that, even at its lowest ratings levels, no one ever accused his *Late Night* of being a Letterman clone. By contrast, Schmidt is a polished, on-air performer (one fan tells me he is "a genuinely funny and competent host, one of an extreme few in Germany"), but he apparently exercised little control over the format of his new show and is now taking a beating for it. A magazine readers' poll revealed that detractors of Schmidt's show outnumber supporters by nearly three to one. One complained, "I want the real Letterman, not an imitation." *(Postscript: Turns out the German knew what he was doing. Die Harald Schmidt Show lasted eight seasons before the host moved on to other projects in 2003.)*

Comedy Boy Tries to Rescue Letterman

'The Most Powerful Man in Show Business' Is Beating Up on Himself and His Viewers;

'The most powerful man in broadcasting'

New York Observer, May 13, 1996

    This article — which marked a fault line in my writing about David Letterman — was several months in the making. My first submission to the New York Observer *appeared in the fall of 1995, shortly after Letterman's* Late Show *had slipped to second place behind* The Tonight Show. *Dave had become fascinated by a woman known only as the "Peach Lady," who was captured on camera in the stands of the U.S. Open tennis tournament eating a very drippy peach. Letterman would not stop showing the clip. Finally, one night he arranged for her image to be displayed on the Jumbotron in Times Square, along with a phone number and the message, "IF THIS IS YOU, CALL NOW!", as the scene was broadcast on CBS. A reader of* Late Show News *who knew the Peach Lady, and was as appalled as I was, passed along the name of her attorney, who was happy to give me an exclusive. I can't remember why I took it to the* Observer, *but an editor there named Jim Windolf was delighted to help fashion it into a front-page story with a double headline:* PEACH LADY QUASHES AN UGLY LETTERMAN GAG; LATE SHOW LOSES VIEWERS, EMMY, AND DAVE TURNS OFF THE CHARM. *Letterman's producer Robert Morton — who had known me up until that point as an unalloyed fan of the show — was furious with the story. But I was right, and Morty was issued his walking papers a few months later, not because of the Peach Lady but because of the malaise that had overtaken the show, both on and off the air. His successor, Rob Burnett, agreed to sit with me and address the show's woes. Windolf suggested that Burnett and I watch an episode of* Late Show *together. While doing that, we were paid a visit by the man himself. It is the only time I have experienced Letterman in the flesh, without amplification, and I must say that man has some fantastic pipes.*

He once seemed so full of life, so effortlessly entertaining. David Letterman embodied his own cliché — he was the "always lovely and talented" king of late night. Already on the rebound from a messy divorce with NBC, Letterman went into a cocoon and re-emerged on CBS as the happiest man in show business. Tuning in at 11:30 became a pleasure again, because we knew that Dave would be waiting for us, waiting, like his idol Johnny Carson did all those years, to put us out with a smile on our face.

And then — it is hard to say when, really — Dave became unhappy. Not grumpy; we'd seen grumpy at 12:30, and it was enticing in its own way. No, this was unhappiness: with losing the late-night derby to an inferior talent, with subpar material fed to him by his writers, with studio audiences whose endless adulation he could not accept. He began shouting his monologues, racing through the comedy like a ninth-inning closer. Though he and his handlers would later blame CBS for driving viewers away, the truth is that millions who once eagerly awaited the *Late Show* opening sequence were now checking to see what was on *Nightline* first, even — egads! — eavesdropping on Jay Leno.

Letterman must have realized that, too, for recently he made a change that many say was calculated to restore some of the lightness and simple pleasure of those first two seasons on CBS. He fired his longtime showrunner, Robert Morton, and replaced him with thirty-three-year-old Rob Burnett, the point man for comedy on the show for the past four years.

In my recent visit to the Ed Sullivan Theater, Letterman's easygoing lieutenant from New Jersey spelled out what it would take to dispel his boss's on-air angst and remind us all of why he wanted Carson's job in the first place. Burnett said his top priority — indeed, his only priority — was coming up with the "smartest, funniest stuff on the air," which in turn would "give Dave the confidence of really strong material so he can relax and perform the way he can perform." He was less concerned about the show's weak monologues, which are not his specialty, and the crushing five-day-a-week taping schedule, which even he had to admit was the mortal foe of quality comedy. Burnett is more concerned with supplying Letterman with solid pretaped fodder and grade-A desk material — "situations where Dave can be Dave," as he puts it. But letting Dave be Dave may simply not be enough, no matter how big of a cushion he is given, as Burnett learned during a broadcast taped not three weeks into his tenure.

The date was Friday, March 29. Burnett was optimistic. He had weathered a storm of criticism that followed his appointment as executive producer, replacing Morton, a man that (as Burnett discovered) had excellent relations with the New York media. And tonight he had the perfect reply to all the naysayers: the first big Friday extravaganza under his wing was about to get underway. First, the show had scored a booking coup when the actor Kevin Spacey, who had won an Academy Award earlier in the week, agreed to read a Top Ten list via satellite from the West Coast. Then there was a brilliant pretaped segment — Burnett's calling card were these tightly-edited, often highly creative video pieces — where Letterman hit the town with his "friend for a day," a middle-aged fellow named Al. Finally, there would be a hilarious candid-camera feature shown in several installments featuring the Late Show announcer, Alan Kalter, playing a weirdo in an elevator with unsuspecting riders. Even after 2,000-plus tapings, this could well be a Letterman show to remember.

And it was — but not for the reasons Burnett had been counting on. The show hit a glitch after the monologue, when Dave decided he wanted to re-tape his introduction to the "friend for a day" bit. The show's relatively new director, Jerry Foley, would simply make an edit after the taping, re-inserting the second version in place of the original. Next, Dana Carvey was to do an unadvertised walk-on. It too was done over, when an extra used in the walk-on did not enter quickly enough for the host's liking. Then the satellite hookup to Spacey failed. When the Late Show band apparently missed its cue following an interview segment with guest Nick Turturro, Letterman became visibly irked. "What's the deal?" he yelled at his bandleader, Paul Shaffer, who avoided eye contact with the host.

Next, he introduced the first part of Kalter's "weird guy" routine. But when the video did not begin in a timely manner, Dave stopped the taping again and redid the intro, although not before commenting, to no one in particular, that the air conditioning must have been cut off to the control room. As Letterman's mood grew darker, his actions became more severe. In a highly unusual move, he decided that the Turturro segment would be redone in its entirety. As his guest settled back into the chair beside him, Letterman asked, "So, when was the last time you were with us?"

"About ten minutes ago!" said a dumbfounded Turturro. "What the hell's going on?"

Next, the two men rehearsed the same anecdote Turturro told in the original segment — with Letterman supplying many of the details himself. Next, it was time to introduce part two of Kalter-in-the-elevator. Again, Foley's crew failed to deliver the video on cue. Letterman leapt up angrily from his desk and yelled, "What do I have to do to get the tape rolling?" The tape rolled again — but this time it was Dave who missed his cue. That did it: Letterman looked into the camera and aimed both of his middle fingers at it. Presumably they were aimed at his director.

In all, miscues forced at least seven interruptions to that evening's taping, and the disbelieving audience did not get out until after 7:15, more than forty-five minutes longer than a normal session. Afterward, the host reportedly stormed down to the control room to confront Foley, whom some thought would be fired on the spot. In fact, he was not, and has since survived other sessions which also went deeply into overtime.

At an outfit which had always thrived on creative tension, the tensions were now threatening to eclipse the creativity. Burnett's comedy staff had turned out two innovative and genuinely funny pieces of video for the program — only to stand by helplessly as the moody and perfectionistic Letterman found some other reason to send this broadcast into the abyss. The show would survive another night; the comedy would still shine, thanks to the miracle of editing. But even the upbeat Burnett must have wondered: Had things just gone from bad to worse?

It is worth bearing in mind that this creative *frisson* has existed throughout Letterman's run on national television. It was, in fact, a slump four years ago, very similar to the current one, that led to the selection of Burnett as the show's new head writer, replacing Steve O'Donnell, who had held that position for nearly nine years. "If it weren't for Dave, I'd be funniest guy working at the car wash, or maybe the second funniest, depending on who was on duty that day," Burnett told me as we sat in his nearly empty showrunner's office, which at the time of our interview he had occupied for all of two days.

Burnett's next promotion made him writer in charge of pretaped segments. "I just loved these from beginning to end," he said. "They're the most sustained piece of complete comedy we do." The procedure for taping these segments has not changed much in 16 years: A writer presents Letterman with a concept for the piece, and then they, along with a producer and crew, go out on a shoot lasting several hours. Letterman is a hands-on participant, supplying ad libs and adding new scenes as he feels inspired. Later, the videotape is shortened to a rough cut of ten or so minutes, and Letterman assists in editing that down to broadcast length. The process is, according to Burnett, "the perfect melding of the writers and Dave."

By the time Burnett became head writer in 1992, Letterman was beginning to shift the show's humor away from the inventive comedy of the O'Donnell years and toward a style he believed would have greater mass appeal. "When we were on at 12:30, there was a certain kind of joke you could do, where you didn't worry about what kind of laugh you got, that remained pure to your own sensibility," Burnett said. At the same time, the late-night host was striving to leave behind his old caustic persona and replace it with one that was more user-friendly, more like that of his idol, Johnny Carson. The buzzword became *accessibility*: proving that the 12:30 host NBC had spurned could put on an 11:30 show, and that the network had erred gravely in casting its lot with Jay Leno.

In the winter of 1994, when *Late Show* was achieving its high-water mark in the ratings and among reviewers, the program's triumphant writing staff was invited to the Museum of Television and Radio to lead a seminar discussing their work and attempt to explain the reasons behind their phenomenal success. One writer, Bill Scheft, cited Letterman's background as a television broadcaster as a point in his favor. "I think that Dave knows the medium he's working in and is more experienced in it than Jay," he said. Another, Gerard Mulligan, was more candid: "At least for the moment," he said, "Dave has a sensibility that people seem to enjoy better than Jay's." Indeed, one can choose a broadcast, any broadcast, from either Letterman's last season at NBC or his first season at CBS, and the contrast between then and now becomes apparent immediately. Back then, he exuded on camera what could best be described as a quiet confidence. His monologue delivery was full-throated but not overpowering; the pacing of jokes steady but not rushed. Overall, his demeanor was bright and spirited, like some of the details of the Broadway-inspired stage that his staff built for him at the Ed Sullivan Theater. By the time Johnny Carson agreed to make two cameo appearances during Letterman's celebrated visit to Los Angeles two years ago, few could argue with the comparisons being made to the once and former king of late night.

But when the point was brought up with Burnett and stated in its converse form — that Leno is triumphing in the ratings because

Letterman's sensibility is no longer preferred by those viewers who once embraced it — the new showrunner bristled. "When we first came over to CBS, I remember it being explained to me very carefully by people who know these things that there was no possible way we could beat the *Tonight Show* for the first year we were on the air," said Burnett. "Of course that's not what happened and we had this incredible fireball. The press was unbelieveable, everything Dave did was incredible. He was on every magazine cover. It grew and grew and grew. Now, interestingly enough, we are sort of where we were expected to be all along. In fact, we still receive ratings bonuses from CBS." He added: "I'm completely confident that if we put this show on NBC and you put [Leno's] show on CBS, these numbers are completely changed."

But would the shows be completely changed? Here Burnett appeared to concede a point. "I think there was a time when the comedy slipped a bit and we got away from putting Dave in situations where Dave can be Dave. And it's difficult to come up with good ideas all the time, but it's possible. We got into a position where I think Dave was being forced to do comedy that was not of him. If there's a big picture, it's not anything visionary, it's more of a return to that thing. Tighten the stuff up, get the smartest, funniest stuff on the air, give Dave the confidence of really strong material so he can relax and perform the way he can perform."

At the request of his interviewer, Burnett selected a recent broadcast which appeared in many ways to confirm his points. It happened to be his second Friday night as producer, a broadcast that became known as "hypnosis night," in which members of the *Late Show* staff performed offbeat tricks while under hypnosis, such as laughing hysterically every time Letterman mentioned his salary. At one point, the host himself accidentally put two of his staffers, who had been hypnotized earlier in the day, into a deep sleep, requiring a call to the hypnotist in Las Vegas to supply the antidote. This was followed by two strong segments with David Hyde Pierce and Scott Thompson. Burnett concluded, "This is a show that seems just about perfect to me, and then something super-spontaneous and unexpected happens on top of that."

Still, there was a seam showing even in this broadcast: the

monologue. When Letterman came to CBS, he insisted on doubling the number of opening jokes he performed. Unexceptional even during the wondrous first season, his standup now seems but a poor imitation of the *Tonight Show* monologue delivered by Leno. On this night, Letterman used the monologue to declare himself "the

most powerful man in American broadcasting" for what seemed the hundredth night in a row. Burnett said, "I have no idea what that means, but it makes me laugh." That was followed by, "Ladies and gentlemen, how about this million-dollar haircut?" — a line he would repeat twice more, each time to peals of applause from his always suggestible audience — before racing through an unfunny collection of topical jokes: "My weekend plans are shot. I was supposed to play golf with the Unabomber ... He was turned in by his brother, the Unasquealer ... Hard to believe this guy was a troubled loner, wasn't it?" Burnett, correctly perceiving that I did not share his amusement, backpedaled slightly. "The monologue to me is always the monologue," he said. "It's never really been my favorite part of the show." The problem seems to come when Dave tries to out-Leno Jay, as evidenced by the nightly onslaught of "How 'bout that Unabomber!" jokes. Various reasons for this are offered, but the most plausible appears to be that Leno does one, so he should do one. Even more likely: if Johnny did one, so must he.

But when the monologue bombs, Letterman can come positively unglued on the air, channeling his broadcaster's angst directly to his viewers. This was most evident during a desk bit on April 11, 1996, when Letterman took a five-foot-tall stuffed dummy — fashioned in his likeness for a viewer-mail gag — and unexpectedly began punching it in the head with great relish. The audience cheered lustily at first, but as he kept wailing away, abusing his own image, the cheers died down. By the end of this bizarre outburst, only the sound of Anton Fig's cymbals punctuating each blow was heard in the Ed Sullivan Theater.

1997

The late-night wars finally subsided, by decree of Jay Leno, and I found myself in unfamiliar territory. It wasn't just the new town, nor the wide-open beat at the *Star*, where I was expected to cover local as well as national television, prime time as well as late night. I was ready for all that. What I was not prepared for were the bewildering customs and overwhelming demands of daily print journalism. To be sure, the job still involved putting one sentence in front of the other, but I had never confronted such a ravenous beast as the morning paper. My 180 bylines that first year exceeded the previous three years' output combined (and would prove to be my *least* productive twelve-month period at the *Star*, including the year I had cancer).

Between the constant clamor for stories, and the learning curve that seemed to extend out into infinity, I often felt I had no time to think — and to my embarrassment, I sometimes didn't. ("Because of a reporter's error, a story about educational TV programs misidentified Jonathan Zimmerman, assistant professor of educational history at New York University, as Jonathan Silverman."). Even when I wasn't producing my monthly correction on page two, I would often pick up the newspaper and read, to my horror, something truly silly under my byline (like when I referred to "the long-running PBS series *Antiques Roadshow*," which had been on the air all of eight months).

I was meeting deadlines and churning out copy like a healthy worker bee, but the inquisitive enthusiasm of the *Late Show News* and freelance years was not translating to print. For the first time since I started writing about television, I was struggling to find my voice. An NPR producer asked more than once if I would contribute commentaries to *All Things Considered,* and finally I had to tell her no. The effort of digging up little facts and building them into little articles — something my coworkers had been doing since they were stringers in high school — ate up every ounce of mental energy I had. The fact that I was not a local didn't help, either. ("Because of a reporter's error, an article described St. Louis as the largest city in Missouri. St. Louis is second-largest, behind Kansas City.") But I survived.

Meanwhile, the abysmal *Suddenly Susan* edged out *Friends* as the third most-watched TV show in the country, behind *ER* and *Seinfeld.*

Ellen DeGeneres' sitcom character followed the real Ellen's lead by coming out of the closet. Princess Diana died, triggering a 24-hour news narrative of global proportions. Tiger Woods won the Masters and set off a Tiger Woods media frenzy that was not equaled until … well, you know. Talk show barker Jerry Springer gave two commentaries on a Chicago TV newscast, and the station's two top anchors quit in protest. Good trade!

Norm!

Late Show News, April 14, 1997

It was such a fine week for Norm Macdonald that when Saturday rolled around and he, in his "Weekend Update" fake news anchor role, let the F word slip on live television, you knew that nothing but good would come from it. The f(a)ux pas was nearly imperceptible, but Norm knew he'd said it, as did some in the studio audience, prompting him to offer an improvised signoff: "Tune in next week to see if I'm still here!" Unlike his predecessor Kevin Nealon, Macdonald inspires strong emotions, mostly positive. *SNL* watchers credit him with spicing up an otherwise predictable season, not just on "Update" but with two bona fide hit characters he created and which paid huge dividends this week. His Bob Dole impersonation got him invited to entertain the White House Correspondents' Dinner on Thursday. And his stunning take on David Letterman's ten most annoying on-air tics earned him a just-as-stunning invite to *Late Show* on Tuesday, where the host treated him as he might an official biographer. At the correspondents' dinner, Macdonald's joke about a news producer who got so drunk at a party, he "actually wound up having sex with his own wife," seemed to cut a little close to the bone. But his trifecta of punchlines about "the most powerful man in Washington … Alan Greenspan," brought down the house, especially the one about Greenspan's recent honeymoon south of the border with his bride, NBC's Andrea Mitchell. As a wedding gift to Mitchell, Macdonald joked, Greenspan devalued the Mexican peso.

This night in history

Kansas City Star, July 28, 1997

Fifteen years ago, on July 28, 1982, David Letterman put on a talk show and a wrestling match broke out. Andy Kaufman, a singular figure in entertainment whose antics both on and off the tube were already legendary, struck a blow for performance art, or rather took one, when he was clobbered by pro wrestler Jerry Lawler during a taping of Letterman's new late-night talk show on NBC. On the same date in 1987, Letterman himself was in the line of fire as a segment with the actor Crispin Glover disintegrated into a kicking exhibition, with one foot coming very near Dave's pricey head. We will likely never know whether these incidents were staged or spontaneous. Kaufman is dead and the other three might not be interested in telling the whole truth. Few things in life are more contrived than a television broadcast, and even in his freewheeling NBC years, Letterman and his crew ran a ship as locked down as any. It is easy to dismiss these as staged "incidents," choreographed to perfection. But here's the funny thing — once the cameras roll, no one is entirely in control of a live-to-tape show, and there is rarely the chance to go back and do it over. If people go even slightly off-script, things can get out of hand quickly, and there is no more effective or compelling theater.

Diana: A sad day ... for TV news

Kansas City Star, September 3, 1997

In the hours following word of Princess Diana's car accident, television relayed accounts that would later be contradicted and instant news analysis that would prove worthless. When word arrived that some paparazzi on motorcycles had been arrested at the crash scene, the electronic media helped concentrate the world's grief and anger onto a convenient target. NBC's Keith Miller in London told anchor Brian Williams that when people "wake up to find out Diana has died tragically in a car accident in Paris pursued by photographers, this nation is going to be shocked and I think angry, Brian." And so it went for more than a day — until details arrived about the driver of the Mercedes, whose blood alcohol level had been three times that allowed by French law and had been driving 120 mph in a 30 mph zone. One would think that in light of recent live TV newsgathering blunders, there might have been more restraint this time around. Two years ago, in the hours after the bombing of the Murrah Federal Building in Oklahoma City, reports of foreign terrorists ran rampant until Timothy McVeigh's arrest. Then there was last summer's media frenzy over the Centennial Park bombing in Atlanta. That proved expensive for news organizations like NBC, which reported Richard Jewell to be the likely suspect and later had to pay hefty settlements to him. One would also think that producers of live news could screen phone calls properly. But shortly after 9 p.m.

Saturday, a prankster kept CNN's Linden Soles on his hook for more than ten minutes before he finally yelled "Baba Booey!", a reference to Howard Stern's producer. The next morning, another caller passed himself off as *Newsweek* Paris bureau chief Christopher Dickey and told MSNBC's Williams that the last stop the princess and her boyfriend Dodi Fayed had made was to a video store to rent *Howard Stern's Private Parts*. Perhaps not surprisingly, the best coverage came from one of the few news outlets whose correspondents were not continually on camera. *60 Minutes* devoted its Sunday broadcast to Diana's death, a superb hour that featured interview subjects chosen for their knowledge, insight, and diverse points of view — and not because they happened to be available at the moment.

Dave, Jay, and Marv

Late Show News, October 7, 1997

Call a ceasefire in the late-night wars! Jay Leno has come to the defense of David Letterman. Since May, Leno has been regaling *Tonight Show* audiences with dozens of jokes about Marv Albert, the now-ex-NBC sportscaster whose sexual practices became the stuff of tabloids following his arrest and trial on forcible sodomy charges. Meanwhile, Letterman has refused to make his friend and frequent guest the butt of even a single joke. Yet it is the loyal Letterman, not the opportunistic Leno, who is being judged harshly. After all, say the pundits, Dave was willing to joke about O.J., Paula Jones and Frank Gifford — why is he giving Marv a pass? *Time* magazine printed a "Harper's Index"-styled comparison of the number of Albert jokes Letterman had told (zero), with the number of appearances Albert made on the *Late Show* (an estimated 100). One person who hadn't been heard from was Leno, so I called him in Burbank for his take. "Dave did exactly the right thing," he told me. "If it were Jerry Seinfeld or a close friend of mine, I wouldn't make jokes about him either." Marv Albert jokes have proven to be such crowd pleasers for Leno that NBC is now using them in promotional ads for the *Tonight Show*. So clearly they're giving Leno an edge. Still, he thinks the whole thing has been blown out of proportion by a news media can't let go of the idea that Jay and Dave are locked in mortal combat. As Leno likes to point out, both men have contract extensions through 2001 and make truckloads of money for their networks. "I don't know if I should be flattered or annoyed that this is still a story six years later," he said.

'I have a right to be here'

Digital Diner, Winter 1997 (unpublished)

One of my last freelance pieces was this profile of Conan O'Brien. It was supposed to run in 1997 as the cover story for the second issue of a new magazine ... that went out of business after the first issue.

They say Conan O'Brien has finally begun to mellow. Calmed down. Taken a chill pill. They — that is, the TV critics who wrote off *Late Night with Conan O'Brien* in 1993, shortly after it stumbled onto the airwaves — they say there's a new man on at 12:30 a.m., a man more sure of himself, more polished on the air. What the critics are saying, in other words, is that since he took over for David Letterman at NBC, Conan has gotten to be more like Dave. And while this probably says as much about the critics as it does the host, the salient fact is that *Late Night's* ratings have, finally, become Lettermanesque again. The show's viewership dropped by half during O'Brien's first year on the air, but now it's nearly back to the old levels. NBC is expected soon to sign O'Brien to his first multiyear contract, ending all speculation about who is the true heir to the *Late Night* throne.

Five minutes before every taping, Studio 6A at NBC's 30 Rockefeller Center suddenly receives a blast of kinetic energy as the host is played out by his raucously retro house band, the Max Weinberg 7. The tune is always the same — "Burning Love" — and the routine never changes. O'Brien bolts into the audience at full tilt with a handheld mike, grabs a female audience member at random and serenades her with terrifying intensity as the woman blushes. It's a weirdly riveting performance, and always seems to drive the crowd wild. Later, O'Brien explains that it's a courage-building exercise. "If I can go out there in the warmup and do something *completely* that Jay would not do, that Dave would not do — if I go hang myself out to dry like that, then I don't care whether they laugh at the monologue, or completely buy the desk piece," he tells me. "It's my chance to walk out without my clothes on."

O'Brien graduated with honors from Harvard, where he edited the *Lampoon* for two years, and had a stint writing sketches for *SNL* with Robert Smigel before joining *The Simpsons* as a writer and producer in 1991. His talent for packing dozens of pop-culture references into episodes became legendary, even by the standards of that show. So did his ability in meetings to get his fellow writers — arguably the toughest of tough crowds — laughing hysterically. By 1993 Fox was ready to pay him seven figures to produce *The Simpsons*, but he balked. "I always felt like, if I could just get out there and be this Conan O'Brien guy that I am in the writers' room, that I am with my friends, that I am in improv sessions at times — if I could just do that, I had this conviction that people would like it," he says. "And if you have that idea, you can't let it go."

As it happened, at that moment *Late Night* was desperately seeking a new host. The biggest names, Garry Shandling and Dana Carvey, had taken themselves out of the running, and as Rick Ludwin, the NBC executive who oversees late night, recalls, it became clear that "the person who got that job would be somebody with nothing to lose." Fortunately, Lorne Michaels, the *SNL* godfather, had found such a person.

Less than 48 hours before NBC was supposed to unveil its choice, Conan O'Brien did his first tryout show for the network. It was a home run. Jeff Ross, the former *Kids in the Hall* producer Michaels had assigned to produce the tryout, approached him during a break. "He said to me, 'You're *killing*,'" O'Brien recalls. "I probably wasn't that funny again for two months." Ludwin says that after the tryout, "Conan leaped to the top of the list."

O'Brien also scored with critics and viewers with his debut broadcast on NBC. After that, however, it went downhill fast. Conan's incessant giggling, horrid ad-libbing, constant sipping from the General Eisenhower mug, and learn-as-you-go interview style conspired to drive away fans of *Late Night with Dave*. After three weeks, the country's leading television critic, Tom Shales, had had enough. "Go Gently Into That Good Night, Already," read the headline of his kiss-off piece in the *Washington Post*.

O'Brien was advised against reading any press during the show's first six months. "There was a part of me that somehow expected it," said Ross, who became the showrunner at *Late Night*. "No matter what we did, we were going to get the shit kicked out of us for a while." One critic even complained that the show had been taken over by "another tall, Waspy male" hired from "the same pool of ex-Harvard *Lampoon* staff members" — a weird observation given that O'Brien hailed from a large *Catholic* family and all but one of his writers hailed from non-Ivy League schools. (Andy Richter, his sidekick, went to Chicago's Columbia College.)

The pummeling NBC took contrasted sharply with the hosannas showered on Letterman and his new program at CBS. It was as though in order for Dave to succeed, his replacement had to fail horribly. So powerful was the spell Letterman had cast over the 12:30 time slot that it seemed only he could break it. Miraculously, that's just what happened on February 28, 1994, when Letterman accepted an invite to return to his old broadcast studio and be a guest on *Late Night*. Less than two minutes after sitting down, he interrupted the clearly nervous host and put his cards on the table. "You guys do an incredible amount of comedy," declared Dave, "and the volume and the quality of the stuff just knocks me out. There's nothing like this show on television and I really, really appreciate that." The crowd burst into applause. "That was a seismic event," Conan says. "Dave came back and said, 'Whatever bad blood there is at the network, whatever crap went down with NBC, CBS, the

Tonight Show, Jay Leno — it doesn't have anything to do with this guy.' I remember thinking after that show was over that if David Letterman thinks we have a right to be here, then *I'm* going to start acting like I have a right to be here."

While it would take several months for the press to come to agree with Dave, *Late Night* found a beachhead in the rapidly growing domain of cyberspace. A group of the show's original devotees starting posting messages to the newsgroup alt.fan.conan-obrien. A young journalist named Allison Bell was working at a Florida newspaper when she joined the fans of *Late Night* on the Net. "I immediately liked Conan because I thought he was doing the show the way I'd do it," she tells me. "He had a literary approach to doing comedy on TV, not literary in the sense of flowery or anything, but trying to filter life through language without being stuffy or snotty." A fan who identifies himself simply as Damone is a fixture on the newsgroup. He started watching *Late Night* for the cutting-edge musical guests; only later did he start noticing the comedy. "I said to myself: *This isn't a Top Ten list I've seen done a thousand times before. This isn't whatever the hell Leno was doing back then*," he tells me by email. "I had no idea what the critics were talking about."

O'Brien says he monitored the alt.fan.conan-obrien newsgroup from the get-go. "It was high school and college students," he says. "They were looking for the *thing* to make their own. They're at that age where they're like, 'Well, what's my thing gonna be?' They were actually very willing to give me the benefit of the doubt."

Forty of the alt.fan.conan-obrien faithful decided to visit New York and take in a taping together — they called it a "Cone-Con." The show's staff, alerted to this fanfest happening in their midst, responded by serving the group pizza and beer on the stage of 6A after the taping. The writers even worked Allison Bell's name into a sketch. "The one law of sanity is that the TV show doesn't talk to us," she said afterward. "And here it did. We'd climbed into the TV show."

1998

If you were Matt Drudge, the *National Enquirer*, or me, 1998 was a better year than 1997. If you were the President of the United States, Keith Olbermann, or Monica Lewinsky, it was worse, much worse. I published my first book, *Barnhart's Unauthorized TV '98,* which got a very nice writeup in *Advertising Age* for "laying bare to average folk the arcane, raveled processes of network programming and agency time-buying." Basically, I explained why shows like *Dawson's Creek* on the WB — a network almost nobody over the age of 40 watched — were considered huge hits.

Seinfeld signed off in May, having edged out *ER* for the ratings crown. They would be the last two shows to average better than a 20 rating in the Nielsens, a dozen years after *The Cosby Show* was the last to achieve a 30 rating. For two weeks in the summer, more people watched cable for two weeks in the summer than were watching network TV — a milestone in viewer choice. Yet network costs kept climbing, epitomized by the ridiculous amounts NBC paid for future seasons of *ER* ($13 million an *episode*) and the prolongation of the unfunny *Mad About You* (a million per episode apiece for Paul Reiser and Helen Hunt). Fred Silverman, the former network chief, declared that the TV business was "moving toward disaster." Tom Snyder moved toward the exit, for the last time, and the *Late Late Show* was handed to Craig Kilborn, who ceded his *Daily Show* chair to Jon Stewart.

Our national outrage: Norm fired

Late Show News, January 13, 1998

My first clue that something strange was going down at 30 Rock was a fax Wednesday afternoon informing me, in the brightest tone possible, that Colin Quinn was replacing Norm Macdonald as anchor of *SNL's* "Weekend Update" — no explanation offered. NBC West Coast president Don Ohlmeyer informed Macdonald that "Weekend Update" wasn't funny and he was taking him off of it. Ohlmeyer later told the trades that viewership among the frat boys and acne victims who are *SNL's* core audience always drop when "Weekend Update" comes on. And we all know why: Norm is too smart for that audience. Dennis Miller, another former fake-news reader on the show, denounced Ohlmeyer. Chevy Chase was quoted by *TV Guide* saying NBC had screwed up. Howard Stern brought in Macdonald and called him the "shining light" of *SNL*. He read a fax from a listener claiming that Ohlmeyer fired both Macdonald and his segment producer because Norm continued to do jokes about Ohlmeyer's buddy O.J. Simpson. David Letterman told Macdonald on his show, "I'll tell you who's taking your place — *nobody* can take your place." And that proved painfully true when Colin Quinn slid into the fake anchor seat. He had good material, but his delivery was inept. Ad libs? Forget it. The funniest part was when Will Ferrell, doing his addle-brained Harry Caray routine, repeatedly called Quinn "Norm."

Mr. Springer's Neighborhood
Kansas City Star, April 25, 1998

Seven weeks ago Oprah Winfrey's show was knocked out of first place in the daytime TV ratings by Jerry Springer's syndicated hair-pulling, name-calling trailer trash circus. That's because each day kids all over the country come home from school and join in the national chorus of "Jer-ry! Jer-ry!" It's a development parents no doubt rue — but because they're at work, there's not much they can do about it. This week I had the opportunity to conduct some in-depth market research on the Springer phenomenon, thanks to Take Our Daughters to Work Day. My office was a stopping point for nine girls, ages 12 to 15, and after they finished asking me questions like "Do you watch TV all day?" and "What are all the videotapes for?", it was my turn. How many of you watch *Jerry Springer*? Eight out of nine hands went up. How many of your parents don't want you to watch *Jerry Springer*? Half of the hands stayed up. Locally, where *Springer* airs at 3 p.m., ratings are up an astounding 106 percent from last year. That sends ripples through Channel 9's late-afternoon lineup, including *Oprah* at 4 p.m., whose ratings are up 26 percent. Not only is Springer watched by more Kansas Citians, if it weren't for his carry-over audience, the gap between his show and Oprah's wouldn't even be close. Channel 9 sent reporter Kris Ketz to Chicago to file a two-part "news story" on the Springer phenomenon. According to a statement the station gave Ketz to read in his report, "Channel 9 does not program that part of the day for children." Right.

Lessons of *The Truman Show*

Kansas City Star, June 11, 1998

The Truman Show, director Peter Weir's unsettling fable about a society obsessed with TV, stands apart from earlier films of its genre, like *A Face in the Crowd* and *Network*, which suggested that Americans would let a mad prophet or a folksy Arthur Godfrey-type tell them what to do. Weir makes no such claim about Truman Burbank, Jim Carrey's cheerful innocent whose  life, unbeknownst to him, has been televised since birth. He lives in Seahaven, a hermetically sealed community staffed with hundreds of extras and monitored by thousands of hidden cameras — all arranged around Truman and his every step, and watched 24/7 by millions of viewers worldwide.

Thanks to the movie's light touch, the creepiness of Seahaven never begins to approach that of Stepford. When a klieg light comes crashing down from the heavens just a few yards from Truman's driveway, the local media spend the next 24 hours hilariously explaining it away. Truman's wife and "best friend" are also on hand to concoct fabulous lies whenever the star of the show has the slightest inkling about the vast conspiracy around him.

Truman Burbank occupies a media cocoon compared with his audience. They no longer live in the world of limited choice that was the context for Paddy Chayefsky's sinister media prophecy *Network.* Rather, *The Truman Show* is making a subtler, but no less disturbing point: that with all the things there are to watch, every moment we spend taking in mediated reality subtracts something from our own lives.

The trouble with access

Kansas City Star, September 11, 1998

When Time Warner Cable took over the old TeleCable operation in suburban Kansas City, few people seemed to notice or care that it shut down Channel 15B, the last place where members of the community could learn to produce television shows. Public access — television by the viewers, for the viewers — was a big deal both locally and nationally in the 1970s and '80s. Hundreds of volunteers learned to operate cameras, run control boards, and edit video, not only at TeleCable's studio but at American Cablevision's  $275,000 public access facility in Kansas City. They created shows that made a point rather than a profit, with unpretentious titles like *The Elderly, Getting Help,* and *Women in Jazz.* The idea was that TV, once the great isolator of Americans, might be used to knit communities together. Cyd Slayton, who started up American Cablevision's public access channel in 1980, remembers staying up countless nights with producers, shooting and editing tape. "These volunteers were so excited about the ability to raise community issues on television, without pay, without even recognition," Slayton says.

But the novelty began to wear off. Interest in American Cablevision's channel had faded 10 years ago when the Klan showed up, wanting to do a show. Then-councilman Emanuel Cleaver led a charge to take the channel off the air. As mayor, Cleaver saw to it that public access was written out of the city's cable franchise.

Meanwhile, in Salina, Kansas, a city of 43,000 two hours west, public access is more than an experiment in cable. It's the one TV station residents can call their own. Access Salina airs at least seven hours of programs every night. More than 100 volunteers this year will produce hundreds of hours of new shows. On a Wednesday evening you might find Eloise Lynch and her crew of seniors doing a live broadcast. Her program, "Oh Say," is the kind of community-service talk show a typical commercial TV station would hide in some early-Sunday-morning time slot. On Access Salina, it airs in prime time.

It's easy to point to the disparity between media-rich Kansas City and media-thin Salina, but the most crucial difference between the two towns is organizational. Kansas City's public access facility was owned by the cable company, which was compelled by city charter to set it up. The people now running American Cablevision aren't going to miss public access. "I liken it to the Internet," says Carol Rothwell, the company's longtime spokesman. "People get so excited — 'Oh, let's get on the Web, let's get email.' Then they get bored and move onto something else. The idea had its time, but that was in the '70s."

Salina, like many cities with successful public access, set up a nonprofit entity to run its channel. Access Salina doesn't take the heat when there is a cable outage or rates go up. And since it essentially acts like any other nonprofit arts group, recruiting actively in the community and building good will, it has been able to weather the storms caused by controversial content. That didn't happen here. After the City Council voted to kill public access, Mayor Cleaver declared that Kansas City had put itself "on a mountain of visibility because we dare to say 'no.'"

He was right. To this day the tale of American Cablevision is taught in public access training seminars across the country as a case study of what not to do. "It wasn't the Klan that was the problem. It was the well-meaning councilmen who are African-Americans like me," says Anthony Riddle, who directs New York City's vast public access facility. "You don't want to stop the Ku Klux Klan from speaking. You want to stop them from setting up paramilitary camps in the woods."

1999

A year of upheavals began in February, when I decided to close down *Late Show News*. It was time to start publishing on the Web and become a full-fledged online television critic-type journalist ... something. (The word "blogger" hadn't been invented yet.) On Feb. 17, *LSN* gave way to TV Barn.

The DVD revolution finally took off as consumers lopped off the head of its rival, DIVX. This idiotic format, promoted by the store chain that owned it (Circuit City, now deceased), made discs unplayable after 48 hours. With DIVX gone, people began buying home theaters — not to watch the handful of HDTV channels but to enjoy their rapidly growing DVD libraries.

Television's quality revolution began with the arrival of *The West Wing* on NBC and *The Sopranos* on HBO. Among the crowd-pleasers, *ER, Friends* and *Frasier* finished win-place-show in the Nielsens for the season ending in May. On August 16, ABC — which, like all the networks, was eager to get viewers to stop switching away during the rerun-heavy summer months — launched a game show that had done well overseas, called *Who Wants To Be a Millionaire*. By November it had become a ratings bonanza and started the homesteading of American prime time by a new generation of low-cost, high-concept reality TV shows.

Stewart to Daily ...

Late Show News, January 12, 1999

The new host of *The Daily Show* called out of the blue, and I'm guessing it had something to do with a report in *Variety* that *The Daily Show's* nightly rating was off by "a sharp 14 percent" since Jon Stewart took over for Craig Kilborn. Turns out, 14 percent is the difference between a 0.7 rating and a 0.6 — and Stewart just wanted somebody to know, preferably a friend in the media. And trust me, Stewart knows who his friends in the media are. When we were introduced at a taping of *Politically Incorrect* in 1996, he amazed me by instantly recalling something nice I'd written a year earlier about his syndicated *Jon Stewart Show*. So, how does it feel doing nightly TV again? "The main focus for the first couple of months was to get the fat guy in shape, which was me," said Stewart. "I didn't want to give people any chance to do anything but focus on the content. You know — 'Do I wear the overalls, or the suit, or the porkpie hat?' You don't want people saying after the first week, 'I cannot stand the overalls.'" We talked about what it was like having to look for new sources of comedy since the Monica Lewinsky well ran dry. "We're probably still suffering from the same kind of thing MSNBC is — you lost your best girl to college," said Stewart. "She was the first thing I saw in the morning and the last thing I saw at night. I miss her, Aaron." Stewart hasn't begun to put his fingerprints on the show yet, but he promised me that would change. "The elections are going to be the next big thing," he told me, "and we're going to try to do some interesting things with it."

... Craiggers to CBS

Late Show News, February 9, 1999

And now Craig Kilborn is on the phone. He's getting ready to take over for Tom Snyder as host of the *Late Late Show.* Tell us about the studio, Craig. "It's the same studio," he promises. "They knocked down a wall." Oh, so it *isn't* the same studio. Actually, it would have been hard setting up five folding chairs in the shoebox Snyder uses. Kilborn's studio, which is being designed by David Letterman's one and only set designer Kathleen Ankers, will hold no more than ninety audience members. "The scariest thing is, they're listening to me on too many ideas." Such as? "I don't want that many lights in the background. I want the moon to be prominent." So, more noirish than Tom's set. "Actually," he adds, "the set I really want is the old *Fernwood 2Night.*" How will you open the show? "We'll do some comedy up front. We're calling it a double monologue; we might do a thing at the top and a little bit later." What else can we expect? "Longer interviews." Longer? "Much as I enjoyed *The Daily Show,*" said Craiggers, "I'm not a big fan of the news parody. I felt really limited. Here I get to ad lib for the whole hour. It'll be a simpler show, sans the sidekick and the band. We'll have a musical guest on Friday. It'll all become clear once the show is underway."

To these dish owners, bigger is better

Electronic Media, May 10, 1999

Clyde Taylor is my kind of satellite-dish owner. He does not own one of those fru-fru, pizza-pie-pan DBS dishes. Oh no. Taylor's dish is a

12–foot supersaucer occupying the backyard of his Kansas City, Kansas, home. He bought the dish in 1985, just as the Kansas City Royals were making their run to a world championship. Rather than tune in the World Series on a local station, Taylor went straight to the network "wild feed," allowing him to watch the games without the commercials and even catch the occasional off-handed announcer's remark during the breaks. Comedian Harry Shearer has a web page full of such classic moments grabbed off his C-band dish: Dan Rather prattling on aimlessly during a commercial, Tom Brokaw taping a Sinatra death announcement months before the fact, Sam Donaldson and Diane Sawyer getting chemistry lessons from their producers, Mary Hart freaking out. While most people today subscribe to a DBS service like DirecTV or DISH, Taylor and Shearer are among the 1.8 million customers still using the old system, known as C-band. It's the ultimate channel surf. Taylor gets dozens of cable channels for free because their signals are unscrambled. Another 60 or so premium channels are unlocked by a subscription service costing just $30 a month. And hundreds more wild feeds are out there for the finding. But learning to navigate a C-band dish involves mastering a remote-controlled apparatus that even ardent dishheads admit is clunky and confusing. Given such obstacles, and the service required on these aging hulks, many C-band dish owners have begun to see the virtues of DBS. Since DirecTV went live in 1994, the ranks of big-dish owners have been been thinning out rapidly. You can probably find someone willing to let you have theirs, provided you haul it away. "I still love C-band," Shearer told me. "As I explain to my friends whenever they let me, it boils down to this: Little dish is buying retail, big dish is buying wholesale. How were you brought up?" (*Postscript: Fewer than 100,000 people subscribed to satellite TV on C-band in 2008 — but it's still around. Many loyalists swear that C-band's uncompressed HDTV picture is the best.*)

TV's wrestling mania

Kansas City Star, August 26, 1999

For the first time in nearly 45 years, a weekly professional wrestling series will air in prime time on a broadcast network when *WWF Smackdown* debuts tonight on UPN, featuring matches taped Tuesday night at Kemper Arena. Pro wrestling has, of course, been a staple of cable TV since the 1980s, and before that it aired in syndication for decades. Going back even further, it was a Saturday-night staple of the DuMont network from 1949 to 1955, with famed Chicago announcer

Jack Brickhouse doing the blow-by-blow. But in recent years wrestling's popularity has soared. Rival leagues WWF and WCW have created spectacles with pyrotechnic displays, thundering music, outlandish characters involved in outrageous "story lines," and enthusiastic fans who know the stories and catch phrases of each character. And it's clear that a huge chunk of those fans are kids, a highly desirable demographic for the UPN network, which is coming off its worst season since it signed on four years ago. Young children were everywhere around Kemper Arena on Tuesday. Brian Johnson and Stephanie Swanson of Ottawa, Kansas, had come to the event at the urging of Swanson's eight-year-old son, Cody. Johnson told me that he doesn't watch wrestling, but he left work early so that the three would be sure to have tickets. Like hundreds of other fans, Cody had made several signs to hold up for the TV cameras, one for each of his favorite wrestlers. For his idol, "Stone Cold" Steve Austin, he chose blue construction paper with red glittery letters that spelled out STONE COLD 3:16 (a biblical reference that has become part of the Austin lore), and dotted the margins with catalog pictures of Austin's action figure. It was a placard the wrestling star would be proud to display on his refrigerator.

You're too old to be watching these shows

Kansas City Star, September 29, 1999

It's another pristine day at Jacqueline Kennedy High School in Pacific Palisades, California. Out on the quad, kids are tossing a football, eating at the outdoor cafeteria, looking out from a second-story railing toward the ocean. It's the kind of idyllic campus scene one might see on TV — which is only fitting, because you will. An actual high school situated in this tony beachside town, a short drive down Sunset from Beverly Hills, has been converted into the set of *Popular,* the quintessential program of the 1999-2000 TV season. Here, twentysomething actors pretend to be teenagers for a show that fortysomething TV executives will market to 12-to-34-year-olds. "Every year there's a particular trend, and this year it's this big blowout of Generation Y," says Ryan Murphy, the co-creator of *Popular.* "Everybody wants on that bandwagon." Indeed, five of the six networks rushed at least one program onto its fall schedule filled with peer-pressure storylines and moist intergender relations. Shows like *Roswell* (aliens mingle with teens), *Wasteland* (college grads in New York), *Safe Harbor* (single dad with teens), *Get Real* (kids struggle with school by day, parents by night), *Freaks and Geeks* (same deal, but in 1980) and *Manchester Prep* (title says it all). And, yes, *Popular,* which ironically may be the least pandering of the bunch but has taken the name that perfectly captures this acne-riddled trend. After all, who gets anywhere in life just by winning popularity contests? Answer: teen-agers and TV executives.

Andy Kaufman

Kansas City Star, December 21, 1999

It's nice to see Hollywood embrace Andy Kaufman now that he has been safely dead for 15 years. Perhaps even the American public — portions of which voted him off *Saturday Night Live* for good in a telephone poll in 1982 — will find a place in their hearts for him, or at least for Jim Carrey's version. With the release of *Man on the Moon,* the feature film based on Kaufman's life, the polarizing comedian has achieved show business immortality, and those stunts for which he was reviled toward the end of his life have been rediscovered as timeless treasures. The reviewer for *Entertainment Weekly* described Kaufman's obsession with wrestling women as "thrilling," although audiences at the time found it revolting and Kaufman couldn't get booked anywhere because of it. The same reviewer also called the lounge act of Tony Clifton, the foul-mouthed entertainer who was variously performed by Kaufman and an associate disguised as Kaufman, "fantastically abrasive" and "mesmerizing," though 20 years ago Tony was better known for driving people out of nightclubs with his verbal tirades. By the time of his death of lung cancer at 35, Kaufman had made himself unwelcome on every TV show but *Late Night with David Letterman.* His manager could not get producers to return his calls. Critics had written him off as tiresome and loony. That's all forgotten now, and the bizarro street theater that Kaufman indulged in, to his career's detriment, is now embraced as a kind of pure artistry. During the filming of *Man on the Moon,* Carrey reportedly continued to "be Andy" off-camera, making himself inscrutable to close friends, just as the master had once done. Well, tribute is something Jim Carrey can afford, having parlayed his shtick on a sketch-comedy show into $20 million paychecks as one of the most bankable movie actors of the 1990s. Kaufman, by contrast, was only able to land a role as a robot alongside Bernadette Peters in *Heartbeeps.*

C-SPAN stirs the pot on race

Kansas City Star, July 17, 1999

The trouble started a few minutes into the first hour of *American Presidents: Life Portraits,* the forty-one-part documentary series about the nation's chief executives that has been airing all year as part of C-SPAN's 20th anniversary celebration.

Brian Lamb, the sphinxlike founder of C-SPAN, had just introduced his guest, presidential historian Richard Norton Smith, and Smith had made a few opening comments about George Washington, in whose colonial home they were sitting.

Then Lamb went to the phones. A caller from Denver, identifying himself as "a descendant of slaves," launched into a tirade against the father of our country. "It is so easy for white people to get on TV and vouch about the character of people they did not know personally who would enslave a whole group of people," he said, his voice rising. "The United States of America *condoned* it, its institutions *supported* it, and until the government *apologizes* for it, in my mind I think Washington is *no better* than Adolf Hitler."

Without missing a beat, Lamb tossed to Smith for a reaction. "What you try to do," Smith began cautiously, "is not so much pass judgment but to turn the clock back and try not to apply the standards of our own time." Folding his arms across his chest, he continued, "This is not to justify the institution, but to try to understand a man of good will who was in many ways trapped in an institution not of his own making."

This scene has played itself out repeatedly on *American Presidents*: African-American callers pouring out their anguish and bitterness at the country's great white fathers, and on-camera experts offering responses ranging from apology to sympathy, usually to no one's satisfaction. "I would agree with the previous caller that most of the guests you have on have a rejoicing attitude toward the suffering of a race of people," said a Cleveland woman during the Millard Fillmore program. A caller from Seattle said, "They're telling us (these presidents) were opposed to slavery, but plainly they weren't." Other viewers were clearly frustrated by the fixation on race. "I enjoy this series very much, but as soon as slavery comes in, the next 45 minutes are devoted to slavery," someone in New Jersey complained during the Franklin Pierce program. To which Barry Paris, the historian on the air at the time, replied, "The reason it's coming up constantly is that it came up constantly throughout this period and obsessed the country."

Paris is one of the few biographers in the series so far to denounce his subject's views on slavery. "What I heard all of my life, and once bought into as a biographer, was that you can't judge a 19th-century person by 1999 standards," Paris told me later. "It's not true. You *do* judge people, not by 1999 standards, but by timeless, universal ethical standards. There were people in 1852 who knew that slavery was wrong."

Despite their criticisms of the presidents and of C-SPAN, many African-Americans are hooked on the series. Tom Feelings, an award-winning children's book illustrator, has phoned into *American Presidents* twice and is taping the three-hour programs. "You cannot get away from slavery if you talk about the presidents," Feelings said from Columbia, S.C. "That goes so far as Franklin Roosevelt, who refused to sign an anti-lynching bill."

So what does C-SPAN's Lamb think about the direction *American Presidents* has taken? "I love it," he said. "I love it when somebody calls in with something that upends everybody. I prefer that to bringing in my own agenda. This issue, which is very much an issue in our society today, has been the most talked-about thread in this series. And if a group of people in this country who are normally not heard from are exercising their opportunity to be heard here, that's great." *(Postscript:* American Presidents *won a Peabody Award.)*

Silencing B92

Electronic Media, July 19, 1999

It's said that in war the first casualty is the truth. That would certainly describe what happened last month to Radio B92 in Belgrade, Serbia's last remaining independent news source, after NATO warplanes began their bombing raids. B92 signed on in 1989, at about the time of Slobodan Milosevic's ascendancy, and has been a thorn in the dictator's side ever since. Twice before, Milosevic has tried to shut B92 down; twice it has returned to the air, the second time through an ingenious system that piped B92 programming out of Serbia via the Internet to the BBC, which beamed it back in. This time, though, in response to the bombing raids, authorities seized B92 and turned it into a propaganda arm of the state. Its editor-in-chief, Veran Matic (pictured), has left the country. The silencing of B92 ought to have sparked outrage among journalists in the U.S., particularly in the electronic media. Instead, CNN, MSNBC and Fox News have fixated on just two stories from the war-torn region: the bombing and the Kosovo refugee crisis. Irony of ironies, TV's craving for visuals has been a huge gift to the state-run Radio Television Serbia (RTS). Its filtered feed is used constantly as video source on American newscasts, resulting in hundreds of hours of free branding for RTS. It is true that American networks take care to point out that Milosevic controls RTS. But they aren't asking the obvious follow-up question: What happened to the *other* Serbian news outlets?

Under Matic, the station's 50 full-time and 120 part-time employees prided themselves on their anti-authoritarianism. (The station's cheeky slogan is, "Don't trust anyone, not even us.") But now, hated by the regime and shunned by the West, B92 is — as Matic ruefully noted to me, "in the most independent position possible." Although he has been urged by friends to stay out of the country, Matic is working with other B92 staffers to set up shop inside Serbia yet again. Considering he once circumvented a shutdown by reading the news over loudspeakers in the streets of Belgrade, one must assume Matic is weighing all of his options.

We met in New York on the day Matic addressed a panel marking the 50th anniversary of the United Nations human rights declaration. A compact and animated man, the thirty-seven-year-old Matic has spent 10 years staying one or two steps ahead of the henchmen who run Serbia, an experience that has refined his morose sense of humor. He recounted trying to cajole Westerners into helping him get the former Yugoslavia online in 1993. "People said the Internet was too sophisticated for us," he said. "They thought we needed tom-toms — *boom boom!* — to communicate with each other." Fortunately he persevered, and with the aid of a Dutch company B92 became Serbia's first Internet service provider.

Pre-shutdown, only about 30 percent of B92's broadcast day was devoted to news and information, the rest to alternative rock and other indigenous genres. Last year the station's popularity among young listeners was recognized with an award from MTV Europe. For Matic, the battle with tyranny is not simply one of truth over propaganda, but of local culture over imported crypto-culture and good taste over appallingly bad taste. "We support alternative youth culture that doesn't have any other outlet for its expression," Matic told me as we lurched toward the UN in a crosstown cab. "Progressive culture is always a threat to totalitarian regimes, which like to promote kitsch. In Yugoslavia the promotion of kitsch is monstrous. They base a great deal of their power on the promotion of kitsch: kitsch culture, kitsch TV, kitsch radio.

"For example, South American soap operas. They are extremely popular in Yugoslavia. And so is this so-called 'turbo folk music' — bad folk music with a techno beat and totally nonsensical, stupid verses. The people who are behind this music, even the authors of the lyrics, have very close ties to the regime. That's why this technology, the Internet, is so important, because it's exactly the opposite of kitsch culture. In the Internet, you always have a choice. You always have an opposite view." *(Postscript: Today B92 is the most-listened-to station in Serbia. But it is still harassed, and in 2008 its TV facility was nearly burned to the ground by pro-government mobs.)*

Remembering Gene Siskel

TV Barn, February 21, 1999

Gene Siskel had been reading me on the Internet for years, having been turned onto *Late Show News* by Roger Ebert. They were my two best-known readers, or at least that I knew of. At the NATPE trade show the year before, I cut into a photo line  to say hi, and they acted like a beloved cousin was paying them a rare visit. I wasn't there for a picture, but as you can see, I got one anyway. Later, Siskel mentioned in an email that he'd like to get together. So, during my next visit to Chicago, I called him up and he invited me to lunch and a screening with a few other people. I had to work on a story and missed our engagement, so I called Gene to apologize and offered to meet up the next time I was in town. He cut me off. "Where are you?" he said. I said I was just about to walk over to Barbara's, the city's largest independent bookseller, to hawk copies of my book, *Barnhart's Unauthorized TV '98*. Gene said, "I'll meet you there in ten minutes."

He walked into the bookstore in a blue hunting jacket and a funny hunter's hat. I wasn't sure at first it was him. But at six-foot-four he stood out like Saul, and once he took off the cap to reveal one of the best-known scalps in the city, everyone noticed.

I told him I was waiting for the book consigner to return from an errand. "When she does," Gene said in a conspiratorial voice, "here's what we'll do. You'll sell her some copies, then I'll go up to her and ask her to sell me a copy." Sounded like fun. I spoke with the consigner, who agreed to take a few copies, which I went to retrieve. By the time I returned to the front desk, Gene had gone up and charmed the consigner into agreeing to be my distributor for the entire Chicagoland region. I heard her say — not to me, of course, but to my self-appointed agent — that she would make sure copies got onto the racks at all the other Barbara's locations.

With that out of the way, the sales pitch evolved into an impromptu session of The Gene Siskel Show. Every employee and customer in the place was now gathered around our star, and he was only too happy to oblige. "Roger claims to have invented 'two thumbs up,'" Gene told the assembled, "but I invented 'two thumbs *way up.*" Gene waited a beat, then added, "And I'm pretty sure I'm the one responsible for 'two thumbs *way,* way up.'" The person who had minutes earlier slipped into this store incognito was striding out of it a recognized celebrity. Gene Siskel enjoyed being famous more than anybody I've ever met. He loved being spotted, loved to recapitulate his reviews, loved filling up college auditoriums around the country with Roger. He loved being caught on camera at the United Center, cheering on his Bulls.

But as he battled the complications that arose after a growth was removed from his brain last May — complications that claimed his life this weekend at the age of 53 — a different Gene Siskel took over. This Gene kept a tight lid on what was going on with him. He fiercely guarded his medical condition, even trying to kill stories in his own newspaper that might indicate how things really were. All the while, with me and with others, he kept up a happy front.

We were at Starbucks, shortly after our conquest of Barbara's, when I brought up the subject. It had been five months since his emergency brain surgery. How was he feeling? Gene said he was fine. He told me about a conversation he'd had with Jeffrey Katzenberg, the former No. 2 man at Walt Disney Co. who had gone on to form DreamWorks with Steven Spielberg and David Geffen. Like Siskel, Katzenberg had been operated on for a brain condition. "Jeffrey had used this phrase, he said, 'I just decided I would *power through it.*' So that's what I'm doing — I'm powering through it." Indeed, Gene resumed his normal routine of five jobs — newspaper critic, *Siskel & Ebert,* and contributor to WBBM-TV, *CBS*

This Morning and *TV Guide* — two weeks after having surgery. (The announcement that he would be setting those duties aside came just seventeen days before his death.)

We had been chatting for an hour when I asked Gene if he needed to be getting home. No, he said, he'd told his wife he would be gone until seven o'clock, meaning we still had another two hours. I chuckled to myself. A man with five jobs has time on a Thursday afternoon for an out-of-town Internet scribe? As I later learned, this was one of the sides of Gene known to few. "He's a very hard man to nail down, but when you do get together with him, it's like the clock doesn't even exist," one of his close friends, Robert Feder, told me. He was devoted to his wife Marlene Iglitzen, whom he met at WBBM, and his three children.

We talked about our favorite topic of mutual interest, *Late Show with David Letterman*. Gene wanted to try something out on me that he planned to say to Dave the next time he and Roger appeared on the show. "When I was recovering from surgery, Dave sent me a collection of baseball essays by Tom Boswell of the *Washington Post* because he knew we both loved baseball," Gene said. "After I'd gotten the book, he called me up and talked for about half an hour. He doesn't like to talk about things like that on his show, but I think it's a side of him people should see more."

Gene proposed that we walk back toward his condo in Lincoln Park, about two miles. Along the way, I saw that he was tilting a little as he walked. I asked him if he'd hurt his foot. Gene immediately became self-conscious about his gait and tried to correct it, with the opposite result — he started listing strangely. He would downplay it with a self-effacing comment every few blocks, and if someone unaware of his condition had seen us that day, she might have thought Gene was re-enacting a classic Monty Python routine. Later, when we entered a Lincoln Park bookshop owned by a friend of his, Gene walked smack into a book cart.

When I got back to Kansas City, I had an email from him. He mentioned the walk home and tried once more to play it down ("Probably a muscle pull"). Later, I learned that Gene had been doing this with practically everyone. Many people who woke up Sunday to the news of his passing had no idea Gene was even seriously ill. And that was how he wanted it. That was his choice, and it was not a wrong choice. But it was a curious choice, given the relationship he had forged over the years with millions of Americans. Maybe Gene Siskel didn't need that kind of public embrace. Maybe he didn't want it. For whatever reason, he chose to play out his last act on this Earth quietly, before the people who mattered most to him, members of his immediate family. For the rest of us, his decision to "power through it" made his loss feel so sudden, as if he had died in a plane crash, and it left our affection for him finally unexpressed.

Afterword

Gene's secrecy shook Roger Ebert, who swore to colleagues that if he ever had cancer, he would make sure everybody knew it. Unfortunately, Roger did get cancer, and complications from surgery deprived him of his voice. But he has been good to his word and kept readers of his blog updated.

In a tragic coincidence, Gene's college roommate at Yale was Tim Weigel, who went on to become a beloved Chicago sportscaster. In 2000 he, too, was diagnosed with the same aggressive form of brain cancer that had killed Gene the year before. But Weigel chose a different tack. He staged a departure as loud as his famous neon neckties, with dinner parties and life celebrations that began the night of his first stay in the hospital. As the *Chicago Tribune's* Steve Rosenbloom later wrote, "Only Tim Weigel would cater a brain tumor operation."

As you will read in the next two chapter introductions, I too was diagnosed with cancer. Hairy cell leukemia is rare, but it is chronic and it is entirely manageable. I also lost my sister-in-law to an aggressive form of brain cancer, and as I look back at this piece I wrote, I realize the tone was perhaps a bit harsh toward Gene. Losing him was a shock, but in hindsight I now know there was little chance of any other outcome. I have also spent several years answering the question, "How's your health?" — and as a result, I am much more able to empathize with anyone's desire for privacy as they grapple with a serious illness.

2000

The year began with a global freakout over Y2K and ended with my lying calmly in hospital with HCL (hairy cell leukemia). In neither case was it the end of the world. That would be next year.

ABC's worldwide ringing-in of the new century on Jan. 1 was one of those spectaculars that made you remember why big-time TV networks existed. On July 16, network and cable news channels set a modern benchmark for futility with their pointless marathon coverage of a search for the missing plane of John F. Kennedy Jr. At the Emmy Awards, *The West Wing* was judged superior to *The Sopranos,* a development that sort of reminded me of *Amadeus.*

Three separate editions of *Who Wants to Be a Millionaire* finished one-two-three in the 1999–2000 Nielsens, and since the people running ABC had no other good ideas, they ordered a fourth night for the fall. That summer, CBS got into the reality game with a competition series called *Survivor.* Fifty million people came indoors on a hot August night to watch Richard Hatch win the million bucks.

Saving more TV, watching more TV
Kansas City Star, April 6, 2000

Get ready to welcome a new abbreviation into the consumer lexicon: PVR, as in personal video recorder. PVRs are minimalist-looking black boxes that save TV shows on a hard drive instead of on videotape. They rolled onto the market in mid–1999, priced at $400 to $800, and immediately became the rage among the nation's "time-shifters," people who are determined to watch their favorite TV shows when they want, instead of when the networks dictate they be in front of the tube. The PVR greatly simplifies the act of selecting a show to record. Three steps and I have Letterman for life — not just tonight's broadcast but every broadcast till kingdom come. No tapes, no times, no weird VCR Plus codes, and (best of all) no coming home to discover the show didn't tape. PVRs also do something VCRs can't: They can pause and rewind live television as you watch it. You would think all of this viewer empowerment would reduce the total amount of time PVR owners spend in front of the tube. So far, though, the opposite appears to be true. "I'm sure I'm watching more TV now," said Kevin Hamburger, producer of *Politically Incorrect* and an ardent TiVo user. *(Postscript: The Brits call them PVRs, but Americans decided to call them DVRs. They were in 34 percent of U.S. homes as of 2009. As DVR acceptance has grown, overall TV watching has, indeed, climbed steadily.)*

Dave, serious as a heart attack
Kansas City Star, February 21, 2000

Tonight marked the return of David Letterman to the *Late Show,* five weeks after he had emergency surgery on a blocked artery in his heart. Much of the program was unplanned and unscripted. Instead of the usual comedy bit from his desk, Letterman simply spoke at length about his ordeal, and fought back tears as he thanked the medical staff that "saved my life." Executive producer Rob Burnett said that he had tried to fly Letterman's mother, Dorothy, to New York to appear on the broadcast but that bad weather in Indianapolis scotched that plan. Last week Letterman was jogging three miles a day and "feeling great," Burnett said. He has, however, been told to switch his coffee to decaf. When or whether he will return to a five-night-a-week schedule are still open questions. For his NBC program, Letterman taped shows four days a week, with repeat broadcasts airing Monday nights. That practice now is carried on by his successor, Conan O'Brien.

Sock Puppet v. Insult Comic Dog
TV Barn, April 26, 2000

The Internet pet-supply startup Pets.com is accustomed to breaking new ground. First in its sector to raise venture capital. First to buy commercial time during the Super Bowl. And now, first to sue a TV comedy writer for making fun of its "spokespuppet." In a complaint filed earlier this month in U.S. District Court in San Francisco and obtained by TV Barn, the e-tailer is charging Robert Smigel, former head writer of *Late Night with Conan O'Brien,* with defamation and trade libel for disparaging the sock puppet that is the center of the company's $20 million marketing campaign. Smigel, as fans of *Late Night* know, is the author and voice of a rubber hand puppet named Triumph, the Insult Comic Dog, whose favorite punchline is "for me to poop on," as in, "This is a fine lawsuit ... for me to poop on!" In effect, Pets.com is

charging Smigel with using his sock puppet to defame its sock puppet.
Its fifteen-page complaint states that Triumph's attacks on its mascot
created "an undesirable, unwholesome and unsavory mental association"
with its Sock Puppet. Perhaps only the people at Pets.com believe that
poop, but its marketing machine has proven itself to be formidable. As
the *New York Times* recently reported, after the Walt Disney Co. bought
a 5 percent stake in Pets.com, the Sock Puppet started popping up on
media outlets owned by Disney, including three within ABC's news
division: *Good Morning America, Nightline* and the Mr. Showbiz Web
site. None of these revealed Disney's financial stake. Both Triumph and
Smigel were declining comment on Pets.com's lawsuit, said Jeff Ross, the
executive producer of *Late Night*. But Ross offered his own: "I think it's
hysterical."

Whatever happened to the V-chip?

Kansas City Star, April 27, 2000

   When it was ushered into the world in 1996 by an act of Congress,
the V-chip was hailed by pro-family advocates and Vice President Gore.
Behold, they said, a three-dollar gizmo that will let parents block any
TV shows that exceed preset thresholds for sex, violence and adult
language. Hollywood cried censorship, while TV set makers grumbled
about having to install something that *prevented* people from watching
TV. Four years later, the V-chip has become television's red-headed
stepchild, ignored despite being built into every new TV set sold in the
U.S. Nearly two out of five parents in a new survey didn't even know
what it was. A new campaign hopes to raise awareness of the device,
with Kermit the Frog acting as the "V-chip spokesfrog." Meanwhile, the
government's "V-chip czar" — who wields only slightly more power than
a "spokesfrog" — sent a memo to the TV networks April 4, pleading with
them to "recommit themselves to educating parents about the V-chip."
Good luck with that! Using the V-chip is dead simple. I've hauled a
TV out to speaking engagements and handed the remote to audience
members. They've figured it out. But the chip is useless without accurate
ratings, and two studies have found the vast majority of shows with
sexual and violent content weren't being tagged as such. Then there's
the problem of cable companies that garble the ratings-encoded part
of the signal. A reader in Wisconsin recently found her V-chip wasn't
blocking *South Park* because the show's "TV-MA" (adults only) rating
had been lost in transmission. Perhaps the V-chip's biggest drawback

is that it is hard-wired into TV sets, unlike the parental controls found on cable and satellite set-top boxes, which can be modified. HBO and Showtime have special content ratings that distinguish between mild and graphic violence; the V-chip doesn't recognize them and never will. When I spoke with Gloria Tristiani, the FCC commissioner who serves as the country's "V-chip czar," she admitted the system would "need time to gauge what the acceptance level is, and by time I mean years." Years? At that rate,"parental controls" will join brightness and contrast another ubiquitous, little-used, and mostly forgotten setting on the TV.

Twice the work, half the pay

Kansas City Star, June 20, 2000

It's 2:50 p.m. in the capital city of Texas, and News 8 Austin's Haley Stavinoha slides into an editing bay with her deadline twenty-five minutes away. She was up at the crack of dawn to shoot video of a juvenile boot camp and do interviews. At other TV stations, two-thirds of her job would be done by others. But at News 8 Austin, a 24/7 local news service set up recently by Time Warner Cable, the reporter does everything. She shoots her own standup, writes and edits the piece, even composes the on-screen graphics. She's a one-woman band. A mantra around the newsroom is "twice the work, half the pay," so jobs at News 8 Austin tend to attract the young and inexperienced, like Stavinoha, who came from the CBS station in much smaller Amarillo. Staring intently at a computer screen, she rapidly slices and dices video of young toughs in fatigues doing push-ups. At deadline, Stavinoha is still composing her script. When she finally hits send at 3:20, her introduction and tagline are fed into the prompter, ready for anchor Bob Branson — one of the few TV news veterans at News 8 — to read. A director makes a video sandwich out of his words and her pictures, and the story is put into the computerized rotation. It will air several times today. The reporters get seasoning; Time Warner gets low-cost product that emphasizes schools, public meetings, and community-minded groups; and everyone gets a respite from the blood-and-guts of traditional TV news. "I think they work harder than their counterparts," says News 8 Austin general manager Brian Benschoter. "But if you want to go home feeling good about what you do, this is the place." *(Postscript: I went to Austin because Time Warner indicated it would soon be bringing its 24-hour news format to Kansas City. The recession changed that. Ten years later, the techniques for newsgathering with cheap one-man bands are being implemented at local broadcast TV stations.)*

On Survivor, *eating their old*

Kansas City Star, June 7, 2000

Tonight more than 15 million viewers are expected to tune in to the second episode of *Survivor,* the $1 million adventure game on CBS that is turning into a morality play about television and the cult of youth. As the first episode unfolded, the inevitable conflicts arose and rivalries emerged among the islanders. Yet one sentiment did seem to unify most of the contestants: These old people have got to go! Thirteen of the sixteen castaways are under the age of forty-five, with many in their twenties. By the end of the first hour, a generation gap had clearly opened up between them and 62-year-old Sonja Christopher, 64-year-old B.B. Andersen, and 72-year-old ex-Navy SEAL Rudy Boesch. Andersen and Boesch, no-nonsense guys from the old school, went all-out setting up their respective camps. When they complained that the others weren't pulling their weight, the youngsters bristled. "Rudy is arrogant," said one woman half Boesch's age. Then there was Christopher, a real-life survivor of cancer and the island's free spirit, who strummed her ukulele and avoided the rivalries simmering around her. But that was before her momentary stumble in a race cost her team a set of waterproof matches. Next thing you know, Christopher was off the island, having received the most ballots in *Survivor's* first-ever tribal council. One of her peers, apparently unfamiliar with the rigors of cancer therapy, called Christopher the "weakest link in the group." The person who came in second in the balloting for banishment was none other than Boesch. And you may see the group dispatch Andersen as soon as tonight; as I reported in March, he arrived back in Kansas City only a few days into the contest. Watching *Survivor* eat its old is as metaphorical as it gets. TV media buyers aim pretty much at younger viewers while shunning baby boomers. At CBS, where the median viewer age is 52, oldest of the six networks, network executives ordered the producers of *Survivor* to cast older contestants to keep the show "multigenerational." For how long they'll keep doing that is anyone's guess. Once the last old-timer is voted off the island, maybe a symbolic tribal gesture would be in order. They could put Rudy on a raft and push it offshore, in the direction of the South Pole. Mountain Dew could sponsor it. *(Postscript: Surprise! Rudy made it to the final episode and became a star, and CBS kept casting older contestants for* Survivor. *But as a result of my story, eliminated contestants were kept on site until production was finished.)*

A forum for all presidential candidates

Electronic Media, August 19, 2000

Since 1987, the Commission on Presidential Debates has decreed that only candidates with at least 15 percent of voter support will be invited to the fall debates. Thus, two well-known candidates for president this year — Pat Buchanan and Ralph Nader — will not be invited. Imagine if the commission's rules had been in effect in Minnesota two years ago, when the ex-wrestler Jesse Ventura was polling 9 percent as a third-party candidate for governor in late September. He was included in the televised debates anyway, and the rest is history. Now let's turn the clock back to 1980. The League of Women Voters, which used to coordinate the presidential debates, had three contenders on its hands that summer, because independent John Anderson was polling above 15 percent. The Carter and Reagan camps couldn't agree on including him in the debates. Finally Anderson dipped below 15 percent in the polls (some say for lack of TV exposure) and the League revoked its invite. So the brand-new, scrappy Cable News Network did something no media outlet has tried before or since: Using satellites and videotape, CNN artificially inserted Anderson into the Carter-Reagan debate. On Oct. 28, 1980, while the "official" forum took place in Cleveland, Anderson sat on a stage at Constitution Hall in Washington. CNN began by carrying the live feed from Cleveland. Then, each time it was Anderson's "turn" to speak or rebut, CNN cut away to Washington. When Anderson was finished, the telecast resumed on tape delay from Cleveland at the exact point where it had left off. CNN received mostly positive reviews for its work. PBS even carried CNN's version of the debate later that night. Imagine if a cable channel with a chip on its shoulder — say, Fox News — did that today. Imagine George W. Bush getting handed a note during the debate, telling him what Buchanan said in his rebuttal. Or Al Gore's earpiece buzzing as aides tell him that Nader is picking apart his vaunted environmental policy — on Fox News, for God's sake! It would be a kick. It would have Washington buzzing. It would be great television. *(Postscript: Nader and Buchanan weren't featured in a debate, yet their presence on the ballots in Florida and Ohio changed the shape of the 2000 election. Had voters been better educated about these fringe candidates, would they have been so inclined to vote for them, accidentally or otherwise?)*

Durst nightmare

TV Barn, March 7, 2000

Poor Will Durst! The San Francisco funnyman usually has to beg for publicity. But after he screwed up the $500,000 question as the Phone-a-Friend for Rudy Reber on *Who Wants to Be a Millionaire* a few days ago, he returned home to find 86 media inquiries on his voice mail. What he didn't know — and it's probably

ich Hollywood figure directed Michael Jackso 1988 video "Bad"?
ven Spielberg   B: Francis Ford Co
rtin Scorsese   D: John Landis

just as well — is that he also became public enemy No. 1 in the *Millionaire* chat room for being such an arrogant bonehead that he cost his so-called friend 218 kilobucks.

So who is Rudy Reber and how did Will Durst wind up as his lifeline on the night of Feb. 17? "Rudy used to be a comedian back when we were all fellow soldiers in the comedy wars in the early 1980s here in San Francisco," the keeper of willdurst.com told me. "Me and my wife Debi had gone over to his house a couple of times for dinner, and versa visa. Then Rudy and his wife Tina split up, and we didn't see much of him. Next time I saw him he was a used car salesman in Portland and was trying to get back into comedy. But they didn't have a lot of open mikes in Portland." Then, last month, "I was in Chicago appearing at Zanies. Debi called me and said, 'Rudy Reber just called. He's going be on *Who Wants to Be a Millionaire* and do you want to be one of his lifelines?' So I said sure. No problem! *What's the big deal?* I didn't think he had a chance in hell of making it through the process." Durst lowered his voice and added, "I was wrong. I was *very* wrong."

On the morning of the taping, someone from the show called. "They say, 'Are you going to be near a phone later today?' I say yes. They say they needed me by the phone from 3 to 6 p.m. Central time. Three-thirty rolls around and there's a call to say, 'Your friend Rudy is on the hot seat.' I answered the phone on the first ring and

I just said 'Durst!', because that's the way I answer my phone. She said to me, 'No, you're supposed to answer it on the third ring like we told you, because the next person on the phone will be Regis.'" Already Durst was feeling uneasy. "I never thought he'd make it through the ten-person speed order quiz," he confessed.

"So the phone rings. I wait three times, but I figure it's been forty-five minutes — no way has my good friend, smart Mensa member Rudy, made it for forty-five minutes. But I hadn't accounted for show stoppages and so forth. Sure enough, it's Regis. I answer the phone, 'Durst!' He says *'Durst? We're looking for Will Durst!'* Then he says it's the $500,000 question."

So at this point you may be wondering, why him? Was Will Durst really the best choice Rudy Reber could come up with after so many years toiling in the comedy and automotive retail industries? As it turns out, no. "He wanted Ben Stein, but Ben wasn't able to, for some reason," said Durst. (The reason is that Stein was ineligible. Disney not only has a stake in *Who Wants to Be a Millionaire,* but the Comedy Central game show *Win Ben Stein's Money* as well. In fact, many of the original *Millionaire* writers were borrowed from *Win Ben Stein's Money.*)

Anyway, Regis asked Will the $500,000 question that he had already asked Rudy: *Who directed Michael Jackson's video for* Bad? Durst didn't have to think about it twice. "I'm not a big music guy," he said. "I have ten presets on my car radio and not one of them is music. But this was a music question I knew! I was so excited for him. I was going to help him out! Oh, man, was I confident. I was *very* confident." Without waiting even a beat, Durst told Reber the correct answer was John Landis. Reber decided to risk his wad and answer the question. He said Landis.

Actually, Landis directed *another* Jacko video, for *Thriller.* The correct answer was Martin Scorsese. "They put me on hold," recalled Durst. "I was able to hear it, but I couldn't say anything. I couldn't go, 'Rudy, I'm sorry.' Plus, Regis took an inordinate amount of time. He stopped for the longest time and then he said, 'No, the answer is C.' And I just screamed. People in the comedy condo heard me screaming. And I didn't have Rudy's number. Meanwhile, I couldn't breathe for 48 hours. I didn't tell people at the comedy

Poor Will.

club. They just thought I was unusually morose. The news media had no problem telling the story in 120 words. But I couldn't." When Rudy finally got ahold of his old pal the next day, "he says, 'Don't worry about it, buddy! I had a great time! I'm getting out of telemarketing! I couldn't ask for any better publicity!' Well, it turns out, *I could.*"

By accepting Durst's wrong answer, Reber waived any chance of keeping his winnings of $250,000.

He went home with $32,000. Durst has already figured out that he can make it up to Reber by sending him $20 a month — for 908 years.

"That poor bastard," Reber said as soon as I got him on the phone. "I felt so crappy for him." I asked him why he called on Durst. Reber explained that he was allowed five Phone-a-Friends. "My brother's a Ph.D., but he wouldn't know a Michael Jackson video from his left foot. My brother-in-law is a lawyer. He knows law, he knows art history." There was also a deejay Reber could call on, but in the hot seat all he could think of was that Durst knew a lot of pop culture trivia. Only afterward did Reber think to ask his deejay friend if he had known the correct answer to the question (he had).

Reber said he will likely use his winnings from *Millionaire,* such as they are, to get a fresh start. Mavis Leno once produced a horoscope for him that predicted he would one day become a writer. He might try that. As for Durst, he's seriously considering the witness protection program. "I haven't seen the show yet. I can't. It's too painful. Someone has taped it for me. Maybe in five, six years we'll look back on this and laugh," he said.

(Postscript: Rudy Reber now lives in Augusta, Ga., according to Facebook. Will Durst is still a standup comedian based in San Francisco. Neither replied to my requests for an update.)

2001

What a year — and 9/11 in some ways was the least of it.

Two thousand one began with yours truly off the air. Hairy cell leukemia sidelined me for nearly two months, beginning at the end of 2000, and it was another five months before I showed my face at work. During that ordeal, a harsh regimen of chemotherapy failed, and when my doctors suggested doing it again, I fired them and found an oncologist I could work with. He got me into a clinical trial at the M.D. Anderson Cancer Center in Houston for a drug called Rituxan that was just starting to revolutionize cancer treatment. It hammered my leukemia without harming me, and once they let us get on airplanes again, I was on my to L.A. to interview the cast of the fall's hottest show, *24*. An indelible memory of 2001 was of standing in the terminal at Houston International after a follow-up visit to M.D. Anderson, watching CNN Airport News as word started to spread of the collapse of Enron. I never heard an airport so quiet in my life.

Of course, there was 9/11, which I liveblogged. Unlike most of the articles you will read in *Tasteland*, the liveblog appears here pretty much exactly as it appeared on TV Barn that fateful day.

In 2001 CBS began to reclaim Thursday, the most lucrative night of network television, after 18 seasons of dominance by NBC. It did this by relocating from Fridays to Thursdays a new series called *CSI: Crime Scene Investigation*, which had been following a much more heavily-promoted series, *The Fugitive*. It was tantamount to a No. 15 seed winning the NCAA tournament. *CSI* might not have made it onto the CBS schedule if the creator of *Everybody Loves Raymond*, Philip Rosenthal, hadn't offered his opinion — at a network meeting he was not even supposed to be in — that *CSI* just looked more interesting than the Tony Danza detective pilot that CBS was about to pick up.

To conclude a very full year, I wrote one of the more personally meaningful stories in this book, about a Kansas City musician whose senseless killing 20 years earlier had been made into an A&E program.

Watching America attacked

Stories I wrote in the heat of the moment.

Liveblogging 9/11

10 a.m. (Eastern Time) Here is what I have been looking at for the past few minutes: a giant factory of death, with smoke billowing from two glassy chimneys. And then, suddenly, the chimneys tremble and sink from view! On the ground level, it is as though a volcano erupted. Watching Fox, I see zombies pass by.

MSNBC's, CBS's and ABC's Internet servers are overloaded. Twelve blocks north, an NBC News reporter did a standup while hundreds of firefighters, clad in black, walked past him to the scene of suffering. Around the reporter the sky was clear. One mile from the factory of death it was a beautiful late summer day.

10:41 a.m. I received this email from a TV Barn contributor who goes by the handle Zen Mondatta: "As I watched the collapse of the first World Trade Center tower live on television, I listened to Blaine Ensley, a talk host on WNEW-FM in New York, say 'Oh my God... oh my God...' over and over again. Phones are scrambled throughout the metro area. WNBC-TV, WPIX-TV, WABC-TV, and FOX-5 are all off the air due to the fact that the main broadcast tower in NYC was atop one of the World Trade Center towers. The only local New York City newscast that is still on the air is WCBS. (The other stations are using Philadelphia feeds.) Fortunately through Instant

Messaging, I have found out that almost everyone I know is OK."

10:45 a.m. Fox was the first to get a fancy graphic up on the screen: DAY OF TERROR. Just before that, Aaron Brown on CNN, standing on the rooftop above CNN's New York studio, was talking and then suddenly stopped. "When we see a plane overhead," he explained, "we get a little nervous." After all, who's to say the bombing is over? Turns out it was a fighter jet.

11:05 a.m. About an hour ago, Fox's Rick Leventhal was as close to ground zero as anyone. It is as though he is on the scene at Pompeii. He is trying to interview every passerby all at once. Most people are on foot, but a van full of hardhats goes by slowly and Leventhal waves it over. The crew was at 25 Park Place, next to the World Trade Center, and saw both explosions. He had buddies working on the 104th floor of one of the buildings. Leventhal asks him how he feels. The driver is slightly incredulous. "Bodies flying out of the sky and I can't do nothin' about it. You tell me."

11:10 a.m. The footage is starting to come in. CNN's Jeff Greenfield is reminding us of a Tom Clancy novel in which the Pentagon is bombed. "I hate to say this, but this may be the day America's luck ran out."

11:13 a.m. Shepard Smith is saying, "For the good of the country, it is time to put the telephone down." Fox has had the most gripping coverage so far. While the other networks contented themselves with the surreal but still-photograph-quality overhead shots of the towers, Fox sent Leventhal and a photographer into the teeth of the action. The photog, I am guessing, was a staffer pressed into camera duty: His pictures bob and weave, he is easily distracted by passing trucks, and even after half a minute he couldn't get the hardhat in the truck into focus.

There is so much news that the news networks are all resorting to stock-market tickers to convey all the data.

11:20 a.m. On ABC I saw footage of an interview with an ABM employee who pulled a man out of an elevator at the World Trade Center and got him to safety. "There was skin falling off his body," he said. Now it's Peter and his yak crew. Only MSNBC and Fox are elbowing their way down to the streets and throwing it live to the TV viewers. CNN has Jeff Greenfield and Aaron Brown, who are great, and Aaron is telling us, "In our reporting, we're going to be a bit conservative ... this is already horrendous and we don't need to make it worse."

11:26 a.m. Al Haig — whom you'd expect to be a faithful Fox News Channel viewer — called in a while ago to say confidently, "This was too broad-based an attack to just be a few crazies."

American Airlines says two of its flights were hijacked: AA Flight 11 (with 92 people aboard) and AA Flight 77 (64 aboard). There is another airliner headed to the nation's capital at a high rate of speed, Brit Hume reports. (Earlier, Fox's Brian Wilson had said a D.C. policeman evacuated him from where he was, saying another plane had been hijacked.) WGN confirmed earlier that the Sears Tower in Chicago was evacuated as a safety precaution.

There is a lull. Fox is showing old tape and talking to Newt Gingrich, who calls this "a 21st-century Pearl Harbor ... I think we need to refer to this as an act of war ... This was a systematic, complex operation of military proportions ... by people with state support." The plane heading at a high rate of speed toward Washington seems to have been a rumor and not fact, according to an ABC News reporter at the Pentagon.

11:36 a.m. It was just about an hour ago that Two WTC collapsed. Rick Leventhal was on the air when it happened. We heard him say, "We need to put it (the camera) down now." And he ran. Then silence. Then Shepard Smith: "America, say a prayer."

Mrs. TV Barn's son is a trader. He knows when the bomb went off in New York because the futures market suddenly stopped.

Tom Brokaw was in high dander, as usual. "There's been a complete intelligence failure here," he said, and began to predict repercussions ahead when Katie Couric butted in. "But can you ever prepare for an attack like this?" Brokaw shifted gears. "This is nothing less than a declaration of war against this country." But by whom? Matt Lauer had some idea but said he didn't want to name names this early on.

CBS can confirm that UAL 175 and UAL 93 were both hijacked and crashed.

There is no choir rehearsal tonight.

Carol Marin is on CBS. She's covered with soot. "Dan, I think

I was in the second collapse." She's rattled. To know Carol Marin is know she has a high threshold for fear. She was knocked down in the collapse. A firefighter picked her up, "threw me into a wall, covered me with his body ... I was sure we were both going to die.... A rain of cinders came down on me ... A police officer named Brendon Duke grabbed my hand."

12:37 p.m. Dan Rather explained a piece of surreal video of the plane ripping into Two World Trade Center saying, "This is not a graphic."

Paul Jay Rodriguez writes, "Bob Edwards is being an amazing comfort, as his clear calm voice just keeps going on, never seeming rattled, even when he was interviewing two people trapped in their building one block from the WTC, with dust and smoke creeping into their apartment."

Fox has retitled its coverage TERRORISM IN AMERICA. At MSNBC, it's been ATTACK ON AMERICA for an hour or so. Same title at CBS and CNN. Now NBC affiliate KSHB-TV is running a ticker. And they've titled it too — TERROR IN THE SKY. Sounds like a *Reader's Digest* "Drama in Real Life."

Only ABC News is refusing to title its live coverage. That more than makes up for the excessive headshots of Peter Jennings. I think that at times like this, you can't get enough video of the destruction. One of the most gripping images of the whole morning, in fact, was a seemingly innocuous one of people fleeing the Pentagon — running, running — an image reminiscent of hundreds of students fleeing Columbine High.

The oddest ticker item of the morning, courtesy CBS News: TOP HALF OF ONE WORLD TRADE CENTER COLLAPSES ... HUNDREDS INJURED.

1:07 p.m. Blogger.com is in meltdown. I'm now posting directly from my HTML editor. Like you care.

Barry Serafin of ABC is reporting that about 10 minutes ago a military helicopter landed, loaded a bunch of people in and then took off. He's speculating that these are senior politicos and intelligence officials being spirited off to a briefing.

MSNBC reported that an ambulance that had pulled to within 500 feet of the first World Trade Center building to be hit exploded from the heat of the second WTC building hit.

Don't bother voting for New York City mayor, flying in a plane, or watching a Major League Baseball game today.

ABC's John McWethy is parroting a bizarre line from his Pentagon sources. "It seems quite clear in this instance that (the terrorists) bypassed the normal methods of communicating and were able to organize this very complex operation in a way that basically escaped American detection." When Peter Jennings questions that assumption, McWethy takes an even weirder turn: "Every time — and you and I know this because we have had conversations with high ranking government officials about how much information we put on the air — every time the news media puts on these details, it helps the terrorists to understand the way the government goes about monitoring their communications ... The terrorists are clearly adjusting."

If John McWethy seriously thinks that the airwaves are promiscuously spreading high-level intelligence in between obsessions with Gary Condit, he needs to get out more. ... Indeed, moments later ABC's John Miller reports that the police command center in New York City has been moved to a secret location, and that the press has been asked not to publicize that location, and that ABC will not.

Elsewhere, the Museum of Tolerance in Los Angeles is closed. So is Knott's Berry Farm. Walt Disney World was evacuated.

1:21 p.m. Peter Jennings is going through the Associated Press's state-by-state reports on reaction to the attacks. In Michigan, the Windsor-Detroit tunnel was closed. North Carolina's military bases are on standby. National Guard units from New York and surrounding states will come in to spell relief workers at the scene.

ABC's John Miller says "no one can put a finger ... on the number of injured and dead." Beekman Hospital "is a M*A*S*H center" because it lost steam power and can't sterilize instruments. We're watching ferry boats transport casualties across the Hudson to hospitals in New Jersey.

1:35 p.m. (Kansas City time: 12:35 p.m.) Why do people applaud at inappropriate times? When President Bush announced that he was going back to Washington and cutting his trip short, the people at the Sarasota elementary school around him clapped politely. Now Kansas City's mayor, Kay Barnes, is stepping up to the mike — and they're clapping for her!

Barnes says something that bears repeating: "It is important not to prejudge people … who represent other nationalities in our community." After she speaks, assistant city manager Rich Noll dispels a rumor of a smallpox virus being spread.

1:41 p.m. Back to Fox News Channel, where Shepard Smith says that "some kind of edgy calm" is descending on New York City now. Fox News is estimating 10,000 dead. We are under "Threat Condition Delta," says Smith, adding with much gravity, "There is no higher state of alert in the USA than there is now." Officially speaking, we're at war. But with whom?

1:49 p.m. The Kansas City mayor is on all four channels, but New York Mayor Rudy Giuliani is even more ubiquitous. And even he's got a story to tell: his emergency command center caved in with him in it. "We were using a ground floor as a temporary command center," explained Hizzoner. "As we were setting up … the building collapsed. We had to evacuate through the basement. It was pretty dicey for a while."

1:56 p.m. Brian Williams on MSNBC is reporting that the number of seats being reserved for journalists aboard Air Force One has been limited to five (one of them is ABC's Ann Compton) and that the rest of the press corps will follow the president in a backup plane to whatever remote location he is heading to. Williams calls this "a fairly ominous sign, but then again, this country is in a state of war. We just don't know who the enemy is."

Now to Ashleigh Banfield, interviewing two firefighters who were there minutes after the attack. "How many did you two treat?" One of them estimates that he saw "approximately 100 to 150 people and the steady flow still coming." The other says that the smoke was so thick that they had to follow the contours of the building by hand. "I don't know where my partner is at," he says. "I lost him in the cloud." Was he ever trained for something like this? "The idea," he says, "but nothing like this."

2:05 p.m. MSNBC's Williams: "We know that a cell phone call was placed — and this is chilling … a man that was locked in a bathroom on the plane" that went down in Pennsylvania "got through to a 911 dispatcher. He said the plane had been hijacked and they were going down."

From a secure military base in Louisiana, President Bush walked grim-faced into a room, stood at a podium, buttoned his jacket, looked off quickly to his right, then said, "Freedom itself was attacked this morning by a faceless coward — and freedom will be defended."

2:11 p.m. "Before we get carried away with theory ..." says Peter Jennings. Amen, Peter. This is one day when TV journalists should have plenty to report without having to sit around in their studios, filling up airtime.

2:19 p.m. ABC News is still the only news organization that refuses to give this horror a catchy title. "I know we can run these pictures to the point of offensiveness," explains Peter Jennings before showing the video of the building collapse again. Now he has John McCain on the phone. "Clearly, we need to look at our intelligence capabilities." An act of war? "Yes." Do you believe that if another country was in cahoots with the terrorists, we should go to war with them? "Absolutely, because they have committed an atrocity on a scale that's unprecedented ... At least (Pearl Harbor) was an attack on military outlets ... This is an outrage."

CBS has live footage, I think, of what appears to be a secondary building with a huge chunk sheared off. Rep. Jim Moran (D-Va.) is estimating on Fox News Channel that the death toll is 10,000 and asking, "Who do we strike back at?"

2:40 p.m. On Fox, Tony Snow says that there is a dispute between the president's bodyguards and political advisers over where he should go. The Secret Service, he says, wants to move Bush to the highly secure NORAD facility in Colorado, best known to television watchers for its annual radar reports on Santa. The president's spinmeisters, however, have objected, saying (in Snow's words) "he will look like, quote, a weenie," if he runs off and hides in the mountains.

Here's a report from the Echo BBS in New York City, which I belong to: "The Times building is on full alert and the newsroom is turning into a M*A*S*H unit of info-gathering with shakey phone lines and reporters and photogs scrambling." In a similar vein, CBS Newspath, a service that supplies news footage to local CBS affiliates across the country, is asking its clients "TO PLEASE LIMIT YOUR PHONE CALLS TO OUR NEWSROOM AND OUR LIVE NEWS CENTER." Newspath is based out of the CBS News HQ on West 57th in Manhattan.

If you're looking for online news, Google is caching reports from CNN.com.

2:58 p.m. Speaking of CNN, Aaron Brown is reporting that no air travel will occur any sooner than noon tomorrow. Now he throws to Atlanta for an update. (Why?) Yeah, like Atlanta has its act together: some goofhead just put up a "Stem Cell Dilemma" graphic, blotting out the news ticker. Joie Chen sounds like she's at the bottom of a well. Throw it back to Aaron!

ABC News passes along this by email: "Rather than present our usual programs today, ABC NEWS will have continuous live coverage with each of the broadcasts contributing. As many of you know, NIGHTLINE had planned to continue our series HEART OF DARKNESS on the Congo this evening. For obvious reasons, that series will be postponed and we will let you know about the new dates."

CNN's interview with George Schulz just went down the toilet in a mess of sound-check tones. He's back now and Aaron is asking the Epochal Question of the Day: Has American life changed today? "No," says Schulz. "We're not going to change our way of life for these people. I reject that entirely." Well, won't it change the way people take airline flights and (Aaron really says this) visit the World Trade Center? Schulz: "I think it'll be a while before they go to the Trade Center."

3:10 p.m. Bush is in Omaha. Is he heading east or west?

The incomparable John Leonard is calling this "the worst sort of TV movie."

3:20 p.m. On MSNBC, Brian Williams says, "It's too early to finger point," and then asks his military analyst, Ken Allard, to point fingers at whoever didn't pick up on this attack. "The thing that troubles me," said Allard, "is we always seem to be reacting to him ... This guy declared war on us two years ago and we seem not have taken that seriously and, if we don't take the war to him, he'll take the war to us."

Which raises a question. If we declare war on Afghanistan, will all Americans support it? Will, for instance, Mavis Leno welcome bombing attacks on the innocent women of that country, who are already victims of the Taliban's misogynstic regime?

Back to the Epochal Question. Allard on MSNBC: "This is a wake-up call ... Our lives changed this morning at nine o'clock and I don't think things are ever going to be the same."

3:26 p.m. I asked an ABC spokesperson why ABC was the only network not giving a "title" to this event. Her response, by email: "This tragedy speaks for itself. No 'title' could explain the story better than the pictures on our air."

3:38 p.m. A former NBC producer has tipped me to CNBC's coverage, which is more international (and, of course, financial) in scope. Investors in Europe, where markets stayed open, were in a panic — it's the biggest-one day selloff since October 1987. The German exchange is down 400 points. Zurich Re off 17 percent. British Airways down 13 percent. Oil and energy stocks, though, are up up up.

From the Echo BBS: 90 West Street (built 1907, 24 stories) is "gone." A New York City TV station is apparently showing footage of people celebrating in Queens, according to various reports on Echo.

3:55 p.m. So, will *Law & Order* producer Dick Wolf go ahead with his triple-crossover five-hour miniseries for later this season, tentatively entitled "Terror"?

4:10 p.m. This is why we have still photography: Go to this MSNBC.com slide show and look at picture 4. Captioned, "Desperate last act," it shows a single body leaping from the smoke and flames of the burning World Trade Center this morning.

4:18 p.m. CNBC reporting that 7 World Trade Center may be on the verge of collapsing. Also, the NYSE, NASDAQ and AMEX exchanges will be closed tomorrow. Perhaps all week.

John Carney reports that Turner is simulcasting CNN's coverage on its entire family of networks, and that home shopping's HSN and QVC have suspended operations. And ABC is simulcasting on the ESPN networks. If your cable provider carries BBC America, BBC World News coverage is there. On the other hand, New York's WABC-TV "is airing only local coverage, bypassing Jennings entirely," says Roy Currlin.

4:25 p.m. CNN has a stunning video taken by one Dr. Mark Heath, who was hard by the World Trade Center when one of the towers collapsed. "We don't know much about Dr. Mark Heath," says Aaron Brown, "but we can say he had extraordinary presence of mind" amid the flying debris and choking dust which filled the sky. Heath breathed into a medical bag. During his video there is a very eerie chirping noise in the background — turns out that's an audio indicator that firefighters wear so that colleagues can find them if they fall.

4:50 p.m. (3:50 local time). I'm getting out of my pajamas and going in to work.

All anthrax, all the time

Kansas City Star, October 23, 2001

For Michael Sipes, it took the powdered sugar doughnut incident to convince him that yes, an anthrax threat is very much like a bomb threat. On Oct. 12, an NBC News employee on the East Coast tested positive for anthrax, setting off a wild weekend in which public health officials across the country were bombarded with reports of suspicious white powdery substances. And wherever the hazardous-materials truck went, TV news trucks were in hot pursuit.

Kansas City was no exception. That Friday, when hazmat responded to a non-emergency call from the *Kansas City Star,* three news crews covered the incident, including KMBC, Channel 9, where Sipes is the news director. (The white substance in a coin wrapper turned out to be a talcumlike powder routinely used to make coins easier to handle.)

Over the next four days the list of possible anthrax reports grew longer and nuttier. Salt found on a restaurant table. Detergent next to a washing machine. The one that beat all, though, was the story of the Overland Park woman who reported an unknown white powder in her backseat just after dropping off her kids at school. Upon questioning, the woman recalled the children had eaten powdered sugar doughnuts that morning.

Though at least two TV stations received that report, neither passed it along to viewers. By then it was dawning on local news managers that reporting every anthrax scare would be like reporting every bomb threat. It makes an already nervous public more so and only encourages hoaxsters. "It got to the point Monday where I was about to pull my hair out," Sipes said. "We were feeding unwarranted concern."

Counting down to 24: Is America ready?

Kansas City Star, November 4, 2001

On Tuesday night the Fox network will briefly suspend its relentless promotion of the premiere episode of *24* in order to actually bring us the premiere episode of *24*. Then, and only then, will we know for sure if a jittery country is ready to watch Kiefer Sutherland try to locate a shadowy terrorist cabal that is plotting to commit what was, until a few weeks ago, considered in Hollywood to be "the unthinkable." As promos remind us seemingly every fifteen minutes, *TV Guide* called *24* the "best new show of the season." So did nearly every TV critic in America, because *24* has all the things critics love: brilliant concept, dazzling visuals, star power and taut, suspenseful writing. This summer it was all anyone in the industry could talk about.

But that was before Sept. 11. Before the unthinkable became thinkable. Before Fox had to revise its definition of "the world's most shocking video" to encompass more than people urinating into break-room coffeepots. Before its promotion department was forced to hastily pull the promos for *24* and remove the scene of the exploding aircraft from its first episode.

A year ago in a different world, Joel Surnow called up an old writing partner, Robert Cochran, to say he had an idea for a TV show, a thriller in which events occurred in real time. The first episode would take place between midnight and 1 a.m., the second episode from 1 a.m. to 2 a.m., and so on until the bad guy was caught, 24 hours later. "I told him, 'That's really clever and ingenious and brilliant, but I don't see how you can do it,'" Cochran told me. "Then he called me the next day and said, 'We can make this work.'" The premiere starts slowly, then picks up steam as it darts deftly in and out of, by my count, six different stories. Throughout, there are reminders on screen that time is ticking away. Stephen Hopkins, the pilot's director, is the person most responsible for *24's* fretful, paranoid look and feel.

The set of *24* is situated on a quiet studio lot on the edge of the San Fernando Valley. I came here to interview Kiefer Sutherland, who is in his first TV series role as Jack Bauer, the no-nonsense counterterrorist at the show's center. Jack is an unambiguous hero, a person preternaturally capable of extreme violence or touching compassion depending on the occasion. As I waited at a patio table on the *24* lot, looking down at my questions, Sutherland suddenly slid into the chair next to me, so softly that it startled me.

"Doing this requires a leap of faith," he said, describing his decision to put on hold a film career that was productive, if not exactly notable. "Basically you're committing to seven years of work based on one hour." In reality, Sutherland cannot even be sure the show will last one year. Fox is airing *24* opposite *Frasier, NYPD Blue* and the new CBS hit *The Guardian.* The network expects great things of *24,* and Surnow and Cochran, who have had success in TV but no megahits, believe that *24* could become the first No. 1 show in Fox's fifteen-year history.

More than any show on television, however, *24* is burdened by the events of Sept. 11. After the attack, the two producers say everything just stopped for about two or three weeks. They were paralyzed — whether by shock or the prospect of watching their big network show go down in flames, it wasn't clear. Surnow and Cochran had collaborated for five seasons of the cable show *La Femme Nikita,* so making acts of evil into entertainment was old hat to them. But this was something new. They knew that CBS had pulled episodes of its first-season spy series *The Agency* that dealt with Osama bin Laden and anthrax. Tidying up *24* would not be so easy. Like every other scene in the premiere, the airplane incident was woven so tightly into the story fabric that pulling it out could cause the whole show to unravel. In the end they decided to make only one change: Instead of a full frontal shot of the jetliner going up in flames, viewers would see a cutaway shot of the terrorist skydiving away from the explosion, with hot cinders of airplane parts flying past.

I've noticed a perceptible shift in the way the show is promoted. The cast and creators have stopped referring to it as an "action thriller," words you will find in nearly every story written about *24* over the summer. "It has the pace of an action show even though it's not an action show," said Cochran. "By the way, the villains were never going to be from the Middle East." Surnow agreed. "What you're buying when you come into our show is big stunts, big action," he allowed. "For the most part, though, what you see is two people in rooms talking."

The star of *24* hasn't found making the adjustment so easy. For three weeks after the attacks, Sutherland said, he was in "this real fog, I'd say depression — real hard to concentrate on anything. I kept seeing the faces of people, desperate, looking for their husband or wife. Outside of that, what could possibly be important?" The change came, he said, when he was approached on the street by an anonymous fan.

"He said, 'Oh man, I can't wait to see your show,' and I was taken aback," Sutherland said. "I almost went, 'How can you talk about that at a time like this?' But I thought about it — about why entertainment has always been so successful, in World War II or the Great Depression or other tragic times. We need to step out of reality. Because reality can be really, really tough."

David E. Kelley's TV trifecta

Kansas City Star, November 25, 2001

From their exterior, the Manhattan Beach Studios look more like an office park than a storied Hollywood backlot. But inside there are rooms you would recognize instantly: the unisex bathroom on *Ally McBeal*; the courtroom on *The Practice*; Winslow High on *Boston Public*. Three shows, all hits, are filmed here on state-of-the-art soundstages. Overlooking them, from his top-floor office, is the man who produces all three. But he is not reading spreadsheets or making conference calls. In fact, he doesn't use a computer. He writes on a yellow legal pad.

Three shows, all hits, all breathed into life by one man: David E. Kelley, the medium's most prolific storyteller. Beginning with *L.A. Law* and *Picket Fences*, the forty-five-year-old former attorney has been responsible for creating more provocative, addictively watchable television than anyone else in the last decade. Of the 66 hours of network television his company produced last year, Kelley wrote or co-wrote all but three. He has solo credit on 39 scripts, including 19 episodes of *Ally McBeal*, a program so idiosyncratic that Kelley has had trouble farming it out to other writers. When Kelley agreed last year to create *Boston Public* for Fox, he wound up writing thirteen scripts by himself, including the first eight episode, and shared credit on another eight.

Camryn Manheim, who won an Emmy Award in 1998 for *The Practice*, has called him an "idiot savant," someone who writes brilliantly without a clue how he does it. Almost unbelievably, he generates all of this material while keeping a regular 9-to-6 routine at work. (The joke I heard was that you'd leave work by 6, too, if Michelle Pfeiffer was waiting for you at home.) And he does it by actually writing, longhand, on special legal pads that are no longer manufactured. (His staff has several years' worth stowed away.)

Pam Wisne, president of Kelley's production company, was hired last year in part to help him cut down on his workload. She told me that won't be a problem, because her boss works well with other writers, some of whom have been with him for years. Kelley must inspire loyalty, because it's a safe bet that few of his employees live near Manhattan Beach, a 20-mile crawl down the 405 freeway from West L.A. As compensation, they get to work for a legend at a high-tech facility with every amenity, including a daycare center. "The best work environment I've ever been in," said Alice West, co-executive producer of *Ally McBeal* and a longtime Kelley associate, as we toured the surprisingly small bar that has become synonymous with song stylist Vonda Shepard. (The bar scenes are filmed with long lenses to give the illusion of size, West explained.)

Robert Breech, the executive producer of *The Practice*, has worked with Kelley since *L.A. Law* in the mid-1980s. He told me about the time that he and another staffer were in Kelley's office, discussing an episode in production. The master was silently immersed in a script when suddenly, he put down his pen to join the conversation. When the subject changed, he immediately returned to writing. "Not *thinking*," Breech underscores, "*writing.*"

Of course, some would use this story as evidence, not of Kelley's freakish powers of concentration, but of why his shows have become so gratingly repetitive.

On the afternoon I was visiting, I happened to come across Kelley in the parking lot, wearing a short-sleeved shirt, faded jeans and white sneakers. He was just out to stretch his legs. I made small talk with him and a couple of associates. Without warning, he then sauntered off in the direction of his office.

Someone next to me said they know a meeting is over when Kelley looks down at his legal pad and starts writing.

Remembering Steve Harvey

Kansas City Star, December 10, 2001

I first heard the story of Steven L. Harvey from a producer named David Wallach. He had heard the story from an assignment editor at WDAF-TV, where Wallach worked after moving to Kansas City. Harvey was a talented young musician and a rising star in the local music scene when, at age 27, he was brutally murdered near the Liberty Memorial. Wallach would cover a lot of crime over the years, including a lot of upstanding people senselessly cut down in the prime of life. But there was something about Steve Harvey. Wallach was also struck by the tenacious effort that Harvey's parents and friends had undertaken to bring the killer to justice — how they hadn't given up after the local jury brought back an acquittal — and how the feds came in to undertake a second prosecution that resulted in a history-making conviction.

Later, when Wallach became a producer for the A&E crime series *City Confidential,* he returned to Kansas City to tell Steve's story, for the first time, to a national audience.

Steve Harvey grew up at 55th and Bellefontaine in Kansas City's working-class Blue Hills neighborhood. He was one of three children in the home of Kathryn and Sherman Harvey, loving parents who would support Steve's career by providing him with room, board and transport for the rest of his life. During his senior year at Southeast High School, Steve took part in a jazz lab where he met the other members of what would become Mass Transit, a jazz-fusion-party ensemble he fronted throughout the 1970s. One day, a teenaged trumpeter from Grandview arrived on the Harveys' doorstep, after hearing that a group was looking for a horn player. Sherman Harvey opened the door, looked the shaggy-haired visitor up and down and then called out: "There's a white boy here!"

His name was Mark Pender. "Steve shows up, pulls his saxophone out, and my jaw drops," he recalled. "I'd never seen a young guy play that well. He was so nice and encouraging to me. He accepted me as a band member from that night." The two became constant companions at the city's many nightly jam sessions. By 1979 they were playing six, seven, eight places in one night.

"Steve would sit in with every band," said Greg Richter, who played piano in a quintet with Harvey. "He always played whatever they were playing: Earth, Wind & Fire, bebop, Sinatra. He knew all the notes." Singer Ida McBeth remembered seeing Harvey at the Phillips Hotel and the old Drum Room. "He was an extremely fine player who was very entertaining when he let the music overtake him," she said.

That was often. More than anything else, it was Steve Harvey's stage presence that people recalled for me, often with great fondness. His soloes electrified the crowd, and he wasn't afraid to wander onto the floor during the song and lead a line dance. He had a whistle he liked to pull out and blow while exhorting crowds away from their cocktail tables. He was the Pied Piper of good times. One friend remembers him walking down the middle of 63rd Street with his saxophone, serenading drivers stuck in traffic.

By 1979 Steve and Mark were looking beyond Kansas City. They accepted an offer to join the traveling band of jazz organist Charles Earland, which played for three months in the Midwest before finishing with some dates in northern New Jersey. The two men hoped their momentum would carry them across the Hudson River and into the New York music scene. But after the band reached Newark, N.J., Earland told Mark and Steve that they could go home.

Steve went. He had two young children in Kansas City, and he missed them. Mark took an apartment in a rough neighborhood in New Jersey. One night he was attacked by some thugs who stole his trumpet. Though he was shaken, he went out and got a new horn and played on. As it turned out, he was the lucky one. "A few days before he died, he called me," Mark Pender said. "He was going to join me out here."

In the early hours of Wednesday, Nov. 5, 1980, Steve left a late-night jam at the Inferno Show Lounge and drove to Liberty Memorial with his saxophone. Ronald Reagan had just been elected president, and friends say Steve was feeling kind of blue. So, as he often did when he felt that way, he went out alone to the park to wail at the moon until sunrise. He went to use a public restroom at the park. A few moments later, nineteen-year-old Raymond L. Bledsoe walked in with a wooden dowel rod, accompanied by two other men, one of whom was holding a baseball bat. They had come looking to crack the heads of gay men who were known to cruise at that bathroom. The sight of a black man — particularly one he assumed was gay — stirred a satanically violent urge in Bledsoe. He struck Steve Harvey with the dowel rod, breaking it. Steve tried to escape, but the three young men pursued him outside. Bledsoe took the bat and smashed it repeatedly against Steve's head until it caved in. The murder weapon was never found.

A tip led police to Bledsoe's accomplices. They flipped, but with only their word against his, an all-white jury decided there wasn't enough evidence to convict Bledsoe. So he walked — and then he talked, boasting to at least thirty people about the murder. He told one friend he'd killed a "nigger queen"; to another, that "a black fag made a pass at me."

There was a community activist in Kansas City at that time named Alvin Sykes, who already had a reputation as someone who liked to right wrongs, even though he was untrained in the law. It was Sykes who found a little-enforced statute in the federal code, 18 U.S.C. Sec. 245(b)(2)(B), which states that anyone who "willfully injures, intimidates or interferes with ... any person because of his race, color, religion or national origin and because he is ... participating in or enjoying any benefit, service, privilege, program, facility or activity provided or administered by any State or subdivision thereof," can be sentenced to a term befitting the severity of the crime.

It was Sykes who pestered the U.S. attorney, Richard Roberts, until Roberts agreed to meet with him. With assistance from the Harvey family, Sykes devoted himself to the campaign to have Bledsoe retried on a federal civil rights charge. In 1983 Roberts took the case and, armed with the additional testimony, got Bledsoe sentenced to a life term in prison. Like many federal inmates, it is expected he will be released after thirty years, in 2013.

Afterword

After I wrote my story, I realized I knew how David Wallach felt. I ordered a framed picture of Steve from photographer Hartzell Gray, who had captured him at an outdoor concert honoring Kansas City native Count Basie in 1980. It's the picture reproduced above, and it still hangs in my living room. In the original, uncropped photo Gray took, Steve is front and center on the bandstand with Basie, while Mark Pender is standing at the edge of the stage. He looks like an uninvited guest.

The Bledsoe victory wound up launching Sykes into a career as a private gumshoe specializing in unsolved civil rights cases. Thanks to his tenacity and his knack for getting government lawyers to return his phone calls, Sykes is credited with having at least a hand in more than 100 cold cases being reopened or bumped up the priority list. That includes two of the movement's most notorious unsolved crimes: the 1955 murder of Emmett Till and the 1964 killings of James Chaney, Andrew Goodman, and Michael Schwermer as they tried to register voters in Mississippi during "Freedom Summer."

Alvin Sykes is a high school dropout who has lived his entire adult life without any visible means of support. But there is unfinished business from the civil rights struggle, and this moral imperative has allowed him to burrow in deep at the Department of Justice and other key agencies. He helped negotiate the passage of the Emmett Till Unsolved Civil Rights Crime Act, even getting the Senate's infamous "Dr. No," Tom Coburn, to remove his hold on the Till Bill.

Early in 2009 I sat in a room with a group of Kansas City civil rights leaders to celebrate the Till Bill's passage, and I'll never forget their stupefied reaction as they watched a videotaped testimonial by Coburn, praising Sykes as "a wonderful man that I am now proud to call my friend" and adding, "Let there be no doubt that Alvin Sykes is responsible for the Till Bill's passage."

That was one of Steve Harvey's legacies. The other was Mark, his musical partner-in-crime. Pender was the shy guy back then, but he was watching. And learning.

In July 2009, I went to see *The Tonight Show with Conan O'Brien*. Just before taping started, the musicians came charging out from behind the bandstand, instruments in hand. As they started into the rousing jump-blues standard "Baby," a couple of band members marched up into the audience seats. Leading the procession was Mark Pender. He has been the band's trumpeter since O'Brien began doing a show in 1993. Horn in one hand, microphone in the other, he would belt out the melody on his trumpet, then lead the audience in an exuberant call-and-response: "Baaaaayyy-beh!" The number is a staple of Pender's live performance, whether he is in a television studio, a nightclub in Kansas City, or a jazz festival he's invited to headline. If I've seen it once, I've seen it fifty times — to this day, though, there is something strangely thrilling about watching Mark work the crowd, the way Steve once did.

Once, I asked him what would've happened if Steve had lived. "I think he'd probably have realized his dream and had a wonderful career," Pender said.

Later in the taping, I looked over at the bandstand, and for a moment I imagined Steve up there, wailing away next to his comrade in horns. I pictured the two of them leading the parade into the seats. Afterward, I imagined them at a jam session on Sunset Boulevard. Saying their good-byes for the night, Mark goes home to his wife and son, and Steve heads for a spot overlooking L.A. He takes out his saxophone one more time and begins to play, something slow and soothing to expel any blues that might still be lodged in his breast. Something to ease the troubled mind, his and anyone else who might be in earshot.

2002

For the third time in four years, an American broadcaster timidly inserted into its summer schedule a reality TV series that had proven wildly popular in other countries. And just as ABC and CBS had done with their sleeper hits, Fox would move Season 2 of *Idol* to the regular-season schedule. And just as *Survivor* trumped *Who Wants To Be a Millionaire*, *American Idol* would go on to outshine both shows in every possible way. For now, *Friends*, *CSI*, *ER* and *Raymond* were the most-watched shows on TV. Other than that, the year seemed to go by quietly. Thank God.

Bias *and Dan Rather*

Kansas City Star, February 24, 2002

Bias, the diatribe by former CBS newsman Bernard Goldberg, has been on the *New York Times* nonfiction list for weeks, yet has failed to inspire the kind of discussion that often accompanies a provocative, idea-driven best seller. Perhaps that's because the book's argument is buried under a multi-chapter attack on Dan Rather, whom Goldberg accuses of sandbagging his career. In 1996, after "complaining privately about bias at CBS News for years," Goldberg took his grievance public, in an op-ed article for the *Wall Street Journal* that singled out for criticism a piece on the *CBS Evening News* that made fun of the Steve Forbes flat-tax proposal. Rather immediately dropped Goldberg as a contributor, and the name of Bernie was soon mud all over the network. So, after 28 years, he called it quits. *Bias* was clearly designed to appeal to Dan-haters everywhere. But Goldberg seems not to have figured out his official story on the matter. He denies having a "feud" with the star anchor, yet five pages later, in the book's most talked-about phrase, Goldberg delivers some smack to Rather's supporters, calling them Dan's "bitches"(this includes the current president of CBS News, Andrew Heyward). He also flip-flops between asserting that Rather "didn't tolerate dissent" and lamely claiming that he never thought his *Journal* piece would put him on the outs with "The Dan." Once he is done unloading this baggage, however,

Goldberg's book gets interesting. *Bias* exposes some of the peculiar taboos of TV news, such as the discomfort network producers felt with "prison stories (that) showed too many black inmates and not enough white ones." A better story would be investigating why prisons were filling up with minorities — but that, Goldberg notes, "would be hard, time-consuming, expensive work" that TV networks would rather avoid. Other chapters, including "How Bill Clinton Cured Homelessness," provide strong evidence that some media trends might be driven by little more than prejudices of a select group of well-heeled news professionals in New York. Alas, it appears *Bias* will be remembered, by supporters and critics alike, for its author's ham-handed tirade against a third-place news operation that has seen better days.

TV, described

Kansas City Star, April 16, 2002

Video description may be the most useful enhancement to the TV signal since closed captioning. So why are the networks trying to kill it? This month several popular television programs began offering an alternate audio track for people who are blind or visually impaired. The service has been around experimentally for years, but will expand widely thanks to an FCC order that took effect April 1. Video description adds the voice of a narrator describing visual elements in the picture. It airs on the secondary audio program or SAP channel. The describer tells people who cannot see a TV screen what they are missing: a facial expression, a car crash, someone spying on another character. The voiceovers are dropped in unobtrusively when characters aren't speaking. They even describe the opening credits. "In a cartoon, words float through clouds," a voice says over the theme music for *The Simpsons.* "Lisa almost runs over her father on a bike. Marge drives straight toward him! In the living room, two men repossess their sofa. As Homer cries, the kids face the TV. Titles appear on a TV set." Hollywood waged a losing legal battle against closed captioning, so it is no surprise that the TV and movie industries are fighting video description. In late March a federal appeals court denied their motion to halt the FCC mandate. They claimed that video description involves "substantial costs." That's rich. Larry Goldberg, who directs WGBH's Media Access Group, the leading supplier of video descriptions, said describing a TV show costs $2,000 to $4,000 an hour. We're talking programs with budgets of $1.5 million to $3 million per hour. Goldberg told me, "We like to say it's the doughnut budget." Mmmm, doughnuts.

They want Moore

Kansas City Star, March 27, 2002

Michael Moore likes to portray himself as a portly slacker who would rather be at home watching ESPN. But lately he has belied that image by conducting a grueling, cross-country tour to promote his book *Stupid White Men ... And Other Sorry Excuses for the State of the Nation*, a 266-page tirade against George W. Bush that has unexpectedly touched a nerve with readers. Moore was in Kansas City Monday for two appearances. After the

700 tickets for his UMKC talk were given away in two days, a late-night program was added at the Uptown Theater, where another thousand people paid five dollars each, with proceeds supporting the Free Speech Coalition.

While the author was being shuttled across town, musical guests Iris DeMent and the Wilders serenaded the crowd with "This Land Is Your Land." Moore's evening ended at 1:15 Tuesday morning — six hours, two performances, and hundreds of autographs later. "Twenty-five cities," he said, "and not one of these has ended in the p.m. Always the a.m."

Moore's book is currently No. 1 on the *New York Times'* list, but this sudden demand to see him in person suggests something more than a publishing phenomenon. It is as though Moore has sounded the alarm that has roused the opposition from its slumber. "People want so badly to support America and do what's right," says Anne Winter, the owner of Recycled Sounds and a member of the Free Speech Coalition. "But we're not necessarily behind the president and what he represents." Moore said, "I had a guy come up to me and say, 'This is the first time in six months I felt comfortable wearing this T-shirt.' The T-shirt said I HATE GEORGE BUSH. This isn't supposed to be a country where you're afraid to speak your mind. This government has had its boot to the neck of the American people. It said, 'If you're critical of George Bush, you're unpatriotic.'"

After the Sept. 11 terrorist attacks, HarperCollins refused to issue *Stupid White Men*. According to Moore, his editors wanted him to rewrite much of the book and tone down the anti-Bush rhetoric. He not only refused, but began campaigning on his Web site to put pressure on HarperCollins. Both the publication delay and Moore's campaign helped fuel the book's juggernaut. *Stupid White Men* has gone through fifteen printings in six weeks.

On tour, Moore eschews the traditional book lecture for a one-hour performance that is part stand-up comedy act, part Green Party rally. He mocked Bush's policies, comparing his anti-terrorism crusade to the "permanent war" of Orwell's *1984*. He alluded frequently to the 2000 election, forming quote marks with his fingers whenever he said "President" Bush. Moore also gave a rollicking, blow-by-blow account of his book negotiations. He recalled how a HarperCollins executive told him he was "out of touch with the American people," a remark that drew derisive laughter. When the publisher asked to come up with a different book title, Moore suggested *Bring Me the Head of Antonin Scalia*.

During the signing session afterwards, a young female attorney asked Moore for advice on making documentary films. He suggested making one about her firm's largest client. "The best documentary you can make is something you know," he said, "You know stuff we don't. You've had a peek behind that curtain." Another fan handed him a book with a waterlogged title page. When Moore asked what had happened, she said sheepishly, "My roommate blew bong water on it."

At 1:45 a.m., Moore was the last man out of the Uptown. He gathered the CDs, T-shirts and zines given to him by appreciative fans. Stuffing them into his tote bag, he laughed. "What am I going to tell the guy at the airport," he said, "when he asks me if any strangers have given me anything?"

The irony of local TV news

Electronic Media, February 11, 2002

When Newton Minow stepped to the microphone of the National Association of Broadcasters annual convention in 1961, he wasted little time getting to the point. "I invite you to sit down in front of your television set when your station goes on the air, and stay there without a book, magazine, newspaper, profit-and-loss sheet, or rating book to distract you — and keep your eyes glued to that set until the station signs off," Minow said. "I can assure you that you will observe a vast wasteland."

One of the supreme ironies in broadcast history is that the chain of events that led to the dumbing down of TV news began right there, with the famous "vast wasteland" speech. Minow — President Kennedy's choice to head up the FCC — in effect threatened to start pulling broadcasters' licenses if they didn't start to repay in public service what they extracted from television in profit. But what exactly did he have in mind? Minow's speech was long on dudgeon and short on specifics, and panicked broadcasters begged for clues from Washington. The agency responded by suggesting "community ascertainment" studies to determine if the stations were serving their interests.

What the stations did, not surprisingly, is bring in consultants — the same consultants who had spent the 1950s applying the latest social science techniques to persuade people to buy more GM cars and Kenmore appliances. At first the broadcasters simply wanted to show the government that they were worthy of license renewals. Later, as the research became more sophisticated, the consultants began to show station managers how they could turn their local news "product" into a profit center.

Craig Allen, a journalism professor at Arizona State with two decades' experience as a local TV news director, anchor and producer, tells this unlikely story in his new book, *News Is People*. What the research uncovered, Allen writes, was a great American class divide. Corporate leaders, by and large, were college-educated and affluent, while their rank-and-file workers, like their customers, were of modest means and education. "For journalists everywhere, the advent of research was a right-angle turn," Allen told me. "It gave Joe Sixpack a direct voice in the news process."

Two former ad men, Philip McHugh and Peter Hoffman, were hired in 1963 by Storer Broadcasting, which owned five stations. All of its stations' newscasts were mired in last place. Oddly, though, when McHugh and Hoffman convened focus groups, they heard viewers complaining bitterly about Storer's top-rated rivals. They were put off by anchors that talked above their heads, or promoted political stories or international news over local news. What ordinary folk really wanted, their research revealed, was to know what was going on in their neighborhoods — and to have news anchors who cared about their concerns. So why did they keep watching those newscasts if they hated them so much? Because no one had yet thought to create news for Joe Sixpack.

Over the next four years McHugh and Hoffman helped Storer do just that, and its stations soared past their competitors, who responded in turn by hiring some of the many other firms that had sprung up to meet the demand. And thus news doctoring was born.

Among the more surprising findings Allen made while looking through decades-old research concerned Walter Cronkite, a harsh critic of dumbed-down journalism and news-by-consultancy. In yet another irony of television news, Uncle Walter came perilously close to being fired in 1963. Consultants had secretly convened focus groups for CBS, and discovered that viewers thought Cronkite stuffy and standoffish — a "history teacher," one called him. Only when he opened up emotionally, while covering the Kennedy assassination, did people warm to Cronkite. That improved his research, and probably saved his career.

2003

My dominant image of the year 2003 is of stacking two brand new Time Warner DVRs on top of my TV in the hours before hostilies broke out in Iraq. They were just two of fifty such devices in the entire area; the rest were in the hands of company beta testers. I had clamored for them, despite the known issues with the software, so I could cover shock and awe simultaneously on four different news channels. As the war progressed, however, I found my interest drifting away from ABC, CBS, NBC, CNN, and Fox and toward the foreign news sources that were readily available for the first time to anyone in the U.S.

On the entertainment front, half of Nielsen's Top Ten was made up of unscripted shows: two hours of *Idol*, an hour of *Survivor*, and the venerable *Monday Night Football* — but the highest-rated was a short-lived dating contest on Fox, *Joe Millionaire*, which finished behind *CSI* and *Friends* as the No. 3 show of the 2002-2003 season.

Can reality TV rekindle democracy?

Electronic Media, January 27, 2003

When I heard that FX was going to stage a competition in which viewers would select a candidate for president, I had visions of Simon Cowell rolling his eyes and telling an idealistic young contestant that was the *worst* deficit-reduction plan he had *ever* heard. But then I learned that the project was the brainchild of R.J. Cutler, the documentary filmmaker who worked on *The War Room*, D.A. Pennebaker's terrific account of the 1992 presidential campaign, and made his own election movie, *A Perfect Candidate,* about Oliver North's run for the U.S. Senate in '94. There's a scene toward the end of Cutler's film in which North's campaign manager, Mark Goodin, has clearly had it with all the sound bites and counterspin and mudslinging. Campaigns, he wearily concludes, "provide daily entertainment. What (they) are not providing is serious solutions to what's going on in the country. Not us ... not Clinton ... not *you*," he says, looking right into the camera. "That's my favorite moment in the film," Cutler told me as we sat in his office in a decidedly unglamorous section of Culver City. "I agree with his lament. I really did feel that there was widespread malaise in the 2000 election. You knew there was a difference" — between Bush and Gore — "but still, it felt so hard to care because it was like the choices were preordained." *American Candidate* will try to rekindle its viewers' faith in democracy through an alternate reality in which anyone can run for president. Already hundreds of people have emailed his office, unsolicited, wanting to be included in the race. Cutler pulled out a fat binder and began reading applications at random. Most of them were touchingly decent. "My family is half-Catholic, half-Jewish, so it never occurred to me to be intolerant. ... My father and grandparents emigrated to the U.S. after the failed democratic uprising in Hungary. ... I'm a common man with common thoughts and everyday ideas. Given a chance I could win this thing and do some good for everyday people in the process."

Kimmel to ABC ...

Kansas City Star, Feb. 4, 2003

In his first week of late-night TV, the talented and likable host of *Jimmy Kimmel Live* often had the unfortunate look of Sisyphus moments after the rock had rolled back over him. Not only has ABC's replacement for Bill Maher been saddled with insignificant guest bookings — the first-week lineup included Tammy Faye Messner, a psychic, and a fry chef — but Kimmel has had to contend with a studio audience that acts as though it were dragged in from Hollywood Boulevard five minutes before the broadcast. For one night he was at least able to ply the crowd with free drinks. Then someone got sick and a nervous ABC yanked the studio's liquor license. Things haven't been the same since. The El Capitan Theater was heavily miked, and much of the time the ambient noise from the audience sounded like Ross Perot's fabled giant sucking sound. For the Jan. 27 broadcast, the writers thought it would be funny to dump fake snow on the set in a parody of a promotion NBC had aired earlier that night called "Blizzard Monday." The studio audience seemed unaware of "Blizzard Monday" until Kimmel brought it up. The snow landed with a thud, and so did the routine. Kimmel's co-host for the week, rapper Snoop Dogg, didn't appreciate imitation flakes falling into his cocktail. Kimmel was a polished sidekick on Comedy Central's *Win Ben Stein's Money* and *The Man Show*, and with his tremendous gift of gab he has the potential to become the next Jon Stewart. But it is worth recalling that Stewart's first late-night talk show was canceled.

... and Maher to HBO

Kansas City Star, February 20, 2003

Being Bill Maher means you have strong opinions about many things, including breakfast. As I enter his office at CBS Television City, he is stirring rice bran extract into a warm seven-grain mixture he prepared the night before. While this ritual is underway, he starts talking about the idiocy of the typical American diet. "Look at the four or five best-selling prescription drugs — they're all chemicals to put out the fire in your stomach from the shit you put in it," he says. "A lot of the health care problems in America could be solved by people changing their habits." The country's most provocative satirist returns has a new weekly program, *Real Time With Bill Maher,* on HBO. Maher was chased off ABC last year, his *Politically Incorrect* the victim of nervous Nellies at the network after the show's fateful broadcast six days after 9/11. Maher's sin was agreeing with his guest, conservative author Dinesh D'Souza, about the "bravery" of the Sept. 11 hijackers, whom he referred to as "warriors" (the president had repeatedly called the hijackers "cowards"). Since his firing, Maher has been showered with First Amendment awards, published a best-selling book, upgraded to HBO and cut his schedule back to one show a week. He even got his old office back, the exact one he used for *PI.* The furniture was still there when he returned. "It's very odd," Maher says, propping his feet on a wobbly coffee table. "I think some people in the building thought I just went on vacation for six months."

Queer show, straight fans

Kansas City Star, August 5, 2003

When the phone lines opened last Wednesday on *The Tenth Voice,* KKFI's radio show for Kansas City's gay and lesbian community, guess what most callers wanted to talk about. Was it: (a) President Bush's declaration that homosexuals should not be allowed to marry? (b) Word that the pope was planning to speak out against gay marriage and adoption? (c) That kicky new show on the Bravo channel? Yep — and gay viewers aren't the only ones buzzing about *Queer Eye for the Straight Guy* on Bravo. "A lot of straight women I know are watching, too," said Mark Manning, host of *The Tenth Voice.* Indeed, Bravo's ratings are soaring among adult women, the channel's target audience, thanks to *Queer Eye.* "I told my husband that he should watch it because he might learn something," said Reuille Green, a fan from Kansas City. The show's style experts, known collectively as the "Fab Five," generously dispense tips on wardrobe, grooming, food, wine, culture and home decor. Their ideas are designed with the clueless male in mind, but their practical approach and good humor appeal to female viewers as well. Jamie Rich, director of the Lesbian and Gay Community Center in Westport, called *Queer Eye* a "revolutionary" program because it presents an image of gays never before seen on TV. "Usually what happens (with gays) on television, it's who can be the most acid-tongued person — like Sean Hayes," said Rich, referring to the actor who plays Will's wisecracking pal on *Will & Grace.* By contrast, the Fab Five "are always doing something nice for people."

Long hot summer

Kansas City Star, August 20, 2003

People are stopping Kansas City's best-paid meteorologists in stores and asking them that burning question: When's this heat wave ever going to end? "By the end of the week it'll be out of the searing 100s," said KMBC's Bryan Busby. But that's not what WDAF's Mike Thompson is telling viewers. "A system like this, it's just stuck," said Thompson, referring to the high-pressure front hovering 30,000 feet above Kansas City. Because the front has baked much of the moisture out of the soil, Thompson said, it's harder for clouds to form and bring relief. KSHB forecaster Gary Lezak agreed that the severe heat will return next week. But he disagrees with Thompson and says a front that is approaching Kansas City will result in a slight cool-off this weekend. "We look at the same data set," said Lezak. "I make up my own mind and Mike makes up his. He thinks it (the cool front) won't make it through here. I think it will." KCTV, Channel 5, chief meteorologist Katie Horner is somewhere in the middle. She too has looked at the computer models issued by the National Weather Service. "I see a little break on Thursday, and then it just gets hot again," Horner said. I asked Thompson about that. "The computer models are wrong," he said. "I just kind of ignore them."

Chuck Lorre's subliminal messages

Kansas City Star, September 18, 2003

There's a heartwarming story behind *Two and a Half Men,* one of the best new shows of the season. The story will be told at the end of the pilot episode — but will pass by so quickly that millions of viewers won't even know they missed it. The 233-word account, written by the show's co-creator Chuck Lorre, appears on his production company's "vanity card" that will flash on screen for all of two seconds after the closing credits. After every show Lorre's company has produced, he's put a message on the vanity card, readable only by people who can pause the video. ("I believe that the Laws of Karma do not apply to show business, where good things happen to bad people on a fairly regular basis. ... Aren't we as a nation sophisticated enough to hunt down and kill our enemies without constantly referring to them as 'evil'?" They're all online at chucklorre.com.) After Lorre's show *Dharma & Greg* was cancelled, his friend Lee Aronsohn approached him with an idea about two brothers who move in together. "Chuck was not excited about it," Aronsohn recalled. "But being a great guy, he went with it." That's because, as it turns out, Aronsohn was desperate not to lose his health insurance. "No matter how much you make in one year, if you don't make enough the next year, your insurance lapses," Aronsohn told me. By helping his friend, Lorre helped himself. CBS gave *Two and a Half Men* the network's choicest time slot. And that led to this vanity card: "When *Dharma* was canceled my heart was broken," it concludes. "How do you mend a broken heart? The Bee Gees never figured it out, but I did. You help a friend keep their health insurance from lapsing."

Fear Factor's *frightening success*

Kansas City Star, September 29, 2003

Because I don't assume the worst about people, I admit I'm mystified by the prolonged success of NBC's *Fear Factor*. The reality show where contestants get to eat bugs and re-enact dangerous movie stunts for a $50,000 top prize is this generation's version of flagpole-sitting, corrupted by teledollars. Host Joe Rogan is a charming fellow who yells at his own staff and trash-talks anyone who dares criticize *Fear Factor*. The producers of *Fear Factor* are the same folks responsible for *Big Brother,* which is to say they are magnets for toxic people. They not only hand-picked Rogan as the show's host, but also decided to play up his abrasiveness toward the contestants. And here's the scary part — it worked. The show successfully crossed over from summer filler to become a prime-time contender.

America's least-loved liberal

Kansas City Star, November 2, 2003

We're here in Manhattan for the first book signing by Fox News Channel's house liberal, Alan Colmes, because we're curious: What kind of person lines up to have a book signed by Alan Colmes? Wes Bigler, a financial planner from Atlanta, watches only Fox News, thinks the rest of the news media is biased, and supports President Bush. He said he likes Colmes because "he asks very good questions and backs them up with facts. He's probably a little left, but you can't really tell." Dave Parker, a heavy construction worker from Queens, was not immediately drawn to Colmes — "When I first started watching him, I hated him," he said — but over time he came to prefer Colmes to Hannity, who Parker now finds to be "too shrill" and "over the top." So it seems the back end of *Hannity & Colmes* is the preferred liberal for millions of right-wingers. After the book signing, Colmes told me about an incident two weeks earlier in Orlando. "This lady said to her son, 'Look, Ricky, it's your first liberal.' Most people want some diversity in their lives. Conservatives want to hear how someone who doesn't think like they do actually thinks. They want to hear a reasonable point of view free of the mudslinging." It's not anything he has to say, but the way he says it, that endears Colmes to the people waiting to purchase *Red White & Liberal: How Left Is Right & Right Is Wrong.* As the subtitle suggests, Colmes's book brims with debaterly earnestness. He spends most of it defending liberalism from the usual insults — that he's unpatriotic, that he's anti-Christian, that liberals control the media, etc. He avoids personal attacks in favor of sometimes clumsy bon mots ("I'd rather hug a tree than a tax cut we can't afford"). On the book jacket, there is a blurb from Newt Gingrich: "Alan Colmes is definitely my favorite liberal with whom to argue." To prominent liberals, such praise from the right just shows that Colmes is kidding himself. Satirist Al Franken has a running gag in one of his books where, every time he mentions the show, the word "Colmes" appears in teensy type. "So they continue to make the case that Fox News Channel is an arm of the GOP," Colmes said of his critics. "The only way they can do that is to diminish my role here. If I'm a potent, strong liberal, then the contention that we aren't fair and balanced has holes shot in it." *(Postscript: Colmes left the show in 2008 and wasn't replaced.)*

War in 3 ... 2 ... and ...

Excerpts from columns I wrote during the invasion of Iraq about media coverage of the war.

Is it on?

Kansas City Star, March 21, 2003

As viewers saw explosions and anti-aircraft fire lighting up the night sky over Baghdad, network anchors and reporters struggled to divine whether this was the opening movement in the American assault on Iraq, the so-called "shock and awe" offensive. They had all jumped in as soon as air raid sirens began wailing in the Iraqi capital, but retreated 90 minutes later. Later, when aides announced that Defense Secretary Rumsfeld would give a press briefing at 10 a.m. Central time, the networks decided the moment had arrived. Instead, Rummy opened the briefing by speaking directly to the people of Iraq — his remarks were being broadcast inside the country.

Hours passed; no war. The networks spent the day talking strategy with their parade of experts and taking video phone calls from their reporters on the front lines. NBC and Fox News Channel, in particular, seemed to have enough retired military brass to fill an officers' club, though their relentless, bunker-busting optimism tended to make them blend together, like Weather Channel meteorologists.

So I flipped around and compared the networks' various graphics packages, created for the occasion. CBS showed off its "America at War" sequence with music that sounded like it had been mixed for a German disco. NBC aired a rather gruesome computer animation that showed a missile corkscrewing into a bunker and going boom. ABC's Peter Jennings seemed less than impressed with all his new bells and whistles. As a three-dimensional map of southern Iraq took over the screen, Jennings dryly referred to it as "one of our technological wonders." And when a cartoon tank cut its way through a berm like it was warm butter, he derisively added, "Well, yes, it isn't quite as easy as that."

The more you watch, the less you know

Kansas City Star, March 23, 2003

There is no question that the presence of journalists alongside fighting units in Iraq has increased the flow of information about the progress of allied forces. But it also has added to the amount of meaningless clutter that already bombards viewers.

Before the outbreak of war, it was unclear how much live reporting the 500 U.S. journalists embedded with combat units would actually be able to do. We now know the answer: a lot. Since Thursday night, each network has been airing various running accounts from its journalists, including some transmissions by videophone from moving vehicles — a technical feat that was impossible until recently. During one remote, CBS's John Roberts was interviewing a Marine gunner from a staging area when word came to move out. Roberts chatted with Dan Rather back in New York as he got into his rig and rode off, the camera following him the whole time. With global-positioning antennas on the roof of the rig, CBS claims, Roberts can go live at 50 mph.

But the giddiness that has accompanied these video adventures does not serve viewers at all. When CNN's Walter Rodgers began excitedly broadcasting from his ride-along with the 7th Cavalry in southern Iraq, his colleagues in New York reacted as if the Giants had won the Super Bowl. After it aired, a Canadian journalist, daring to say what Rodgers' American counterparts would not, called it "cheerleading."

News anchors keep telling us what a wonderful thing the embed program is, but there has not been much discussion of whether all the reporting is helping viewers. Indeed, judging from messages posted to my message board, the addition of the embeds is making it harder, not easier, to understand this war. "I consider myself a news junkie," one wrote, "and I find that my eyes glaze over when trying to synthesize what the television gives me." Some people have begun seeking refuge with Web sites and public radio, which are less of an assault on the senses. Others have simply stopped watching. On Thursday night NBC and CBS went back to regular programming, giving ABC broadcast ownership of the war. When the Nielsen ratings came in Friday, it was a reminder that no matter how good a show a news organization puts on, it still can't beat a rerun of *Friends*.

Where are voices from the battlefield?

Kansas City Star, March 25, 2003

Before U.S. soldiers began moving into Iraq with journalists riding shotgun, the Pentagon's chief PR flack promised that "the spokesmen for the war will be the kids next door in America, not the General Schwarzkopfs." That lofty ideal, however, has yet to be realized. Television coverage of the war has instead been dominated by the same people who commanded most of the air time during other recent wars: journalists and generals. The Pentagon holds special briefings with military experts so they will have talking points when discussing war strategy with Brit or Wolf.

On Monday evening, Thomas McInerney and Bob Scales, both ex-military, were on Fox News with a fancy map graphic showing how the Americans had moved the distance from Normandy to Belgium in a mere four days. McInerney praised the "brilliant strategy" of commanding Gen. Tommy Franks and said it had been "executed extraordinarily." Scales agreed, noting that U.S. forces were superior to Iraq's "in technology and morale and leadership."

So where are the soldiers? Mostly, they are showing up in newspaper photographs — breathtaking portraits of grace under pressure, whether involved in the grueling push toward Baghdad or the firefights near Basra. TV has not figured out how to tell these stories of suffering and strength through pixels and sound.

World media sees a different war

Kansas City Star, April 20, 2003

The war in Iraq became a watershed event in the annals of media, as the first where Americans could see and hear what the whole world thought in real time. Take April 9, the day cameras carried images around the world of U.S. troops helping pull down Saddam Hussein's stubborn statue in Baghdad. "This scene," said Paula Zahn on CNN, "should certainly leave very little doubt in everyone's minds today that if the regime isn't all but gone, it certainly is in disarray." On Lebanon's independent NBN network — in an excerpt featured on the American satellite channel LinkTV's daily news digest *Mosaic,* the moment was also rife with symbolism: "This is how the Americans ended the era of President Saddam Hussein in Iraq after decades of cooperating," NBN's correspondent said. "When he became useless to them and an obstacle to their plans, they eliminated him so they can rule Iraq themselves."

Americans wanting off the bandwagon of domestic war coverage have been turning to the BBC, which offered amusing contrasts with the coverage of Fox News, the most-watched cable news channel in the U.S. When looters pillaged the National Museum in Baghdad, the BBC termed the incident "a disaster" and gave wide coverage to an official, Donny George, who declared the museum's treasures "gone" and "lost." But on Fox News, reports quoted that same official saying that the museum's most precious goods might well have been removed before the fall of Baghdad. Fox's top anchor, Brit Hume, harrumphed, "Well, really, did it happen?" By contrast, when 1980s terrorist Abul Abbas was captured, Fox was all over it with triumphal coverage, while the BBC's Humphrey Hawksley dismissed it, saying, "Abul Abbas is seen very much as a has-been and out of the loop of those planning today's war on America."

'You the man, Bob!'

Kansas City Star, June 24, 2003

Bob Werly, the 66-year-old *eminence grisé* of Kansas City TV reporters, is retiring Friday after three decades at KMBC — but as I chased after him on a muggy afternoon earlier this month, I found him anything but retiring. On camera, Werly looks and acts more like a middle management type: he's silver-haired, bespectacled, and wears a striped tie that, no joke, he bought after seeing on an episode of *Law & Order.* But the Bob Werly I got to see was someone who relished the process of putting a story together in the hours leading up to his live shot. This, I had to conclude, is what explains his longevity in broadcast journalism. "He always seemed more like a newspaper guy than a television guy," said Fred Wickman, former *Star* columnist and longtime friend of Werly's. "He was thorough. Asked good questions. Wasn't very handsome." Jim Overbay, who was responsible for Werly's hiring at KMBC in 1971, called him "a throwback, an old-fashioned high-energy reporter." I wouldn't have thought to use the word "high-energy" until I saw him in person, moving in on a scene to claim a scoop. The sheer volume of his exclusives, his willingness to try anything, and his spare, evocative writing style have made him Channel 9's go-to reporter on the hard news of the day.

He had started this particular day making calls to Overland Park police, but after lunch he called me to say that I should meet him on the other end of the metro, at LaBenite Park in Sugar Creek. A decomposing body had gotten caught in the backwash of a jetty just east of the Highway 291 bridge. The fisherman who saw it called 911 and his brother. Then he and his fianceé went back to fishing, the body floating just a few feet away. The brother called Channel 9 with the tip. About an hour after that, Werly and photographer Mark Lea pulled up in a news truck. Various law enforcement officers stood around a boat trailer at water's edge. A black body bag lay on the ground.

A man came up to Werly and told him that the fisherman was still out at the levee, about a half-mile east. Werly suddenly got a spring in his step. Moving quickly, he and Lea grabbed their gear and headed toward the river. "For TV, this fisherman will make or break the story," Werly said as we moved in on the scene. "I know it's not the highest form of journalism, but this is the only thing that would make it interesting."

Werly walked up to a bank overlooking the river and yelled, "Excuse me, sir! Are you the guy who saw the body?" A man sitting on the far end of the jetty stood up and started to head toward him, but Werly shouted, "Just stay there! Go back to fishing. We'll come to you." After shimmying down the incline (on a bum knee), Werly introduced himself to the couple. Lea set up his camera while chatting with the eyewitnesses. Werly whispered to me, "See? So much of this story is the photographer. He's putting them at ease." When Werly started out in TV, cameramen weren't considered journalists.

In fact, a lot has changed since his first full-time job in Elkhart, Indiana, in 1963. Stories were shot on film and hand-spliced. Editors decided what the news would be, with no input from viewers. As TV news evolved, so did Werly. He adapted to live shots, viewer research, and even a major professional setback.

When Brian Bracco became KMBC news director in 1987, Werly was the medical reporter — a nice gig. "We still call him Doctor Bob," said Peggy Breit, his colleague for the last twenty-one years. Bracco gave the job to someone else. "He had fallen into a pattern," explained Bracco, who's now an executive with KMBC's parent company. Demoted and discouraged, Werly refused to take a hint. He returned to general-assignment duty and started to take on stories that showed his versatility and aggressiveness — qualities he knew the new boss valued.

"The great thing about Bob is that he's been through five news directors here, and he's been able to adjust his style to each one," Gary Roberts, the longtime assistant news director at KMBC, told me. Werly wanted me to know that there was no pressure put on him to retire. But when he learned that at age 65 he was entitled to his full pension and Social Security, in addition to his salary, he decided to "triple dip" for a year, then get out and move to a lake house with Kathy, his wife of twenty-four years.

He has a wealth of stories, and nearly all of them, as far as I can tell, include at least one embarrassing detail about Bob Werly. In 1964, he was the person who broke the news to Richard Nixon that his old sparring partner Nikita Khrushchev had been ousted as Soviet premier. "It's not as impressive as it sounds," Werly added, explaining that at the time, Nixon was a two-time election loser working in Indiana for the Goldwater campaign. He called a press conference, and Werly, who had just learned the news about Khrushchev, was the only reporter who bothered to show up.

Back at the levee, the fisherman and his fiancée gave Werly everything he needed and then some. Basically they talked his ear off. He listened patiently, as though he had nothing better to do all day. As Lea was packing up the camera gear, Werly asked the couple: "None of the other stations have been down to see you, right?" *No,* they said, *and we've got to leave in forty-five minutes.* Shortly after Lea and Werly made their way back to the park, at 2:50, an NBC Action News truck pulled up. "Do *not* tell him about the fisherman," Werly told me sternly. To Lea he said, "Let's go behind the tree and talk."

Afterward, Werly began "logging tape," playing back the interview and listening for sound bites he could use. Lea wandered around, eyeing his rival while shooting "B-roll," video wallpaper that Werly could talk over. The NBC reporter interviewed a patrolman who either didn't know about the fisherman or was in silent cahoots with Werly. One of the men who had helped him get the exclusive walked by. "Hey Bob," he said, "we ain't giving up no information to the other station. You the man, Bob!" At 3:34, the fishing party rolled by in their car and stopped briefly to talk with Werly. The NBC van disappeared and a truck from KCTV arrived. By this point, even the talking heads from the police were gone. The KCTV shooter photographed the river. Werly had his scoop. Lea could hardly contain his glee.

At 4:19 a second KMBC truck pulled up. There was a laptop-sized editing machine inside and a microwave link for live shots. By then Werly had selected the sound bites he would use and was finishing his script. Lea recorded Werly reading the script, sat down at the laptop and began merging the audio, sound bites and B-roll into a taped piece. In his spidery longhand, Werly wrote talking points for his live shot. He worked through the five o'clock newscast; the newsroom had decided to save his exclusive for the six. At 5:45 Lea fed the taped piece back to the station while Werly watched. There was the woman, telling him what it was like to be fishing next to a dead body. There was the man, saying that once the water patrol took the body away, he thought the fishing got better. "Good," was all Werly said.

At 5:59, as he stood before the camera in the park, he saw KCTV's Sandra Olivas at the top of the hill, also preparing for a live shot. "They may have something I don't," Werly said. "Maybe he was murdered." In fact, Olivas was going to report — as happens so often on TV — that there was little to report. Werly and Lea chatted until 6:04, then fell silent. Then: "Larry, the body was found ..." By 6:07 it was over.

"Did you see?" Werly said. "It fell out." He grabbed his dangling earpiece. "It fell out while I was on the air." Werly had scored the tip, the eyewitness, the exclusive, and the embarrassing detail to make the story complete. "This is the first exciting day I've had this week," Werly said, not sounding excited at all. "The part where you feel good about it — that's the part I'll probably miss the most."

2004

One of the wonders of television is how a single bold new show can make or remake a network. It happened to ABC — twice — in the fall of 2004, as both *Lost* and *Desperate Housewives* dazzled critics and viewers. Meanwhile, a puzzling new phenomenon arose: the microhit. Shows like *Arrested Development* and *Veronica Mars* wowed critics and practically no one else, yet networks kept them afloat in the hopes that viewers would catch on, as happened those many years ago with *Seinfeld*. Speaking of erstwhile NBC hits, *Friends* exited stage right in May, and not even the arrival of Donald Trump and *The Apprentice* was enough to stem the bleeding of viewers that has continued at NBC ever since.

Producer Robert Greenwald tried to rip the lid off Fox News Channel with his el cheapo documentary *Outfoxed,* that people mostly watched at house parties. It demonstrated that a business model based on viral marketing could work — but Fox News was barely scathed by Greenwald's hatchet job. In fact, it was a pretty good media year for the right, with the Swift Boat campaign helping to undo Democratic nominee John Kerry.

From the Super Bowl to *The Daily Show*, it was hard not to write about TV this year without writing about politics. Thank heavens for Conan O'Brien, Internet sex stings, and Ken Jennings.

CBS unmoved by MoveOn's ad

TV Barn, January 21, 2004

The heart stirs as soon as the lonesome guitar music starts. From a few feet away, through a dark and dismal restaurant kitchen, we see a boy no more than ten years old spraying off dirty dishes. The music quickens as a procession of solitary children performs other mind-numbing adult jobs: hauling garbage, changing tires, scanning groceries. Near the end of this thirty-second TV commercial, a message appears: "Guess who's going to pay off President Bush's $1 trillion deficit?" Titled "Child's Pay," the amateur ad last week won the contest sponsored by MoveOn.org, an advocacy group that wants

Bush out of office. It won over the judges with its understated appeal to every parent's worst fears. Large budget deficits are, to many, an abstract evil. But a Dickensian vision of a future in which our heirs atone for our fiscal sins (toiling, the ad suggests, in the only jobs that haven't been shipped overseas) hits people where they live. You can watch the winning ads online — but not on TV during the Super Bowl. MoveOn's $2 million buy was rejected by CBS because, a network executive explained, "We have a policy against accepting advocacy advertising." *(Postscript: CBS revised its policy. As this book went to press, the network accepted an anti-abortion ad for the 2010 Super Bowl.)*

If Nipplegate had happened on cable ...

Kansas City Star, February 8, 2004

When Janet Jackson's breast popped out on live television last Sunday, America's top media regulator, Michael Powell, launched a federal investigation. But when a naked, albeit blurred, breast appears on MTV, or a BET music video features sexually explicit lyrics and scenes — or any number of other everyday occurrences on cable TV shows supposedly OK for all ages — who makes a fuss? Almost no one. According to Nielsen Media Research, the most popular choices among young viewers include MTV, Cartoon Network, Comedy Central, BET and VH1. If you were to have sat down this past Tuesday and surfed those channels during the prime viewing hours for kids — 4 p.m. to 10 p.m. — here is some of what you would have seen: aging rock star Ozzy Osbourne and his wife, Sharon Osbourne, yelling bleeped profanities at each other. "Splash Waterfalls," the popular video airing daily on BET, in which rapper Ludacris and his female companion strip bare, their private parts pixellated. On MTV, the new Britney Spears video shows her nearly naked while getting it on with at least four men. A *South Park* rerun at 8:30 p.m. featured copious profanity, much of it unbleeped, followed by *Chappelle's Show* with Dave Chappelle and others using the N-word repeatedly. But Congress doesn't regulate cable TV the way it does broadcast TV. It can't. Previous attempts to restrict indecent programs on cable have been struck down by the U.S. Supreme Court, most recently in the 2000 case *United States v. Playboy Entertainment.*

Internet sex series is talk of the town

Kansas City Star, February 14, 2004

A weeklong series on Internet sex has produced impressive Nielsen ratings for KCTV, and become water-cooler topic No. 1 around town. Channel 5's controversial sting operation lured 16 local men to a rented house, where they found not the underage sexual partners they apparently were seeking, but KCTV reporter Steve Chamraz and a camera crew. The series gave Channel 5 its highest viewership numbers at 10 p.m. since 1995 and its first chance in years to beat KMBC in the ratings book. With the help of a Web site called perverted-justice. com, KCTV tapped into the power of undercover journalism, a genre many news organizations have sworn off because it often involves deception. Broadcast news experts interviewed this week, however, said Channel 5's strong Nielsen numbers virtually ensure that its formula will be copied by TV stations across the country. Viewer Scott Beaubien said he was channel-flipping when he went by KCTV's report Feb. 5. He and his wife normally watch news on another station, but they were so riveted by the investigation, they wound up following it for two more nights. "We were shocked and disturbed, not only because of the number of predators they got, but because they were such normal people," said Beaubien. Perverted-justice.com was started in 2002, according to a statement posted to the site, in order to "root out and bring to light those who would use the Internet as a way to sexually abuse children." Those who contribute to the Web site, about two dozen unpaid volunteers, essentially take part in an elaborate role-playing game. They create the personalities of their underage characters — male and female - then hang out in Internet chat rooms and wait for strangers to strike up conversations. If a stranger proposes sex, the volunteer pretends to be receptive to the offer. Afterward, volunteers confirm the identity of the sexual predator and post it to the Web site — full name, address and phone number — along with the full transcript of the chat. Over the course of four days, thirty men made appointments to come to the house in Independence where Chamraz was waiting. Of those, seventeen showed up and sixteen were caught on camera. "It was a much bigger threat than I ever imagined," Chamraz said. FBI spokesman Jeff Lanza said perverted-justice.com was, at best, "a temporary solution" to a growing problem. "A permanent solution is to put people in jail," Lanza said. "If you just embarrass them, they can move to another city." *(Postscript: As of January 2010,* Perverted-Justice.com *stings have been linked to 502 convictions.)*

Strip Search, *the film too hot for HBO*

Kansas City Star, May 18, 2004

Strip Search, a button-pushing movie from HBO Films, brazenly equates the state of freedom in post-9/11 America with that of China under its notorious regime. Directed by Sidney Lumet from a Tom Fontana script, it stars Glenn Close and Maggie Gyllenhaal. But it seems to have spooked HBO. The network that's usually happy to put on edgy, high-profile entertainment has aired this unsparing film only a handful of times, always in minor time slots. What's more, according to my colleague Alan Pergament of the *Buffalo Evening News,* HBO at the last minute whacked the running time from 88 minutes to 56 minutes, eliminating performances by Ellen Barkin and Oliver Platt. *Strip Search* interweaves two stories — one of a young American (Gyllenhaal) being interrogated in China, another of an Arab male seized by U.S. agents in New York City. Each person is identically grilled, head-gamed and, yes, strip-searched. They aren't charged with anything; each is told only that homeland security is at stake. The point, made with all the nuance of a pistol-whipping, is that this can happen anytime, anywhere. I'm not saying you'll like or agree with *Strip Search.* But the subject of civil liberties during a "war" on terrorism couldn't be timelier. And the film's no-holds-barred approach will at least get you thinking and talking. You'd think HBO would welcome that. *(Postscript: Lumet did two TV projects in the past decade, this and the A&E series* 100 Centre Street *— and neither is available for viewing today.)*

Reality KOs the scripted show

Kansas City Star, May 22, 2004

Two dozen young men have shown up at the Trinity Boxing Club in Manhattan's financial district, lured by the $1 million prize being offered to the winner of *The Contender,* a new competition show from *Survivor* and *Apprentice* producer Mark Burnett. But on this morning, you're more likely to bump into a publicist than a pugilist. Today is media day, and the Trinity gym is packed with sports reporters and celebrity hounds who have come here to see the two big names that have agreed to appear each week on *The Contender:* actor Sylvester Stallone and former middleweight champion Sugar Ray Leonard. Of course, Burnett is also holding forth, just down Broadway from where people used to line up to see P.T. Barnum's latest freak acts. With characteristic modesty, Burnett says *The Contender* is about to "reinvent the heart and soul of boxing." Isn't reinventing the heart and soul of prime time enough? With the fall season previews underway in New York, reality shows are no longer the undercard for scripted programs — they're the main event. Twelve of the top 20-rated shows this season were unscripted, led by the two editions of *American Idol* at No. 1 and No. 2. And there's more to come. Thanks to *The Apprentice,* which propelled Donald Trump back to cultural relevance, dot-commer Mark Cuban and British billionaire Richard Branson are each getting their own reality shows. Two more Burnett projects, *The Casino* and *The Restaurant,* will add to the growing subgenre of reality TV series set at sexy, high-pressure businesses. As for *The Contender,* it will have to contend with another new boxing show, *The Next Great Champ* on Fox. Though one or two of these shows might prove a knockout with viewers, most will join the bum-of-the-month club — but not to worry, there are plenty more palookas lined up to take their place. Reality TV ideas are a dime a dozen, and if one of them catches on, it becomes that network's ATM. Which is why NBC president Jeff Zucker stood in front of thousands of media buyers at the network's upfront presentation this week and smugly informed them that cheap nonfiction TV was here to stay. "This," he said, "is no passing fancy."

Leno hands off to Conan: Why? Why now?

Kansas City Star, September 30, 2004

Monday's announcement that Jay Leno was turning over *The Tonight Show* to Conan O'Brien in 2009 surprised most people. Why would the comedian known as Robocomic for his legendary work ethic freely give up one of the top jobs in television? And why announce it half a decade before the fact? "When I took this show over, boy, there was a lot of animosity between me and Dave," Leno said Monday on his show. "Good friendships were permanently damaged. And I don't want to cause anyone to go through that again." He added, "This show is like a dynasty. You hold it and you hand it off to the next person." And then he reiterated, "I don't want to see all the fighting," as the studio audience broke in with applause. This all happened because O'Brien — standing at the same career crossroads David Letterman faced in the early 1990s — made a couple of key tactical choices that Dave didn't. Letterman had an awkward relationship with NBC executives that kept him from actively pursuing the *Tonight Show* job he dreamed of having. And he was too shy to talk to Johnny about it. By contrast, as far back as 1996, when I interviewed O'Brien for a story, he suggested that he expected someday to be offered Leno's job. Earlier this year, a curious story appeared in the *New York Times*, ostensibly a less a profile of the late-night host. But early in the story O'Brien dropped this bomb: "A big question is looming," he said. "What's next?" And with that, he quietly turned the tables on NBC. After all, the network had strung him along for nearly two seasons of *Late Night*. As late as August 1994, when O'Brien had been on the air more than a year and won over many of his early critics, NBC would not sign him to a one-year contract. Now it was O'Brien who could afford to be coy and the network that was nervous for a long-term deal. It was the kind of public relations maneuver Letterman was incapable of performing.

Ken Jennings: The end is nigh ... right?
Kansas City Star, October 6, 2004

If you have been watching *The Jeopardy Show Starring Ken Jennings* this week, you may have noticed that something has changed. Suddenly KenJen's opponents aren't wussing out like they used to. That's because, until the game that aired Monday, the ten-week reigning champion was enjoying an unseen advantage over his challengers. The thirty-year-old software engineer from Utah, whose game show haul is $1.6 million and growing, has wiped out his competition with relative ease, almost seeming to settle into a zone — a KenJenZen, if you will — by the second commercial break. And those shows that aired last month? According to two eyewitnesses I spoke with, they were actually taped back in the spring, before news of KenJen's exploits had begun to circulate. A former contestant said in July that she found it impossible to recover from the shock of finding out the champ had been there for more than a month. As a result, she went quietly, like most of the other 100 deer-in-the-headlights that faced Jennings. But this week's shows are stocked with challengers who have been following the freak act all summer long and steeling themselves for the test. On Monday's game KenJen trailed after the first break. By the second break he had alpha-dogged his way into the lead, but one opponent charged back and actually made him sweat right to the end. Jennings' reaction made it clear that he had guessed his Final Jeopardy answer, but the guess proved to be correct. Had it not, Mr. Roboto would have lost by $101. Surely the end is near. *(Postscript: Surely not. KenJen beat back all comers for two more months, taking home $2.5 million in winnings.)*

Obama takes national stage, networks take night off

Kansas City Star, July 31, 2004

ABC, CBS and NBC continue to reap the benefits of free broadcast spectrum. So how is it they were able to weasel out of covering one of the essential moments in a free society? Their failure to cover a single minute of Tuesday night's proceedings at the 2004 Democratic National Convention meant that millions of people missed out on what was the biggest political debut of the year, as Illinois state senator Barack Obama delivered an electrifying address to a cable-and-PBS audience.

Obama, a self-described "skinny kid with a funny name," came into the convention as the presumptive next U.S. Senator from Illinois. He left as the brightest new star in politics. The son of a Kenyan father and Kansan mother, Obama made his biography the centerpiece of his rousing fifteen-minute address. "I stand here knowing that my story is part of the larger American story, that I owe a debt to all of those who came before me, and that in no other country on Earth is my story even possible," he said to huge cheers.

The next day ABC, CBS and NBC were left to scramble to cover the story. How did they not see this coming? Certainly it wasn't because their affiliates in Chicago (who pre-empted their networks to cover the speech) had failed to alert them to Obama's oratorical skill and rising profile. "They had every advance notice that this guy is going to be a star," Robert Feder, the veteran TV-radio columnist for the *Chicago Sun-Times,* told me.

As always, the broadcasters were ready with the same rehearsed defenses they've given in years past. The top executive at ABC News, David Westin, tried to blunt some of the criticism with an op-ed piece in Friday's *Washington Post.* "With the advent and expansion of cable and, more recently, the Internet, there are just too many alternatives available to the audience at all times of the day and night," Westin wrote. "Now you'll attract an audience only if what you have to offer is seen to be better than hundreds, indeed thousands, of alternatives."

Excuse me, but didn't ABC — along with CBS, NBC and Fox — televise the funeral of Ronald Reagan in June? In network prime time? For two hours? According to Nielsen, more than 35 million people tuned in to see the Gipper laid to rest. And while it was a public service to air the ceremony, nobody, not even David Westin, could argue that a funeral was more visually compelling than a political convention. The big networks aired it because there would have been a congressional investigation if it hadn't. As a result, 35 million people were able to see the Reagan funeral instead of the fraction of that number who would've watched had it only been shown on cable.

There was a time when the big networks thought big, even about news. I'm thinking about the late Roone Arledge, who a quarter century ago took his production wizardry from the sports division of ABC, where he had concocted *Monday Night Football,* to the news division, reinventing the news magazine and creating *Nightline.* Today's news executives are grateful to Arledge because he showed that news could make big money. But they don't have a clue how he did it. If Arledge were running ABC News today, I imagine he would be ordering some of those "up close and personal" profiles (which he pioneered with ABC's Olympic Games coverage) to accompany each of the speakers just before they stepped to the podium. He would cut down on the chitchat, because anybody can do chitchat. He'd kick the graphics up a notch — in short, he would be figuring out how to make his convention coverage stand head and shoulders above everybody else's.

The networks won't do that because they're fixated on the bottom line. For them, that's profits. Congress needs to step in and remind them that another bottom line exists: public service at a time of national decision.

Sinclair's 'right' kind of news

Kansas City Star, October 22, 2004

A furor erupted last week over Sinclair Broadcast Group's plan to air a documentary attacking presidential candidate John Kerry on many of its 62 owned-and-operated stations, raising concerns about whether a single network could circulate falsehoods and innuendo so that they started to take on the authority of fact.

Sinclair has been in full damage-control mode for two weeks after word got out that it intended to broadcast — without comment, rebuttal or reaction — an angry, forty-minute jeremiad against Kerry called *Stolen Honor: Wounds That Never Heal.* Made by a Vietnam veteran, *Stolen Honor* rips Kerry and his fellow antiwar activists, quoting American POWs who are still incensed at Kerry after more than three decades because his words were used against them when they were held in Viet Cong prison camps. In response to the public furor, Sinclair now says it is planning to air a "news special" about the power of documentaries, kind of a clever response to its critics.

Sinclair is a company that has fascinated me for years. Not just in its promotion of conservative politics (something TV and radio stations used to do all the time back in the days of mom-and-pop broadcast ownership), but in virtually every aspect of its business, Sinclair pursues a dogged determination to go its own way. Earlier this year, I had a chance to hear about the Sinclair philosophy directly from its president, David D. Smith, whose family owns a controlling interest in the company. For more than an hour, Smith held court in the lobby of his corporate offices in suburban Baltimore, answering my questions about Sinclair and its unusual approach to local TV and television news.

"Our news media have intentionally dumbed down the news,"

Smith told me, "and we all know why they do: because they have a political agenda." Since when is reporting on crimes, fires and other local news of the day political? Smith smiled when I asked him that. "What would serve you better," he asked me, "a story about a house fire, or a story about the Supreme Court?" As he sees it, news is dumbed down because the companies that own TV stations don't want people questioning the institutions running the country. That, in Smith's mind, includes the media corporations that his more entrepreneurial-minded company is challenging with products like News Central, an experiment in reinventing local TV.

From its Maryland-based nerve center News Central sends out a daily stream of video content: national news, sports, and features, along with weather locally tailored to each of its markets. It's piped into each Sinclair city, where a skeleton crew takes care of local news. This hybrid allows Sinclair to offer "local" content at a fraction of the usual cost. Whether it will pay off is anyone's guess. The company has slowed its rollouts of News Central in St. Louis and Kansas City, and Sinclair's stock took a hit following the protests over *Stolen Honor*. Crisis management has become routine at Sinclair. In May, critics attacked it for refusing to air an edition of *ABC News Nightline* on its eight ABC affiliates, because Koppel would be reading the names of soldiers and Marines killed in Iraq and Afghanistan. ("We do not believe political statements should be disguised as news content," spokesman Mark Hyman hilariously opined.) Industry publications had been hammering the News Central model for months when I visited, and it showed.

"We're not doing air crashes, we're not doing fires," complained co-anchor Jennifer Gladstone. "I feel like I'm doing stories that matter. People try to make a big deal of our national coverage, but the big deal is our local coverage."

Sinclair is not new to the local news business, but doing centralized news, with a generous side helping of right-wing commentary, is something that only one cable network has tried before. Smith openly admires what Fox News Channel has done in a handful of years on the air. "I'm tired of watching biased, distorted, sometimes made-up news on television," Smith said. "It's time for some of us to do the right thing, which is to tell people what the facts are and let them make up their minds." He assured me that critics "won't like us any more than they like what Fox does."

But make no mistake — Sinclair is in this for the money. Three out of every ten dollars spent on local TV advertising, he points out, are earmarked for news. Stations without news can't stick their hands in that cookie jar. With his lower-cost newscasts, Smith thinks his stations eventually will turn a higher profit during that hour than they do now with syndicated shows.

One media watchdog who's sold on News Central is Carl Gottlieb. A veteran news producer in New York and Washington, D.C., his last job was rating local newscasts for the well-regarded Project for Excellence in Journalism at Columbia University. Today Gottlieb is the managing editor and second-in-command at News Central. To hear him tell it, Sinclair not only represents the future of local news, but a bright future indeed. "We are getting local relevance back into the news," Gottlieb said. "We try to avoid everyday murders, 'chalk line journalism,' call it what you will, and get into the issues."

I sampled a recent newscast from Sinclair's Flint, Michigan, station. It led with the story of a suburban fire department dispute and followed with taped pieces on health care costs for city employees, rising prices at the pump and a school janitors' strike. The Baltimore-based national segments had more of a Fox flavor to them. Last month, anchor Morris Jones introduced an upbeat story about the U.S. occupation of Iraq by asking, rhetorically, whether Americans were getting "the real message" about that country's turnaround. "Frankly, centralcasting is not a new idea," said Jones, who has been anchoring local TV news since the 1970s. "What's different is that we're free of the built-in political correctness and bias that viewers see from the East Coast networks."

(Postscript: News Central was abandoned beginning in 2006, as Sinclair started to sell off stations.)

Another weird election night

Kansas City Star, November 4, 2004

Four years ago Fox News Channel seemed to move the mountain on election night by projecting George W. Bush the winner, even though his lead over Al Gore in Florida was microscopic (if not illusory). On Tuesday Fox was at it again. Anchor Brit Hume announced at 11:41 p.m. local time that the state of Ohio belonged to Bush, putting him at 266 electoral votes. Alaska's three electoral votes would raise the total to 269  a few minutes later — one vote shy of guaranteeing the president a second term. MSNBC followed eighteen minutes later. No one else followed. "We are not in a great hurry," murmured ABC's Peter Jennings at 12:43 a.m. Wednesday. In fact, after the scorching the networks took in 2000, no decision desk seemed up to the task of awarding Bush the decisive 270th electoral vote. Neither Fox nor MSNBC could summon the nerve to hand him five crucial electoral votes from Nevada. It was a fitting end to a most peculiar night. Early in the evening the momentum seemed to be going Kerry's way. One of the surest signs that Bush was in trouble came from his most trusted mouthpiece, CNN's Robert Novak, who declared at 7:54 p.m. that "the Republicans need to count on losing Ohio." Ninety minutes later, though, an incredulous-sounding Novak reported, "The word I get is Ohio ... is coming back to Bush!" With regular news in turmoil, I turned to the fake newscasters of *The Daily Show* for perspective. And there I heard Stephen Colbert nail it. "Tomorrow morning, regardless of who wins, we'll have the opportunity to come together as a nation," he began. "This is an opportunity we must reject." Colbert explained: "Ours is now an *anger*-based economy. I look forward to a glorious tomorrow, when hybrid vehicles run half on gasoline, half on seething hate. ... Remember, a house divided against itself — is what we here in New York call a duplex."

2005

The television show of the year was Hurricane Katrina. The devastation that followed the storm not only showed cable news at its best, but local news at its best, as the New Orleans powerhouse WWL streamed its gripping coverage over the Internet after its studios and tower were destroyed. FEMA director Mike Brown was thrown under the CNN bus, and then the *Nightline* bus … when it was all over he must have known how Wile E. Coyote felt. In hindsight, though, it was one of those media frenzies where the most convenient target, rather than the most deserving, was put in the crosshairs. When we look back at the undoing of the Bush Administration, I think it will be the straight shooters like Dan Verbeck and Shep Smith, with no political axes to grind, who did the most damage.

Speaking of damage, CNN cancelled its long-running shoutfest *Crossfire* after Jon Stewart came on the program and told co-hosts Tucker Carlson and Paul Begala they were "hurting America." Johnny Carson passed, and with him an era. ABC started selling its TV shows on iTunes, and other people started uploading and watching TV for free on a little site called YouTube. Martha Stewart got to remove her ankle bracelet, but by then she had shackled herself to Mark Burnett, who sweet-talked her into doing her own *Apprentice*, a decision almost as dumb as fibbing about her stock trades. *CSI*, *Idol* and *Idol* were the three most-watched shows on TV.

Fake Kansas a favorite of Hollywood

Kansas City Star, April 9, 2005

If you've been watching ABC's new adaptation of *Little House on the Prairie*, you've no doubt noticed the familiar-looking backdrops, those gently sloping mounds of brown grass acting as a catch basin for all that pale-blue sky. Even today, the area surrounding the Flint Hills of Kansas retains much of its ancient beauty, like it did when the Ingalls family settled there in 1869. But this *Little House* was actually filmed on a patch of land west of Highway 22 near Calgary. Plied with Canadian tax incentives, ABC opted to make the six-hour

miniseries north of the border. Hollywood loves to drop references to
Kansas into scripts as shorthand for Midwestern and rural life — but
rarely do producers feel the need to supply geographic authenticity to
TV shows or movies set in the Sunflower State. The original *Little House,*
for that matter, was filmed in Southern California. In the pilot episode
of *Summerland,* currently on the WB network, Lori Loughlin's character
adopts three orphaned children from Kansas. For the Kansas scenes,
megaproducer Aaron Spelling used exterior shots of a fancy house in a
rural setting near L.A. For the hometown of Superman, the producers of
Smallville, used the small town of Merritt, British Columbia, northeast
of Vancouver, the hub of Canada's $1 billion entertainment export
industry. Lately, the incentives that pushed so much business north of
the border are being adopted in more than 30 states. Texas and New
Mexico recently had a mini-border war over where the film *Every Word
Is True* would be shot. The outskirts of Austin were ultimately chosen as
the location for the film, which is based on George Plimpton's screenplay
about the writing of *In Cold Blood* — which, of course, was based in
Kansas.

Katrina: Where is the coverage?

TV Barn, September 1, 2005

I am certain that the big networks would be paying a lot more
attention to the aftermath of Hurricane Katrina had it devastated New
York City, or Chicago, rather than New Orleans. If not for President
Bush holding another press conference this afternoon, the networks
would have gone blissfully on with their entertainment schedules. CBS
is airing repeats tonight, with no plans for Katrina coverage. Where is
the urgency? Where is the concern? Where is the social responsibility?
At this point during 9/11, or the Iraq War, broadcast TV was overrun
with news coverage. To be sure, cable coverage has been unstinting. I've
preferred Fox News' coverage to the other two, just because it seems
more compelling and urgent, but all look like they're doing their jobs.
But when broadcasters pass the buck to cable, they are commenting on
that story's newsworthiness. By ignoring Katrina, they are saying it is
not that much of a concern for the rest of America. By contrast, after
9/11 dozens of broadcast and cable channels aired continuous coverage
for three days, some for nearly a week, before returning to regular
programming. As I argued in 2004, it doesn't matter if the coverage

can be found somewhere else. When it's offered by broadcast networks, more people are informed and the overall sense of urgency rises. Coverage equals importance. That corollary is what makes broadcasting broadcasting. What exactly is at stake here? Those screamingly high viewership levels during the last week of August? Broadcasters that air a single repeat this week should be ashamed of themselves when the magnitude of this disaster is so painfully clear.

Colbert Report: *Too much of a good thing?*
Kansas City Star, October 20, 2005

Monday's premiere of *The Colbert Report* was one of the most nearly perfect half-hours of television I've ever seen. Stephen Colbert delivered a blistering manifesto modeled on the show's touchstone, fatuous ranter Bill O'Reilly. "This show is not about me," Colbert declared Monday. "No, this program is dedicated to you, the heroes. And who are the heroes? The people who watch this show. ... You're not the country club crowd. I know for a fact that my country club would never let you in." Later he and his guest, actual anchor Stone Phillips, read local news teases out of context to prove they could make anything sound dramatic ("If you have ever sat naked on a hotel bedspread, we have got a chilling report you won't want to miss"). But the meat of *The Colbert Report,* so far, is his send-up of O'Reilly. Exactly how long Colbert can stay in character — basically as a parody of another TV character — is the question, and Tuesday's show, with another long opening rant, didn't do much to dispel it. Fans have come to adore Colbert's put-on smugness. Still, he was only on *The Daily Show* once or twice a week, doing bits like "This Week in God" that were less about him and more about God, a slightly higher power. I can't imagine tuning in *The Colbert Report* four nights a week just to watch a caricature. Stewart invited the real Bill O'Reilly onto his show Tuesday night, no doubt to give fans of *The Daily Show* who wouldn't be caught dead watching Fox News a glimpse of the devil. Amazingly the devil took the bait, came on the show, was mocked by Stewart and jeered by the partisan crowd. O'Grumpy fought back, calling Stewart a "pinhead" and refusing to mellow on France or any of his other oddball peeves. I wouldn't want to be his next-door neighbor, but O'Reilly is undeniably his own man. That's more than can be said of the host of *The Colbert Report* so far. *(Postscript: Boy, did I underestimate him.)*

Dave and Oprah back on speaking terms

Kansas City Star, December 1, 2005

For twenty years there have been two constants in American television: Oprah and Dave. Yet for most of that time there's been a palpable chill between the King of Late Night and the Queen of Daytime. At last our long national nightmare is over. Tonight, Oprah Winfrey is the guest on *Late Show With David Letterman*. It's not entirely clear why Winfrey refused to appear on Letterman's show all these years. The two most likely reasons are his repeated jokes about her weight problems, beginning with a 1987 reference to her as "Mrs. Butterworth"; and the nasty reception she got in May 1989, the last time she appeared with him. He was airing his *Late Night* show from Chicago, where a noisy, boozy audience visibly frightened her. (Someone in the audience could be heard yelling, "Rip 'er, Dave!") Since then, Winfrey has allied herself with his rival Jay Leno, appearing several times on *The Tonight Show*. Letterman's attempts to humor her back to his guest couch have only made the situation worse, like his Academy Awards "Oprah-Uma" routine and, more recently, the running bit on his show where he would write forlornly in his "Oprah Log" that Winfrey was not returning his calls. So why end the feud now? Maybe because Letterman's program, which is based in New York, is the logical choice for her to promote *The Color Purple*, the musical she's producing. Or ... maybe it's that *The Color Purple* will be playing at the Broadway Theater, one-half block south of the Ed Sullivan Theater, where *Late Show* is taped — setting up a lovely remote outside his building.

Dubious defender of decency

Kansas City Star, February 13, 2005

When Michael Powell assumed the chairmanship of the Federal Communications Commission in 2001, many in the media industry thought they had gained a friend in high places. Here, after all, was a bright young Republican lawyer who had won First Amendment awards for his outspoken defense of broadcasters' rights. By all indications, he was eager to start slashing the rules  governing station ownership that he and many others said were out of touch with the current media marketplace.

So who could've guessed that as he prepared to leave office four years later, Powell's greatest legacy would be Nipplegate? The son of Gen. Colin Powell may be proud of the FCC's role in arcane matters like certifying cellular phones, but his final year as chairman has been a complete effing disaster. After last year's Janet Jackson incident at the Super Bowl, Powell decided to become the 21st century's answer to Thomas Bowdler, the 18th-century English physician who published an edition of Shakespeare from which he had excised "every thing that could give just offence to the religious and virtuous mind." The onetime defender of deregulation began to impose his agency's power on the country's television stations in ways his predecessors scarcely imagined. Under Powell, the FCC has handed out more indecency fines than were levied under all previous chairmen combined.

If there is one area of communications policy long overdue for review, it's the broadcast indecency code, which has not changed since the three-network days of the Carter administration. But that would have landed Powell in the middle of a very public and contentious debate over what exactly constitutes indecency, a matter on which the FCC's rulings have been slightly more predictable than coin flips. Powell, who ignored his critics when he wasn't belittling them, never had the stomach for that fight. Explaining why he rarely held public forums, he once said, "In the digital age, you don't need a 19th century whistle-stop tour to hear from America."

Speaking of relics, let's turn to the U.S. Supreme Court's landmark 1978 ruling, *FCC v. Pacifica Foundation*, which upheld the agency's right to penalize indecency. That decision also established the criteria by which all future cases would be judged: "... language or material that, in context, depicts or describes, in terms patently offensive as measured by contemporary community standards for the broadcast medium, sexual or excretory activities or organs."

After largely ignoring this statute for three years, Powell began enforcing it with a vengeance after the 2004 Super Bowl. Predictably, panic and overreaction ensued. Recently, I went to the studio of KCUR-FM for my monthly appearance on *The Walt Bodine Show,* and discovered that the show had been put on a six-second delay — a direct result, I was told, of the FCC crackdown. Anyone who has listened to Walt's (or anyone else's) show on KCUR knows how silly this level of caution is. But when the current FCC regime shows no qualms about a levying a crippling fine on a small California PBS station for airing a naughty word in *The Blues,* a Martin Scorsese documentary that played without incident throughout the rest of the country, then truly no station is immune from the terror of uncertainty that Powell's capriciousness has fueled.

Powell's rumored successor as FCC chairman is his fellow commissioner Kevin Martin, who has indicated he would like to widen the indecency net beyond "the broadcast medium" — namely, to cable and satellite TV. Unfortunately for him, the courts have already established that the FCC's power in the area of content regulation is very limited indeed.

Adam Thierer, a telecommunications analyst for the Cato Institute in Washington, D.C., and unlike Powell a true libertarian, would like to see *Pacifica* overturned. He'd like the government to get out of the content-nanny business completely. "ABC has a steamy show like *Desperate Housewives* that they can't say or do certain things on," Thierer said. "However, if ABC streamed that video from *Desperate Housewives* on abc.com, there's nothing Congress can do about it." Thierer understands parents' concerns that their kids are inundated by news, information and entertainment like never before. "That is not a curse," he said. "It's a blessing. But it does have some side effects. Some mature and even disturbing material will be released in public and be overheard by children. But that is why parents need to sit down with children. That's a tough conversation I think most parents don't want to have. It's part of the maturing of a society. And we don't have any choice anymore but to do it."

A somewhat different tack is taken by Nicholas Johnson, a storied FCC commissioner who battled the corporations almost continuously for his seven-year term in the Johnson and Nixon administrations and once graced the cover of *Rolling Stone*. Currently a teacher at the University of Iowa law school, Johnson has no problem with the government telling broadcasters and cable companies what they can put on the air. But he can think of a hundred concerns more important than decency, and none would do as much harm to free speech.

"Take, for instance, the matter of regulation of commercials," Johnson told me. "Commercial clutter is something everybody complains about, and it's an issue that the FCC long ago used to regulate. Nowadays, though, it's the Federal Trade Commission that calls TV sponsors to task, usually in their marketing to kids. So the FCC steps back, as though from a rattlesnake, and says, 'Oh, no, we have the FTC to regulate commercials.' Well, we also have a Department of Justice that has indecency laws on the books. When I was a commissioner I always said to the others, 'Hey, if you have any problems with indecency, why don't you refer it to Justice and see what they think?' It's just rife with hypocrisy."

Ultimately, the final word belongs to that wise man who once said, "It is better to tolerate the abuses on the margins than to invite the government to interfere with the cherished First Amendment."

That man was Michael Powell — in 2001.

Adult Swim: The edge of night

Kansas City Star, July 24, 2005

Aaron McGruder's comic strip "Boondocks" took the funny pages by storm in the late 1990s with its mixture of social comment and political incorrectness. It also made McGruder a star and got him what he had lusted for all along: the chance to make an animated *Boondocks* series for Fox. A dream, right?

"We wrote the script, we did a six-minute presentation and it died," said McGruder. "Fox wanted a sitcom with an 'A story' and a 'B story,' and there were just very rigid creative rules that work on some shows and don't work on others." Enter Mike Lazzo, the head of Adult Swim, the late-night lineup airing on cable's Cartoon Network that is wildly popular with young viewers. With his longish beach-blond hair, leather jacket and jeans, Lazzo might be television's most unlikely big shot — a high school dropout who started out in Ted Turner's mail room. Even today he looks more like an aging roadie than a top TV executive. But this is the dude who more or less invented the format that now prints piles of money for Cartoon Network. Lazzo saw the six-minute film McGruder had put together for Fox and, not surprisingly, thought it "too networky." He suggested that the young artist forget about the sitcom formula, bring his comedy ideas over to Adult Swim and start over.

These are the kinds of decisions that Lazzo, the Quick Draw McGraw of the cable business, has been making for more than 20 years as an executive in Turner's empire. He created the prototype for what would become Adult Swim in 1994, more or less out of boredom with his job, which at that time involved caretaking some

8,000 Hanna-Barbera cartoons that Turner had used to launch Cartoon Network. "We were like, 'Another *Huckleberry Hound?* Don't we have anything new?'" Lazzo recalled. Turner made it clear that there wouldn't be any money for new shows on Cartoon Network for a while. Other than that small obstacle, Lazzo and his small Atlanta-based staff were free to try anything.

Every afternoon at the CN staff meeting, Lazzo would hear the big, booming sound of Gary Owens coming from a television monitor. He loved that voice. It meant that CN was airing its daily repeat of the 1960s cartoon *Space Ghost.* From that inspiration, Lazzo one day got the idea of making Space Ghost a talk show host — the late-night wars were white-hot at the time — and *Space Ghost Coast to Coast* was born. It featured the superhero on a cheaply drawn background, interviewing celebrities like Susan Powter and Kevin Meany — "whoever would talk to us," Lazzo said. The humans appeared in the cartoon via a small TV screen that was lowered from the ceiling. Space Ghost would talk to the screen in non sequiturs: bragging about how strong he was, or blasting his creepy bandleader, a life-sized predatory insect named Zorak, with a laser ray emanating from his wrist. The guests would chuckle nervously and make oddly off-kilter comments that suggested their segment had been taped much earlier. Soon the bored host would zap them and move on.

At first few people noticed. Cartoon Network was in only 10 million homes when *Space Ghost Coast to Coast* made its debut in late nights, after the kiddos were in bed. "We all had day jobs," Lazzo said. "Our writers weren't writers; they were schedulers. I think people who loved television instantly responded to it. They got it. But it was only on 15 minutes a week. Nobody knew about us, nobody talked about us, but I could see that people were watching."

Lazzo and Co. then revived *Sealab 2020,* except in the new version (*Sealab 2021*), the people living in the futuristic underwater city were hilariously self-absorbed idiots. More bargain-basement hits followed, like *Aqua Teen Hunger Force,* a crudely animated cartoon featuring the exploits of a talking milkshake, a talking meatball and a talking side of fries superimposed on old scenes from *Scooby-Doo* and other shows. It was funnier the less you tried to make sense of it. *Harvey Birdman, Attorney at Law* recycled a staggering number of old Hanna-Barbera characters in service of TV's daffiest courtroom show. In one episode, Speed Buggy — the wheezing 1970s jalopy from my youth — hires Birdman to defend him against charges of reckless driving. While that goes on, his dashing driver, Mark, seduces women in the next room. "We were just all TV-obsessed," Lazzo said. "We thought we were doing cartoons that reflected what we liked to watch."

Lazzo told Turner's sales staff that if they'd just let him buy reruns of *Fish Police* and a couple other animated shows for grown-ups, plus make more *Space Ghosts*, he could rule the evenings. "Sales kept saying, 'We don't need it, and we don't think you'll make money,'" said Lazzo. "But by 1998, '99, we were pretty much *C'mon-let-us-let-us-let-us*, and we did that every minute until they said yes." Adult Swim debuted, two nights a week, two hours a night, in 2001, with *Futurama* rather than *Fish Police,* and it took off from there. Lazzo bought the rights to a prime-time cartoon that Fox had cancelled. That show, of course, was *Family Guy,* which found a devoted audience on Adult Swim and ultimately convinced the Fox suits they'd made a mistake getting rid of it.

Ironically, Lazzo obtained the services of McGruder by telling him not to make *Boondocks* like Adult Swim's biggest hit. "Our show is not *Family Guy,*" McGruder says. "The element of race changes everything." Lazzo says he gets that. And that leads McGruder to pay his new boss a compliment: "It astounds me," he said, "that good, responsible white people paid for this show."

(Postscript: McGruder made 30 episodes of Boondocks *for Adult Swim over two and a half years. Two never aired, because Black Entertainment Television threatened legal action if they did. In one of the unaired episodes, a character obviously based on BET chairman Debra Lee tells a staff meeting, "Our leader Bob Johnson had a dream. A dream of creating a network that would accomplish what hundreds of years of slavery, Jim Crow and malt liquor couldn't: THE DESTRUCTION OF BLACK PEOPLE!" All 30 episodes are on DVD.)*

'FEMA was ineffectual ... to the point of criminal'

Kansas City Star, September 8, 2005

Radio reporter Dan Verbeck was one of the first people on the scene of the 1981 Hyatt Regency skywalk collapse that killed 114 people. He thought he had experienced the depths of human suffering there. Then he went to New Orleans to cover Hurricane Katrina. The veteran KMBZ-AM reporter got a call Aug. 27 asking if he was willing to help his employer, Entercom, provide extra manpower at WWL-AM in New Orleans as Katrina bore down on the Gulf Coast.

After arriving late on Saturday, he awoke, filled his hotel bathtub (in case he needed drinking water), then headed out. The city was under an evacuation order, but as he toured the neighborhoods in a police SUV Sunday morning he saw little evidence that residents were paying attention to warnings delivered over the loudspeaker. Instead, he saw people preparing to ride out the storm. He even covered a small riot at a store that had jacked up its prices on water and ice.

Katrina rained heavily on New Orleans, then subsided. Verbeck went out in his cruiser, where he told me he saw nothing more than "knee-deep flooding and siding torn off buildings." Then the levees broke. With other radio stations knocked off the air, and those stranded by the rising waters relying on battery-powered radios, WWL became a lifeline to the community. He broadcast from the Jefferson Parish Emergency Center for four days straight. He interviewed elected officials, emergency officials, law enforcement, whoever came in. He anchored the news from 2 a.m. to 5 a.m. Conditions were primitive. "If you had to relieve yourself, you used a plastic bag, knotted it and then found someplace outside to dispose of it," he said.

I have always found Verbeck to be a careful, detail-minded reporter. He gets upset when listeners can't tell the difference between news and commentary. So he plays it straight. And as he saw it, the local officials in and around New Orleans responded calmly and effectively to the crisis.

"On the parish level, things were superbly well organized," he said. "The sheriff's patrols were detailed — where they were to go, when they were to go, it was very well done. You could tell someone had put a lot of work into planning it and practiced it."

The Federal Emergency Management Agency was another matter. "FEMA was ineffectual at best, shamefully lax at worst, almost to the point of criminal," said Verbeck.

It was WWL that aired New Orleans Mayor Ray Nagin's emotional outburst last Thursday, chiding federal officials: "Don't tell me 40,000 people are coming here. They're not here. It's too doggone late." Earlier in the day, Jefferson Parish President Aaron Broussard broadcast a plea for drinking water. Verbeck told me, "At one point on Wednesday a FEMA man had finally shown up, spent 15 minutes with (Broussard) and said everything was going to be fine and that a field representative would be back to take over. And by Thursday that FEMA field rep had never shown."

Verbeck learned that a Wal-Mart truck carrying water had been stopped and refused entry into the area by FEMA. Verbeck called Heart to Heart International in Olathe and asked if it could ship water down there pronto. And when the relief organization said yes, Verbeck decided not to broadcast the news, "in case some petty bureaucrat was listening."

There were the terrible calls from residents trapped in their homes. One caller, whom he put on the air at 3 or 4 a.m. one night, haunts him now. "She said, 'I'm in my house and I'm up to my chest in water.' ... 'Can you save our lives? Can you save our lives?' ... There was nothing we could do to save her life. But she asked us anyway, with dignity." For days afterward Verbeck and the news director of WWL would exchange glances. "His eyes would seem to bore into mine," he said. "I knew what he was thinking. The day before I was pulled out of there he said, 'I have that address.'"

2006

In a year when the future of the nightly network news was being openly debated, two of the three newscasts undermined their own futures. In January, ABC's Bob Woodruff was injured in Iraq, mere days after his boss, David Westin, trotted Woodruff and Elizabeth Vargas before the press as a new breed of TV anchor who would go anywhere to get the story. In Woodruff's case, that meant a road outside Baghdad notorious for IED attacks. Over at CBS, network chief Leslie Moonves guessed, incorrectly, that former *Today* show host Katie Couric could smoothly transition to telling us the hard news of the day. Couric's ratings soon slipped down to the levels of her predecessor, Bob Schieffer.

American Idol won the season ratings race — a first for Fox — while the best NBC could manage was a tie for 15th. And last but certainly not least, networks finally started offering full episodes of their hit shows on the Web.

What would Murrow think of Stewart?

Kansas City Star, March 5, 2006

Officially, it's a coincidence that Jon Stewart, a comedian specializing in "fake news," was named host of the Academy Awards the same year that *Good Night, and Good Luck* was nominated for best picture. The producer of the Oscars, Gil Cates, has said that Stewart was chosen as host because "there are big culture issues in these films ... and he's about as issue-oriented as a host can be." But to many of us who work in the news business, the symbolism couldn't be more obvious. *Good Night* is the story of Edward R. Murrow, the newsman's newsman, who used the emerging power of television in the early 1950s to bring down Joe McCarthy, the rampaging anti-communist senator. And now, look who gets to introduce Murrow to a TV audience of millions: a guy who gets paid to make fun of the news, its overamped hysterics, its live-late-breaking theatrics and, above all, its allergy to asking tough questions of people in power. Come to think of it, Murrow probably would've approved the choice of Stewart.

The patron saint of CBS News had many of the same misgivings about network news back then. And that was when the news divisions didn't have to show a profit. Were he around today, who knows, maybe Murrow would count himself among the New York cognoscenti who are big fans of *The Daily Show* and use it to balance out their daily diet of news. What Murrow probably would find disturbing are recent polls finding that young people consider *The Daily Show* a perfectly adequate substitute, not supplement, for actual news of the world. Back in Ed's day, the idea of a comedy show becoming people's sole source of news would have made no sense. You might as well have asked a woman to anchor the nightly news.

Idol *is No. 1 with a bullet*

Kansas City Star, March 21, 2006

From the minute Season 5 of *American Idol* began in January, its ratings have been way up. About three million more are watching it this season. At this rate its two nights will be TV's No. 1 and No. 2 shows — a first for Fox. In January *Idol* forced President Geena Davis out of ABC's White House and into an undisclosed location. Last month it reduced NBC's Winter Olympics to a three-ring circus. It's unheard of for a reality show with *Idol's* mileage to be gaining steam. Why is it? Not even Mike Darnell knows. The Fox network's dark prince of reality TV (besides *Idol,* he has *When Animals Attack* to answer for) recently said that the growing appeal of *American Idol* was "an almost unanswerable question." Here's my theory. *Idol* has grasped a basic truth: Mass taste didn't go away when the CD burner was invented. With no help from the recording industry or radio, it has replicated the hitmaker environment that we all took part in during our youth. The difference between then and now is that Arthur Godfrey or Ed Sullivan wouldn't let anyone on their shows until the talent was ready. With *Idol,* the stars are no longer delivered to us shined up and prepackaged. That's also part of the show's genius, realizing that we like to watch the sausage getting made. Simon Cowell is the show's one crucial presence. As a successful producer and businessman, he acts as *Idol's* economic conscience. He is forever reminding the singers not to choose "safe" songs — a far more withering rebuke than his better known, "That was just horrible," because failure to take risks often fails to sell records. And selling is the only way to measure stardom.

Product placements the $tar of the show

Kansas City Star, April 2, 2006

On Thursday HBO will air *All Aboard! Rosie's Family Cruise*, a documentary filmed aboard America's "first-ever gay family cruise," which was chartered by entertainer Rosie O'Donnell and her partner Kelli O'Donnell in 2004. After watching the film I was left with the uneasy feeling of having just sat through a slickly produced sales pitch, since I knew the O'Donnells had used this voyage to launch their family-travel business. "Was I making a commercial for Rosie?" said Sheila Nevins, HBO's documentary queen, who seemed taken aback by the question. "I certainly didn't make it for that reason." Also, she reminded me, "we don't take commercials on HBO." Be that as it may, the number of on-screen "brand occurrences" for consumer goods and services on network TV jumped 30 percent last year. Such placements (the vast majority of which were paid for) averaged eleven minutes per hour in prime time, not counting the seventeen minutes or so of plain old advertising. Last month I wrote a column about an episode of the UPN sitcom *Half & Half* that was supposed to raise awareness about HIV and AIDS. It was more memorable, though, for the number of times the show's characters shamelessly lavished praise on a certain brand of hand lotion. That column caught the attention of Patric Verrone, head of the Writers Guild of America-West. Verrone isn't opposed to product placements, particularly if the unions get a piece of the action. But he told me that product bombardment, if not carefully monitored, will have "a souring effect on viewers." Ironically, it's HBO that's currently in the news for its copious product shots — namely, the Porsche Cayenne that threatened to steal the season premiere of *The Sopranos*. HBO's no-commercials policy must have come as news to Porsche's marketing team after it learned that *The Sopranos* needed a Cayenne ($110,000, loaded) so Tony could give one to Carmela. She is transported in both senses of the word, rhapsodizing about her new ride early and often. That episode also included a closeup of a Nesquik branded car on Bobby Baccala's model railroad; the Philips logo on Uncle Junior's TV; Armani glasses; a Members Only jacket; and other unpaid placements. A network spokesperson explained that bling is an integral part of the *Sopranos* characters' identities, so all the brand-name-dropping adds "realism" to the script. Only in Sopranosland, the argument went, would such a wildly overpriced SUV be regarded as a status symbol.

Mr. Smith goes to Kansas

Kansas City Star, November 6, 2006

Shep Smith was in town, leaning over a laptop as he waited for the Fox News Channel to come out of a break. He was broadcasting his midday show, *Studio B,* from the sidewalk underneath the farmers' market clock tower in Overland Park. Not fifteen feet away, a white pickup truck drove by the crowd of 50 crew members and onlookers, slowed down, gave a good long blast of the horn, then drove off. Without looking up or smiling, Smith said in a loud voice, "Hi!" People laughed. "They're so nice in Kansas," he said. "Let's go someplace with a little more of an attitude. You get more than a horn honk." When the show was over, though, all Smith got was love. A mother with her young children in tow tried to present him with a gift basket. He graciously declined. Later, as Smith warmed his hands inside a satellite truck, I observed that Fox was the only cable news channel with a fan base. "It's weird, isn't it?" Smith said. "At least, it is to me." Smith, a forty-one-year-old Mississippi native, has been with Fox News Channel since its inception ten years ago. He was hired as a reporter. "There was a live shot I did during some story I was covering on the West Coast. They came to me and said, 'What's going on?' and I said, 'Well, there's not really much going on, but we're here and if something happens we'll get back to you.' " Roger Ailes, the founder of Fox News Channel, saw it and called Smith to say that was the most honest thing he'd heard from a reporter in a while. "He said, 'If you can do that in the studio, we want you. But I'm not going to give you this job. I'm not going to give you any guarantees. We'll let you try it for a while and call when you mess up.' And he didn't call for a while." Smith's other show, *Fox Report,* is now the third-highest-rated show on Fox News, and thus all of cable news. But ratings for Fox News have plateaued of late. Ailes reportedly is not happy. Smith, though, thinks that's to be expected. "This war in Iraq is a mess, bordering on a disaster," he said. "People are depressed, they're confused, disillusioned in many cases by what's happening in this country right now. And they don't want to see it every day. So they're not watching as much. They're not watching our competition as much, either."

John Higgins

TV Barn, May 17, 2007

My career as a journalist was barely underway when Higgins first barged into my life in 1994. (Everyone called him Higgins, never "John," other than his immediate family.) He was a reporter and editor for the trade publication *Multichannel News* and had been emailing me his thoughts about late-night TV for months. When he came to Chicago, he looked me up. That was a first for me — drinks with an actual ink-stained wretch. He looked and acted the part, too: baggy trousers, rumpled coat, hangdog appearance, kinda gruff … but once we started talking he was complimentary of my little e-newsletter and had even brought me a little gift to cement our friendship: a scoop. Higgins had come to town to cover a trade show and had been chatting up a TV executive about another matter when this suit let slip that Greg Kinnear, then the host of NBC's *Later,* was leaving to pursue a movie career.

Higgins moved to the more prestigious *Broadcasting & Cable* magazine about the same time I moved to Kansas City, and the larger profile better reflected Higgins' knowledge of the television business and his access to its movers and shakers. I used to go to New York to cover the network upfront presentations. I would stay with Higgins, who insisted on putting me up. He must have known he was saving my company buckets of money, although I would always take him out for dinner at least once. He'd lend me his MoMA membership card and offer advice on where to go if I had a few hours to kill. One year, my flight was scheduled to arrive two hours before the NBC upfront in Radio City Music Hall. Higgins told me to go across the street to the Hilton, tell the bellman I was planning to check in later and needed a place to stash my bags, and tip him $10 on the spot. It worked just like he said it would.

He had three qualities that served him very well, both in work and in life. One, he knew the schmooze. He seemed to know everyone at industry parties. He sent his friends mix tapes, cards and flowers. He showed up at their weddings. Two, he was brilliant. Training himself on the job, Higgins learned to read a company's balance sheet and SEC filing as well as anyone at that company could. As Judy McGrath, the longtime MTV executive, mused at his memorial service, when you got a phone call from Higgins, you never quite knew if he was calling to shoot the breeze, or if he had the goods on you. Three, even as journalists go, he was admirably independent. The very last thing Higgins wrote was a commentary on the notorious O.J. Simpson *If I Did It* special for Fox and its related book deal:

Does anyone find News Corp.'s decision to cancel O.J. Simpson's "confession" disturbing? It's pretty scary to see a a major media company as powerful as News Corp. cowed into cancelling a program and a book just because a lot of people who have seen neither product find it inappropriate. ... O.J. is unimportant to me. I am in complete control of my exposure to what he has to say. I could choose not to watch the TV special; I could choose not buy the book. Critics had the same options.

Higgins cultivated a larger-than-life personality: aggressive reporter known by most people for his kindness and generosity. When I took ill in 2000, Higgins (who lost a sister to cancer) offered to fly out and be with me. But he could also be strikingly self-conscious. If he wasn't the coolest dude in the room, he gravitated toward whoever was. One time he and a friend walked into a restaurant for lunch wearing matching black suits, white shirts and sunglasses. The clerk looked them up and down and said, "And what would the Blues Brothers like today?" Without missing a beat Higgins shot back, "Four fried chickens and a coke, ma'am."

That was the Higgins we knew and loved — a man of character who *was* a character.

He died Thanksgiving week of 2006 of a heart attack. He was just 45. Three weeks later, hundreds of people packed into the MTV Lodge overlooking Times Square to pay tribute to him. CEOs sat next to journalists and marketers. Many kind and hilarious things were said about Higgins that night.

"The qualities that made him a great researcher also made him a great friend," said Marc Rosenthal.

2007

Twelve thousand members of the Writers Guild of America went on strike, throwing the 2007–2008 season into chaos. *The Sopranos* went out in style, winning best drama at the Primetime Emmy Awards after receiving a special honor earlier in the evening. The final episode ended controversially, as fans panicked when their screens went black in the show's final scene. *30 Rock* won the Emmy, and Tina Fey redefined sex appeal as brainy, funny and vulnerable. Nielsen revamped its television ratings to include DVR viewing. Many shows began offering their entire seasons online for on-demand viewing. But because the networks didn't want to pay residuals to the writers, TV had a strike.

For the first time in history, the five most-watched shows in America were unscripted: two hours of *Idol* and three hours of *Dancing With the Stars*.

When weather attacks

Kansas City Star, March 7, 2007

I have a solution to one of Kansas City's most vexing civic issues. I'm referring, of course, to weather interruptions on TV. On Tuesday I told you about FireKatie.com, an amusingly vicious Web site that ripped KCTV meteorologist Katie Horner for her marathon coverage of severe storms, her tendency to dramatize things, and her station's insistence on steamrolling network programs. But all news stations in Kansas City do this to some degree, as the Web site's creator conceded. Here's another inconvenient truth: When local stations go wall-to-wall with storm coverage, people watch. At 9:30 p.m. last Wednesday, when four local stations were doing little more than showing I-35 underwater, 48 percent of viewers were tuned to local weather coverage — not counting the three additional options on cable. So if the people upset at Katie Horner and her fellow pre-emptologists are just a small, if highly vocal, minority, do we really have a problem here? The answer is yes. Whether broadcasters want to admit it or not, the virus of weather rage is now loose. But there is a vaccine, and KMBC introduced it last week. The morning after the ABC affiliate pre-empted *Lost,* its schedulers were on the phone with the network, which gave permission to re-air the program three days later, after the Saturday late news. That gave KMBC, the newspaper and the electronic listings guides enough time to get the word out. By contrast, KSHB and KCTV simply re-aired their pre-empted shows as quickly as they could, which means almost no one had the chance to set their DVRs. Instead of adding insult to injury, all stations could follow KMBC's lead and devise a sensible pre-emption plan that respects the viewers who aren't affected by severe weather. Mother Nature has a mind of her own, but this is a storm front broadcasters can do something about.

Al-Jazeera English: A world of difference

Kansas City Star, July 1, 2007

After 9/11, the American media's gaze turned beyond our borders in a way it hadn't since World War II. Since then, cable news has reverted — like Robert De Niro's character in *Awakenings* — to its pre-9/11 state. Meanwhile, a new wave of international news channels has sprung up to expand viewers' horizons. One of these upstarts has a familiar-sounding name: Al-Jazeera English. Launched last fall by the same oil-rich emirate of Qatar that runs the Arabic Al-Jazeera, it was offered free to cable companies across America. Exactly one took up the offer — a tiny carrier in Vermont serving fewer than 2,000 households. Even at no charge, it apparently wasn't worth the potential backlash from customers who consider Al-Jazeera the official network of Osama bin Laden. I've been monitoring the new channel for several months over the Internet, and I am convinced it is the most important English-language cable network since Fox News. It's everything our news isn't: global, meaty, consequential and compelling in the best sense of the word. I called Reese Schonfeld, the first president of CNN to get his take. Still going strong after 50 years in the business, the ageless Schonfeld is active as a consultant and writer. He's also an occasional guest on Fox News Channel and an Iraq War supporter. He had sampled Al-Jazeera English online, and told me he considers it to be "a legitimate news service. They've told me things I never knew before, which surprised me. Their reports are much longer than American news reports. They pick their stories carefully. They're as straight and narrow as Fox is." You may not agree with Schonfeld's last assessment, but this much is undeniable: Fox's critics haven't done a thing to dent its growth. By contrast, the minuscule opposition to Al-Jazeera English has effectively kept it off American cable and satellite systems, even as our allies scoop it up. (It's in about 80 million homes worldwide and already a success in Israel, Pakistan and Germany.) Until everyday Americans can sit down, turn on their TVs and watch Al-Jazeera English, most of them will have no clue that one channel can make a world of difference.

Reality TV, aka strike insurance

Kansas City Star, July 24, 2007

Up on stage, top executives at the Fox network were fielding questions about their fall lineup from a roomful of TV critics, while in the back of the room, by the coffee service, lurked a small, wiry dude in denim who might hold the real power at Fox this season. His name is Mike Darnell, and his name and profile — well under five feet tall, with long, biker-chick hair — are familiar to anyone who covers the industry. Since 1998 he has been Fox's head of alternative programming, and he is widely considered the king of American reality TV. He is every bit the pioneer that William Paley was, only instead of Jack Benny and Lucille Ball, Darnell gave us *Joe Millionaire* and Paris Hilton. He has made money off the middlebrow (*American Idol, So You Think You Can Dance*) and lowbrow (*When Animals Attack, Are You Smarter than a 5th Grader?*). There is widespread fear throughout Tellywood of a crippling writers' strike this fall. But Darnell's world would actually begin spinning faster, because reality shows, which require no writers or actors, would become the only game in town. Darnell has not renewed his contract at Fox, and other networks are said to be wooing him to bring his special brand of strike insurance their way. Fox entertainment chairman Peter Liguori was asked about Darnell's future. "We look forward to having Mike for a number of years at Fox," came the reply. *(Postscript: Liguori is gone, but Darnell is still there.)*

TMZ *is H-O-T*

Kansas City Star, July 26, 2007

Lindsay Lohan's latest worst day ever turned out to be a good one to visit the headquarters of TMZ.com, which will double as the set of the new *TMZ* TV show. LiLo was pulled over early Tuesday morning; within minutes tipsters had set the Web's hottest celebrity news site in motion. An email titled "Lohan Busted for DUI ... Again!" was followed 23 minutes later by "Lohan — It's Allegedly Worse than Alcohol" and then, seven minutes after that, by "Lohan Charges — Coke Found." Harvey Levin, the 55-year-old attorney who started TMZ (industry slang for the thirty-mile zone surrounding Hollywood) and will appear daily on the *TMZ* show, said his troops get their scoops by reversing the industry's usual power relationship. "If you're doing a traditional entertainment show and you want an interview with Tom Cruise, when the publicist calls you up and says, 'If you do that story, we're not going to give you Tom Cruise,' it means something," said Levin. "We don't want the interview with Tom Cruise. We're going to be fair, but we're not going to fear publicists." Twice during the news conference Levin's cell phone went off and he had to take the call. In one instance a well-trained aide stepped in front of Levin so no one could read his lips. "You will so like this story," Levin said afterward, though he added, "I'm not sure we're going to be able to deliver it." TMZ seems to do journalism every bit as hard-nosed as any news organization — but why bother when it just helps people poke more fun at Britney and Lindsay? "These are people that human beings invest in," Levin responded. "They invest in them by going to movies. They invest in them by buying DVDs, by buying their clothes. They follow these celebrities, and they want to see what they look like when they're not wax figures on a red carpet."

Meet the Press *at 60*

Kansas City Star, November 18, 2007

Ask Tim Russert how much *Meet the Press* has changed in 60 years, and he'll tell you of sitting down with one of the NBC show's creators, journalist Lawrence Spivak, after Russert got the job. "Spivak told me the mission in 1947 was the same as it was in 1991 — learn as much as you can about your guests and the positions they take, and take the opposite stance. And though I do it in a persistent way, I try to do it in a civil way. I don't think I've changed very much." However true Russert feels he's being to *Meet's* origins, it's not true that he didn't change the show. Before his arrival, *Meet* was a dour half-hour that looked like it was being shot in a closet at NBC's Washington bureau. The moderator presided over a panel of journalists, and they did most of the questioning. ABC, not NBC, was the network that changed the Sunday-morning TV game. David Brinkley was paid a fortune to leave NBC in 1981 and start a one-hour interview show on ABC built around him. Meanwhile *Meet the Press* was churning through five moderators in seven years. On air the show exuded "funereal peace and quiet," as the *Washington Post*'s Tom Shales put it. When NBC promoted Russert, a burly former aide to Sen. Daniel Patrick Moynihan, he knew what he had to do. "I thought it was my role to reinvigorate the show," he told me. Spivak had reminded him that Sunday morning TV used to be more of a bare-knuckle brawl. "So we reverted back to the original *Meet the Press:* Put a guest in the seat, turn on the lights, turn on the camera and go at it," said Russert. Some people think that his approach's effectiveness has faded over the years. *Slate*'s Jack Shafer wrote a piece called "How to Beat Tim Russert" that showed how guests like ex-Klansman David Duke and then-Sen. Carol Moseley Braun were able to walk through the *Meet* minefield unscathed. "If people are paying attention, I think that's extremely helpful," Russert said. "It's a sign of respect for the tradition of the program."

Sorry, NFL Network, but you're greedier

TV Barn, November 28, 2007

As we have learned from the current writers' strike, making moral choices in a less-than-life-and-death situation is really not as hard as it looks. Yes, it is true that a lot of millionaires are out on the picket lines fighting for eight-cent DVD residuals on a $20 sale, but all you have to do is look to the other side of the dispute, to the multi-billion-dollar companies that don't want to share eight cents on a $20 sale, and that settles that. In that same vein we turn to the crucial National Football League matchup that will pit the Dallas Cowboys against the Green Bay Packers. Outside of those two cities, the game is being televised exclusively on the league's own NFL Network, which most cable systems in the country don't carry. That, says the NFL, is because of the greedy, greedy cable monopolies. The monopolies blame the NFL. The league wants NFL Network on basic cable. Comcast, Time Warner, and Charter are crying highway robbery over the fees the NFL has demanded. In response the NFL has tried to mobilize fans, urging them to switch to satellite if their local cable operator won't give in. Now, while this may look like two billion-dollar behemoths exchanging blows over nothing, keep in mind this one key detail: If the league gets its way, it will be able to charge the cable companies 70 cents per subscriber — that's you — for the privilege of carrying NFL Network. That's not 70 cents per year, but per *month*. Even in the off-season. Even if you couldn't care less about football. It is one of the highest rates of any cable network. The

NFL argues that its channel offers much more compelling product than the college lacrosse and rodeo offerings often found on ESPN and FSN — and those channels cost a lot more than 70 cents a month. That logic doesn't hold up, though, for one simple reason: The NFL Network is not an independent cable channel. *It is owned by the content provider.* The reason FSN and ESPN charge so much money to be carried on your cable system is that they spent billions to acquire content. The NFL Network has no rights fees to pass along. That makes this a cash grab, pure and simple, and if the NFL pulls it off, the price will be paid, in its entirety, by you.

Striking writers, in deep freeze

Kansas City Star, December 15, 2007

On a miserable Thursday morning this week, the Writers Guild of America-East picketed in Times Square outside the headquarters of Viacom, the media giant that runs MTV, VH1, Comedy Central and other media outlets. Out in L.A., talks have reached a stalemate between the writers and entertainment conglomerates. Everybody is losing buckets of money, and things look grim on paper. Out on the pickets, though, the Californians at least look like they're having fun. They wear color-coordinated T-shirts and make up creative chants like, "Peter Chernin, what you earnin'?" In New York, the weather is a better fit for the overall mood. "It's the end of the world," said a female striker as she struggled to repair her sign, which had been pulled apart by the wind and freezing rain. "It's like somebody's sneezing on us," said Eric Stangel, who is co-head writer of *Late Show with David Letterman* along with his brother Justin. While thousands have shown up for daily strike duty in L.A., the Viacom picket — one of just two scheduled this week — attracted 170 hardy souls who sloshed in a circle on Broadway for four hours as temperatures dipped into the low 30s. There was no chanting. Most of the writers here work in late-night TV. They've been off the air since the strike began in early November. The day before, I was a guest on MSNBC's *Hardball,* where Chris Matthews tried to convince Howie Kurtz and me that the strike was having an impact on the 2008 presidential race, because candidates like Mike Huckabee weren't getting torn apart on a nightly basis. Out on the line, *Daily Show* writer Scott Jacobson mocked Matthews' lament. "I pity you guys," Jacobson said. "I've had to keep my Huckabee jokes to myself. The world is really missing out."

God made him a gypsy

Montana Quarterly, May 2007

It's forty minutes before showtime and I am backstage at the
Acuff Theatre, a modern, 1,800-seat auditorium on the Grand
Ole Opry campus in Nashville. John Bohlinger, the bandleader
on *Nashville Star,* the country-music talent competition seen
by three million people a week on USA Network, is showing me
around. The namesake and son of Montana's lieutenant governor
keeps introducing me to everybody like *I'm* running for something.

We approach Meg Allison, a forty-two-year-old singer-songwriter
from Chicago. John was accompanying singers at the tryout
when Meg walked in and asked to do Patsy Cline's "Walkin' After
Midnight." A dozen girls had already covered it that day, but he
remembered that she had asked him to play the song in a bluesy,
slow way, which he did, and it knocked the judges' socks off. So
what if it wasn't country? John starts kidding around with Meg
and me. We laugh. Meg relaxes a little. I ask if she's enjoying her
ride on *Nashville Star.* "It's fun," she says, not very convincingly.
"But I want it to be over." Her wish is about to come true. There is
a folded-up sheet in John's back pocket, and it contains the run-

through for tonight's live broadcast. He showed it to me just before the secret ritual with his band, the one he calls the come-to-Jesus meeting. The sheet has the names of the five contestants who will be performing on the show that night. Her name is not on it, which means she was eliminated. For the past six days John and Meg have been rehearsing the Trisha Yearwood hit "The Wrong Side of Memphis." John has known for an hour and a half that all their arranging and rehearsing would be for naught. But he smiles and humors her like it's all good. He's not paid to be the bearer of bad news. He's just here to help every contestant look, feel, and sound great on *Nashville Star*, before the biggest audience most of them will ever know.

"We went through several iterations of the band," says the co-creator of *Nashville Star*, Howard Owens. "We were being very TV-producer about it. But at the end of the day, John held the band together." To the amateurs trying out, he is gracious and soothing; to the pros, his attitude gets them through the dry patches in the day, when jealousies and resentments can spring up like weeds and take over everything. "John has a unique personality," says Jon Small, *Nashville Star's* producer. "To hang five years with a guy and not see him drift a different way is very unusual, let me tell you."

You can know John Bohlinger 35 years and it won't change your opinion about him. (That's John and me in the 2007 photograph above.) Still, it *is* curious how he made it to Nashville. "I think John would've made a wonderful, kick-ass attorney," says his father. "He loves to debate, loves to argue, loves to defend the underdog. Most musicians who try to do this as their life's work, they're poor, they struggle financially. We were afraid we had doomed him to a life of poverty." When I ask John about that, he shrugs. "If God makes you a gypsy," he says, "then be a gypsy."

John's parents met in a bar in 1962. Bette was two years older, with four small children from a recently-ended marriage. They married in 1963 and Bette soon gave birth to Nick and John Jr. In elementary school, I often went over to the Bohlingers; later, during a rocky patch at my house, I lived with them. They seemed like a real family, and I both envied and idealized their life inside their beautiful home on Mountain View Drive, overlooking the city.

In eighth grade, the most powerful forces in John's life —
parents, music, and faith — converged at the Billings Newman
Center, a Catholic parish that met in a house on North 30th
Street. For years Bette and John had chafed at the strictures of
the downtown church, St. Patrick's Co-Cathedral. The first ten
years they were married they weren't allowed to take communion,
until finally John complained and the monsignor worked out an
annulment of Bette's first marriage. "We are more progressive, more
ecumenical, more inclusive than many of our faith tradition are,"
John Sr. told me recently, doling out his words in a warm, measured
baritone. "We feel the Holy Spirit led us to Newman Center, where a
more progressive message was being preached."

The Billings Newman Center had a living-room area that
extended in an "L" from the kitchen in the back all the way to the
front and was covered in shag carpeting. As people gathered around
them, three or four musicians with acoustic guitars sat in the vortex
of the "L" and played folkie hymns like "Yahweh, You Are Near" and
"Be Not Afraid." Their leader was a fun-loving strummer named
Dave Kreiter. "He had a great big Guild acoustic, biggest guitar I've
ever seen," John recalled. "My mom wanted me to play like he did.
I think she had a crush on him." His folks bought him an electric
guitar. Not long afterward, his dad heard "Sultans of Swing" on the
radio and picked up the LP. John played it over and over, trying
to imitate Mark Knopfler's effortless-sounding intricate stylings.
Senior took Junior to hear Eric Clapton's band. John was blown
away by Albert Lee, Clapton's virtuosic frontman, who could play
R&B and rock with the best of them, but specialized in country. "He
just kicked Clapton's ass," John said. "That was the best country
guitar I ever heard." He raided his parents' record collection for
Charlie Christian, Les Paul, Mary Ford, and other legends, and
started working out their arrangements on his guitar.

During John's sophomore year in high school, the dean's office
would periodically call the Bohlingers to ask if he was at home. At
night, John Sr. would ask his son where he'd been. "John never
lied. He said, 'Well, I went down to Hansen Music and worked on
my guitar licks.' He'd do this a lot. One day he came home and said,
'Dad, I've got an invitation to join a rock and roll band. We're going

to travel the country.' I said: *The hell you are.*"

Concerned about John's future, his parents started looking into prep schools. Someone recommended the Hun School of Princeton, and that's where they shipped off John until he graduated.

After graduation, he earned a full academic scholarship to Columbia University. While visiting Billings on Christmas break, he got his girlfriend Sherrie pregnant. They decided to get married. Sherrie came to New York to stay, but it was midway through the school year and Columbia didn't have any family housing for them. When I visited John, Sherrie, and August in the winter of 1988, they were living in a walk-up apartment building on 127th Street in Harlem. "Here, I want to show you something," he said, drawing me over to the window. "When Augie gets a little older, we're going to let him play down there" — and he pointed to the courtyard, which was filled two feet deep with garbage. We laughed hysterically.

He graduated *magna cum laude,* and the family moved back to Billings. He got a job teaching English composition and played in the clubs at night. When the time seemed right, John and Sherrie piled their worldly possessions, and Augie, into a 1977 VW microbus and headed to Nashville.

John started writing songs under contract. That didn't quite pay the bills, so he started to tour. The money was OK, so long as he found work all the time. Which meant he was on the road all the time. At one point he was gone 260 days out of 365. He didn't make it back to Montana for five years. Sherrie and Augie would make visits without him. Even gypsies usually travel together, but John wanted his family to have a normal life. As if. "I regret it," he said. "I was trying to build a career. I had to make some money and that's how you do it. It was kind of a bait-and-switch deal. When I was living elsewhere I'd see this guitarist on TV and I'd think, 'Wow, they've got it made, rich and famous.' But when I was on the road and wanting to be with my kid, sitting in some shitty hotel room, I'd tune in CMT and see this clip." It was him, playing in the background on a video for a Major Recording Artist. "And I'd look at that, and I'd think, 'Well, I'm on TV, and I'm on the road and I'm completely anonymous and poor.' "

In the spring of 2002, as the reality-TV craze was kicking into high gear, two former William Morris agents named Ben Silverman and Howard Owens were getting into the game. They had already sold one show, *The Restaurant,* to NBC, and were on the prowl for more ideas. They had been monitoring the success of *Pop Idol,* the hit musical-talent-search show in Great Britain. They wouldn't be able to create *American Idol,* of course, since the company that owned *Pop Idol* would be doing that. But imitation is the sincerest form of television, and nothing was stopping them from starting up a show like *Idol.* "We wanted singers and songwriters, people who were multi-skilled talents," Owens told me. "People in bar bands down the street — that was the kind of contestant we were looking for." As part of the competition, each entrant would have to submit one original song. Owens and Silverman wanted to base the show in Nashville, the songwriters' capital.

They flew to Music City and took a meeting with Jon Small, a veteran producer who made Billy Joel's first music videos for MTV before becoming a fixture on the country scene. Silverman and Owens had planned to use prerecorded music on the show, even for the songs that the contestants wrote themselves. (*American Idol* used music tracks for the first two seasons.) To Small, that was karaoke, and he argued strongly against it. "I explained to them that this is Music City, and there are great musicians here," he said. "I did the numbers to show that a live band would work."

Small's first choice to lead the ensemble was an accomplished studio musician who "knew the guys in Nashville who can make records." But those guys didn't make road trips. What Small hadn't factored in was the auditioning process. The road to *Nashville Star* would have to pass through a dozen cities every year, so USA Network could build excitement for the show. Problem was, the names Small wanted in his band were all highly in demand as studio musicians. Every cattle call meant time away from Nashville — which meant missing out on more lucrative recording gigs. Small had touted his industry connections to Silverman and Owens in order to sell them on the live-band concept. Those connections weren't panning out. "So now I'm stuck," Small said.

And that is how a show that was looking for unknowns to turn into music stars first had to find an unknown as its music director.

Small found him through Tracy Gershon, the record executive. John is the only member of the original *Nashville Star* band who is still with the show. And he still works like a fiend. During the off-season, he goes on the road with the Nashville Star Tour, featuring finalists from the show. He'll be the opening act this summer for Alabama's Randy Owen, who's embarking on a solo tour. And it seemed like every time I called him while working on this story, regardless of what night it was, he was heading out to some local club for a gig. When I ask why he doesn't let up a little now that he has TV work, he laughs. "I'm like one of those people who grew up in the Depression," he finally says.

John and I never talked about his divorce while he was going through it. "Things were falling apart," he says now. "I was angry at my wife, and God seemed so distant. For a couple years there I just shut down." There's a pause. "But I'm fine now."

As I was finishing this story, however, something happened that would upend his world again. John was in Bozeman, Montana, promoting his upcoming CD release, when Sherrie called from Nashville. She had discovered their nineteen-year-old son's body in her house. The coroner later determined August Bohlinger had died of an overdose.

Four days later, in a shady picnic shelter at a state park southwest of Nashville, 200 mourners gathered to say goodbye. "I feel like everything I've done in life is derivative," John said in his eulogy. "Augie was original. He was a wonderful, sweet creative force. I learned so much from him." I stood next to John Sr., whose face was shiny with tears and perspiration, while his son humored the crowd with stories about Augie — a boy who, much like his father, marched to his own beat. There was the time John urged Augie to try his regimen of vitamin supplements and a healthy diet, noting how fit-looking it had made him. "But, Dad," the son said cheerfully, "I already look like you *now*." And he was always urging Augie to get a job. Invariably, the son replied that there would be time for that someday. "I gotta hand it to him," John said. "He beat the system. He didn't have to work a day in his life." There was a bit of wonder in his voice.

2008

As in 2004, I found myself writing more media analysis and even political analysis, as television was the stage for the most remarkable campaign of my generation. At the end, there was an election night scene from Chicago's Grant Park as celebrities and everyday people stood shoulder-to-shoulder and cheered on the new first family — unlike any we'd seen on TV before, real or fictional — as they took the stage and brought an end to TV's most thrilling reality show.

Late-night TV comedians proved once again in 2008 that they often can speak truth to power better than journalists. Tina Fey surrendered to the demands that she play Sarah Palin. David Letterman wound up playing an unexpectedly pivotal role as the man who exposed McCain's claim to be "suspending" his campaign to be the empty vow it was. Letterman flipped a switch and showed viewers the candidate, instead of flying to D.C., getting powdered up for an interview with CBS' Katie Couric, a few blocks away from the Ed Sullivan Theater.

Tim Russert's death stunned the capital and left NBC with a huge void to fill during election season. Jay Leno made history as the first late-night talk-show host to get his own nightly prime-time program.

Once again, two *Idols* and three *Dancings* were the five most-watched shows — though advertisers were paying more attention to *House,* which drew more 18-to-49-year-old viewers than *Dancing With the Stars*.

Mad Men: *It's brilliant by design*

Kansas City Star, July 27, 2008

Two days before the first season of *Mad Men* was nominated for seventeen Emmy Awards, the show's creator Matthew Weiner gave a personal tour of Don Draper's home and office on an L.A. studio lot. "These are all New York colors," Weiner said as we gaze around the offices of Sterling Cooper. He pointed to a desk phone with bulky wires that extend down to the floor. "You will never see a telephone in a movie with these wires. They'd cut the wires and take them off." Weiner studied industrial films and amateur photos for clues about the East Coast palette. "You can't use the movies for research," he explained, "because even if they shot for weeks on location in New York City, everything inside is completely from California." Just then January Jones who plays Betty, materialized in a yellow and blue print party dress that flares out, with shoes made of clear Lucite, all courtesy of *Mad Men's* costume designer, Janie Bryant. Between Bryant and set decorator Amy Wells, this mid-century playground is the envy of tastemakers everywhere. Bryan Batt, who in real life runs a design store in New Orleans, joked, "They have to check my bag when I leave the set — there are *so* many things here I would kill for." Season 2 takes place in 1962, a year of station wagons and Drexel Heritage furniture. Americans were buying more, yet the styles lacked imagination compared with European products, because manufacturers entrusted design to engineers. Writing in the *New York Times* that year, the chairman of Tiffany & Co. lamented that consumer products in the U.S. lacked "what is commonly called taste." Inside the Draper home, for instance, there's a washer-dryer unit and gas cooktop in the kitchen in a familiar dull gold color. "There was a big, big design boom in the '50s which was commercially motivated," Weiner explained. "If you came up with a new color for a stove, you could reduce the time that you replaced the stove from eleven years to seven years." The most elegantly designed appliance — a chrome-and-black toaster — was hidden under a dorky slipcover. The living room was dominated by a cream-colored sectional with throw pillows colored burnt orange (to match the drapery) and turquoise (to match the wallpaper). There's a formality to the *Mad Men* set that lends everything an air of quiet desperation. "Really, it's not about the products," Weiner said. "It's about how you change. Everyone can remember someone who, senior year of high school, just *froze*. And that is as interesting as the person who the first time they heard about the civil rights movement, got on a bus and went to Mississippi. How many people lied about going to Woodstock? That's the story about history. We get the juicy parts. It's really so much more complicated."

The John Edwards love-baby story

TV Barn, July 31, 2008

Who knew that the biggest story to break at the television critics' tour would happen while we were all in our rooms getting some shut-eye? In the wee hours of July 22, former U.S. senator and presidential hopeful John Edwards was confronted by reporters for the *National Enquirer* outside a men's room at the Beverly Hilton, the very hotel where our summer press tour had concluded a few hours earlier. The *Enquirer* believed he was there to pay a visit to the child he had fathered out of wedlock and the baby's mother, an ex-campaign staffer named Rielle Hunter. Nine days later, the story finally started to trickle out into the mainstream, beginning with a news story in our sister paper, the *Raleigh News & Observer*. Given the *Enquirer's* stellar track record in reporting such things, why was the media so slow? It's not like a liberal conspiracy of silence kept this story under wraps. It wasn't even under wraps. In December 2007, the *Enquirer* reported that Hunter was pregnant and living in a gated community near a close Edwards confidant, who was insisting (not very persuasively) that the baby was actually his. Edwards was still running for president then. Why didn't the story get any traction? Because vigorous denials from campaign staffers, threats to put reporters off the bus if they persisted, and the absence of any follow-up reporting from the *Enquirer* helped take the air out of the story. Yes, I'm well aware that there were several bloggers chattering about the Beverly Hilton incident days ago. These same bloggers love to talk about the MSM's irrelevance, but the reality is that mainstream media coverage was indispensable to getting Edwards, and the Democratic Party, to finally treat this open wound.

Oprah's ratings crater; what went wrong?

TV Barn, August 11, 2008

What a stunning development for the so-called Queen Of Talk. *The Oprah Winfrey Show* finished fourth in its time slot here in July, despite airing on a powerhouse ABC affiliate. In fact, *Oprah* is losing its time period across the country this summer: third in Houston; third in D.C.; third in Pittsburgh; third in Miami; second in New York, Dallas, St. Louis, Atlanta ... OK, you might say, but those were repeats (though her reruns have been whupping her competitors' reruns for years). Well, I decided to go back and look at the May ratings book in all 53 metered markets tracked daily by Nielsen. Here's how it's supposed to work: *Oprah* comes on the air, creates a rising tide, and all boats are lifted. Simple! Except when it doesn't happen ... and that's what happened last May. In more than half of the metered markets where news follows *Oprah,* the show wasn't lifting the newscast's rating at all. And that was when *Oprah* wasn't in reruns! Why isn't this trend being noted? I think it's because *Oprah* is doing well in the big cities (New York, L.A.,

Atlanta and D.C.). Once you start getting into smaller markets, though, the *Oprah* effect vanishes, and that makes her an expensive drag on those smaller stations' budgets. Why is middle America rejecting *Oprah*? Responses from my readers suggest that at least some white evangelical women have stopped watching because of Winfrey's endorsements of New Age spirituality and Barack Obama. "I was a supporter for Hillary, who would have made the best President," said former viewer Reba Williams. Perhaps the most damning response I got was from a longtime reader of mine, C.D. Thomas. She said that Oprah's embrace of Marianne Williamson and James van Praagh, "and her hosting the huckster mysticism of *The Secret*," was too much for many of her women friends, all of them African-Americans like herself. "If her audience believes she's laughing at them behind their backs because she no longer believes in Jesus Christ as her personal savior," Thomas said, "she'd lose audience share, even if she backed the second coming of Jesus for president."

What's missing from presidential debates
TV Barn, September 11, 2008

Here's a little-known fact I uncovered while looking up other things: Since 1992, the presidential and vice-presidential debates have featured *no* questions from reporters, only anchorpeople and "uncommitted voters." In 1992, two of the four debates featured panels of print and television journalists in addition to the moderator, but since then the Commission on Presidential Debates has hewed to the single-moderator format. And that person has been a news anchor, not a reporter — mostly the *NewsHour's* Jim Lehrer, who has moderated eight of the past eleven presidential debates. Because all moderators have to have the tacit approval of both parties, the people who ask hard questions have been effectively squeezed out with bipartisan consent. Now, you say, what's wrong with that? You do have a journalist on stage, and the whole point of a debate is to sway uncommitted voters, so why not hear from them? Two problems with that reasoning. First, the moderator has to play the part of both impartial judge and hard-nosed prosecutor. That's hard to do, and it's probably why Lehrer gets the gig as often as he does ... because he errs on the impartial-judge side of things. That's his job. But let's say a Brit Hume were available (as he was for the 1988 Bentsen-Quayle debate) or Helen Thomas (Bush-Clinton-Perot, 1992) to lob a firecracker or two on stage. Wouldn't that create a little more drama, make things a little more unsettling for the candidates? And isn't that why we don't see journalists in the debates anymore? Second, these "uncommitted voters" (who are chosen at random by Gallup from poll subjects who say they haven't decided) are no substitute for professional question-askers. When non-journalists get to ask the questions, they rarely get to ask a follow-up. Helen Thomas recently observed in her HBO documentary that the follow-up is where you really get to nail your subject on his or her evasiveness. Just the other day Ted Koppel, now at NPR, took down a wily Republican operative over the question of Sarah Palin's foreign policy experience. That would never happen in a town-hall setting.

Those town halls Obama wouldn't do

TV Barn, September 26, 2008

In previewing his presidential debate tonight, Sen. John McCain groused to Charlie Gibson that he had challenged his opponent to a series of town-hall debate meetings way back on June 4, but "he refused to do it." Yes, this tune is getting old — but McCain is right. All summer long, Obama ran away from any kind of direct encounter with his opponent. When pressed, Team Obama fell back on three easily refuted myths. *Myth No. 1: John McCain likes the town-hall format, so this will only help him.* No, McCain likes *Republican* town halls. When his candidacy was in the doldrums, he went and held informal meet-and-greets with people who were wondering which GOP candidate to support. In a town-hall meeting with Obama, the crowd composition would be entirely different — and far less partisan. *Myth No. 2: Obama is more comfortable with formal debates and McCain is more comfortable with town halls.* Says who? With Obama up there, McCain would be forced to account for his ridiculous, over-the-top TV ads attacking Obama. Of course, McCain would have been free to question truthiness claims in his opponents's TV ads as well, but that, to steal a phrase from Obama, is a debate the Democrat would like to have. *Myth No. 3: Obama was leading McCain in the polls, so there was no reason to engage him directly.* For three months after the primary season ended, Democrats nervously waited in vain for Obama's poll advantage to climb higher than seven points. After McCain brought out Sarah Palin, the polls flipped and Democrats were in a panic. Who in that party could honestly say they were glad Obama didn't expose himself to the public this summer with hours of free television time?

Maddow: the future of news?

Kansas City Star, June 15, 2008

Commentator Rachel Maddow has seen her star take off on MSNBC this year. On *Countdown with Keith Olbermann,* she even fills in when the anchor is gone. "She's terrific," Olbermann told me. "Totally prepared, forceful, and yet respectful." Also young, gay, geeky, and one of the few unapologetic left-wing voices in mainstream media. Maddow attended Oxford on a Rhodes scholarship, earning a doctorate in political science. Her next step? Logically, she said, it would have involved "either Yale Law School or McKinsey," but instead she went to work as an activist in HIV-AIDS and prison reform issues, supporting herself with odd jobs. One day a local radio station in Amherst, Mass., held a tryout to become the morning zoo's traffic reporter. She entered and won. "It just bit me and interested me far more than I thought it would," Maddow said. She joined Air America Radio in 2004. Tucker Carlson first booked her on MSNBC, but it was Olbermann who put her on the map. After he asked her to be his sub, she agreed on one condition: that he show her exactly how a teleprompter works. After ten minutes, said Olbermann, "she had clearly mastered it." On MSNBC she often debates Pat Buchanan, the old Nixon hand and hard-line Republican, whom she treats kindly on the air, like a blustery uncle. Perhaps that's because she doesn't feel the need to over-defend the presumptive Democratic nominee. "Honestly, there's enthusiasm for Obama as the guy running against McCain," Maddow said, "but it's not like what he's putting out in policy proposals is energizing the left." The future of television news might involve more people like Rachel Maddow, clever nerds who don't believe in information overload and are fluent in irony.

2009

The year started with the Screen Actors Guild, in a lousy economy, threatening to shut down Hollywood for the second time in two years. The hardball tactics of its soon-to-be former leadership backfired. The next threat on the horizon was the Feb. 17 deadline to shut down analog TV signals — a date that had already been pushed back three years from the original DTV switchover goal. Fearful of millions of voters being caught without converter boxes, the Obama White House got Congress to move the deadline to June, by which time America's attention had turned to more important matters, like whether it was time to stop watching *The Tonight Show* now that Jay Leno was no longer host.

Technology became more than just a way to watch *The Office* on the bus. Cell-phone videos of the crackdown in Iran were broadcast to the planet, including the heartbreaking death of a young woman named Neda from a stray bullet. YouTube conveyed the white-hot anger of "tea parties" protesting the stimulus package to news organizations that had failed to cover them.

The marriage of Jon and Kate Gosselin came apart, and millions of people watched right to the bitter end. If these were the highlights, then you know 2009 was a pretty crummy year. *Mad Men* took home the prestigious Best Drama Emmy for the second year in a row, but *Idol* continued to rule the ratings roost. Among scripted shows, *NCIS* took over the top spot. We lost Walter Cronkite.

Bravo eats cake

Kansas City Star, February 28, 2009

When the economy goes into the toilet, what happens to a cable channel devoted to chronicling the lifestyles of the rich and famous? Bravo — the upwardly mobile, gay-friendly lifestyle channel — reported that ratings for February were the highest in Bravo's history. A record two million viewers watched the fourth season of *The Real Housewives of Orange County*. Bravo has used the ironically-named series about shopaholic trophy brides to create a franchise, with spinoffs filmed in New York City, Atlanta and, coming in April, New Jersey. More than two and a half million viewers tuned in for the latest *Top Chef* competition, in which aspiring gourmets cook the kinds of meals that would cost the average American the equivalent of a week's worth of groceries. And Kathy Griffin, the onetime sitcom sidekick whose career was so perilously close to obscurity that she turned it into a Bravo series, *My Life on the D-List,* just signed a book deal to write her memoir for a reported $2.2 million. While the media have been almost uniformly brutal toward Bravo since Wall Street started to go south — one blogger wondered "if Bravo's wealth-based programming has jumped the Louis Vuitton-monogrammed polo pony" — Lauren Zalaznick, who oversees Bravo, thinks otherwise. Zalaznick told me that she and her top lieutenants have been "relentlessly, maybe obsessively, talking about the notion of affluence and what our programming is really about." Their takeaway, so far, is that people who like Bravo are less interested in the shiny things that money could buy than in the type of person whose career made it possible to acquire those shiny things. "We really program to people who esteem the notion of jobs and careers," she said. "We program to people who enjoy thinking about what their lifestyle of hard work is going to yield in terms of personal relationships and stuff they appropriate."

Paul Harvey ... good-bye

Kansas City Star, March 4, 2009

There was a time in my life when nothing excited me so much as a Paul Harvey news and comment. No one invested a newscast with such thrilling vigor and optimism. When Harvey gave up the fight on Saturday at the age of 90, it truly was the end of an era, in politics as well as media. Paul Harvey was a conservative who didn't feel the need to rip viciously into those who believed differently from himself. His is a type of broadcaster who has gone away and is not coming back. Idiosyncratic doesn't begin to describe the combined effect of his voice, phrasing, news selection and worldview. In the America where I grew up, Paul Harvey was a uniter, not a divider. And yet he was anything but a centrist or a moderate. At times he would sound wildly out of the loop, while other pronouncements now seem prescient, like his unfailing enthusiasm for biofuels, which were key to his vision of national self-sufficiency. The flagship of *Paul Harvey News and Comment* was the noon newscast, which could have taken on import only in the Heartland, with its captive audience of farmers and housekeepers. In the years before Rush Limbaugh, this midday missive to the faithful allowed him to become hugely influential while, at the same time, remaining unnoticed by most of the mainstream news media. Keith Olbermann was Paul Harvey's official fill-in from 2001 to 2003. When he got a chance to return to MSNBC, Olbermann pitched his bosses a new format for a fast-paced program that combined news and comment, with a few oddball items to lighten the load. He had no doubt that it would work, because it was Paul Harvey's format. "I stole it almost entirely for *Countdown*," he said.

Super un-size me

Kansas City Star, July 19, 2009

What kind of person drives 550 miles to sit in line for eleven hours to try out for a reality show? In the case of *The Biggest Loser,* it's not someone primarily interested in fame or even the $250,000 first prize. "I've been heavy my whole life," said April Cowan of Connersville, Indiana, who had been in a large camp chair since 10 p.m. the night before. "My weight's affected my marriage. It's affected my children. I'm not stopping until I get it. I need it." By "it" she means the regimen of grueling workouts, sensible diets and endless encouragement made famous by *The Biggest Loser,* NBC's weight-loss competition megahit. Every few months, people like April are chosen by casting directors at open calls like this one. Almost all contestants are at least 100 pounds overweight. Many are experiencing diabetes, heart trouble and other ailments that they know will kill them at a young age. These lucky few are sent to "the ranch" in Arizona, where collectively they shed thousands of pounds during the competition, not to mention their feelings of hopelessness, fear and self-loathing over a lifelong failure to beat back weight gain. More than 300 people lined up for the chance to spend a minute or so pitching their case to a *Biggest Loser* casting director. The odds of being selected are extremely remote — Marty Wolff was the sole contestant chosen from the last tryouts held here, in 2006 — but at least it is something a person can do after the dieting, even the gastric bypass surgery, has failed. One hopeful said she would lose her job if her employer knew she was trying out for a show that would take her away for three months. But if chosen, she would quit and go to the ranch. "It's the only reality show that changes lives," she said.

The wind brings it back

Kansas City Star, May 4, 2009

There's a Ford Escort in the yard of a house at Iowa and Sycamore streets in Greensburg, Kansas. It rests there in a V, crushed in the middle like an aluminum can. At first, you think it's one last piece of unpicked debris from the EF-5 tornado that swept through Greensburg two years ago — a sad reminder of the fury that destroyed 95 percent of this town and scattered its 1,600 residents

That crumpled car, however, actually is a symbol of Greensburg's vision for the future. And so is the house. It's called the Silo Eco-Home. Inspired by the grain elevator on the other side of the highway — that withstood the tornado — the Silo Eco-Home has rounded, eight-inch, steel-reinforced concrete walls that will keep the occupants cool in the summer and warm in the winter. It also can withstand 180,000 pounds of impact. To prove it, last month the home builder hired a crane to drop that Escort onto the roof from a height of sixty feet — twice.

On the night of May 4, 2007, three large, violent tornadoes emerged from a massive supercell parked over the Midwest. One of them, a 1.7-mile-wide flying wedge, charged into Greensburg, 100 miles west of Wichita. But today, a different storm is sweeping through Greensburg. It started days after the tornado struck, when civic leaders committed to turning the city into a model of sustainable living with architecture that drew energy from the wind, sun and earth. Their timing was ideal. Not only was green technology emerging, so was a media movement to promote it. Combined with the tremendous largess that follows a major disaster — and, let's face it, the dumb luck of having "green" in its name — Greensburg began generating publicity and support rarely seen in a town this small and remote.

Today, some of the most energy-efficient buildings in the country are in Greensburg, and 100 of the 300 rebuilt homes use green technology. It has the first all-LED streetlight system in the country. Volunteers continue to pour in to help, as have media outlets that are eager to tell the story of "the greening of Greensburg." Last month at a ribbon-cutting outside the city's new business incubator, an event covered by the ever-present crew of Planet Green's TV series *Greensburg*, Mayor Bob Dixson declared, "We in Greensburg are new pioneers in the twenty-first century."

In the solar-lit showroom of BTI-Greensburg, the family-run John Deere dealership, co-owner Mike Estes pointed out the building's many features. Out in the parking lot were two wind turbines that supply energy to the dealership. One is a five-kilowatt model donated by a company in Canada. Now BTI has a spinoff business, marketing those turbines throughout North America. It's an opportunity that would not have come about except for the EF-5. "The wind took it away," he said. "The wind could bring it back."

Congressman Emanuel Cleaver of Kansas City recently led a delegation on a 300–mile bus trip to Greensburg to get ideas for a new "green impact zone" back home. Cleaver said he intends to pump millions of stimulus dollars into the urban core to make low-income housing more energy efficient and affordable. Daniel Wallach of the local advocacy group Greensburg Greentown told me that he envisions the town serving "as a continuous trade show" for other communities. "You can come to Greensburg and have these new technologies demystified for you. You can make better decisions for sustainability. Something like this doesn't exist anywhere else, and there's a real hunger for it."

Willie's money makeover

Kansas City Star, November 5, 2009

In our last episode of "Willie Aames Confidential," the onetime star of TV's *Eight Is Enough* and *Charles in Charge* was holding a yard sale in front of his foreclosed home in Olathe. Eight months have passed since then, and the forty-nine-year-old Aames has since begun an extreme makeover, not of his house but of his life. He's training to be a financial adviser. That's right. Aames, who has filed for bankruptcy twice since 1997 and was selling his possessions in March just to make ends meet, has stabilized his finances and is well on his way toward learning this new profession. He hopes his story will inspire others who find themselves in similar straits. "How do you start over from scratch?" Aames said last week. "I didn't know. But I thought that if I made it, maybe, just maybe, it would be helpful to some people."

The VH1 cable channel took an interest in the former actor after he hit bottom. But so did Thomas W. Butch, the president of Waddell & Reed, a locally-based financial advisory firm and mutual funds seller. Since coming under Butch's tutelage, Aames has passed two of the three tests required to qualify as a financial adviser. Not unlike a contestant on *The Biggest Loser* who decides to become a fitness trainer, Aames could find himself hanging out a shingle with Waddell & Reed by 2010. "He will still have to do what all of our advisers do — become adept at financial planning, at knowing our products and understanding how to ascertain products that are best for clients, marketing himself and acquiring a client base," Butch said in an interview. "I think he will have the capacity to do that very, very well."

The VH1 special, *Broke and Famous,* is hosted by corporate trainer Sarano Kelley, who describes himself as a "financial literacy advocate." He visits Aames at his foreclosed home not long after his wife and eighteen-year-old daughter, Harleigh, have moved out. It opens with a heated exchange over some questionable decisions Aames had made in recent years, such as getting $3,000 worth of tattoos. "It's stupid!" Kelley says. Aames, who has also done *Celebrity Fit Club,* knows how TV gets made, and up until that point, things were proceeding more or less as he'd expected. Then, he said, "one of the producers said, 'You're on the radio in ten minutes.' I said, 'For what?' 'We're throwing a garage sale.'" He didn't see that coming, and initially objected. But he had little leverage at this point, so he went along. The sale netted more than $5,300. Aames agreed to stick with Kelley's plan for financial accountability, which included moving into a $760-a-month apartment. VH1 rewarded Aames with a $25,000 check.

Once the cameras were shut off, however, that was when the real makeover began. "The approach I take is real and lasting change," Kelley told me. "They've got to confront their demons, their challenges, around making the change. And then they need to accept the help to execute the change. And in the case of Willie, one needs the necessary support to sustain the change." Kelley, who has extensive ties in the financial industry, called Tom Butch at Waddell & Reed. "Sarano and I have known each other many years," said Butch. "He called me and asked me point blank if I'd be willing to serve as a mentor to Willie. And I reflexively told him I would if he thought there was something of value I might impart."

Aames entered the Career Readiness Program at Waddell & Reed. Butch supplied career guidance and Kelley held a weekly conference call with Aames, giving him a support system few homeless people have. "Here I found myself in this position, completely undeserving, with people willing to reach down and give me a hand and mentor me," he said. "No guarantees. They gave me the opportunity to learn if I would take it."

Aames, who admits he never paid much attention to his studies as a young actor, has been preparing five to ten hours daily for his exams. He still lives in his budget apartment and has become financially adept for the first time in his life. (*Postscript: He passed all his exams and was taking on clients by the beginning of 2010.*)

Epilogue: 2010

Tasteland took more than a year to complete, and just as I was preparing to write a bookend piece summarizing the state of late night television, out of the sky dropped Late-Night War II. Here are my thoughts from the opening skirmishes, along with an assessment of which hosts are worth watching in late night. For balance, I decided to end this section with one last thought about the news.

Lessons of Late-Night War II

Kansas City Star, January 18, 2010

In the year 2027, when Jimmy Fallon is trying to wrest control of *The Tonight Show* from its 76-year-old host, Jay Leno, he would do well to study the lessons of history. Laugh if you will, but mark your calendar for seventeen years from now, when Leno — he's half cockroach, half cicada! — ignites the third round of Late-Night Wars. Then he will recall how, in the opening days of Late-Night War II, the world learned that Jay Leno would do and say anything to keep his famous chin in front of the cameras.

Of course, Leno's survival skills became legendary in Late-Night War I of the 1990s, when he somehow held onto his job after blowing a big lead to CBS. He did this, in part, by eavesdropping on NBC executives and stealing elements of David Letterman's show as he pleased. But in 2010, Leno outdid himself.

Remember how he once made such a big deal of the fact that he was handing the 10:35 job to Conan O'Brien? Last week he was shamelessly mocking O'Brien's ratings in his monologue — even though *The Jay Leno Show* has turned into his own Nielsen crater. Oh, and remember how Leno's best bud, Jerry Seinfeld, advised him to step aside and give the spotlight to the heir apparent? Now

Seinfeld belittles O'Brien for being upset that the spotlight is back on Jay. "I don't think anyone is preventing people from watching Conan," Seinfeld sniffed last week.

And remember how executives at NBC spent years promising O'Brien *The Tonight Show*? Now, as they circle the wagons around Leno, they're trashing O'Brien because he dared to criticize their brilliant scheme to reinstall Leno at 10:35 and move O'Brien to 11:05. One network suit, Dick Ebersol, called O'Brien an "astounding failure" because he could not beat David Letterman in seven months of head-to-head competition. Ebersol — who hasn't had a good idea since he fired himself as the producer of *Saturday Night Live* in 1985 — knows full well that it took Leno twenty-three months to beat Letterman, even though at the time NBC was No. 1 in prime time, and viewers did not have the late-night options of Stephen Colbert, Adult Swim, DVRs or Hulu.

The final proof that Leno would do anything to survive is when he killed off his alter ego, Mr. Nice Guy, who was last seen in 2004 telling his *Tonight Show* audience why he had agreed to retire in 2009 at the age of 59. "There's only one person who could do this job into his 60s, and that's Johnny Carson," Leno said at the time. "There was a lot of animosity between me and Dave (over) who's going to get it, and quite frankly, a lot of good friendships were permanently damaged. I don't want to see anybody ever have to go through that again. This show is a dynasty. You hold it, and then you hand it off to the next person. So here it is, Conan!"

Here it comes, and … there it went. At that time Leno made the above grand gesture, it was clear that O'Brien had gained the upper hand, by learning the one important lesson of the Leno-Letterman war: Do not be coy about your ambition. He asked NBC for *The Tonight Show* in 2003 because he saw what happened when Letterman kept his yap shut. Now, by writing a public letter to his fans explaining how and where exactly NBC screwed him, O'Brien proved once again that he has from Dave, not to mention the Rolling Stones: If you can't get what you want, you get what you need. And when all's said and done, he may wind up at Fox, not only hosting the 11:30 show but producing a 12:30 as well.

The "People of Earth" letter was a *tour de force*: funny, self-effacing and direct, with a breathtaking leap at the end, as O'Brien publicly liberated himself from the show he had spent his adult life dreaming of. "I sincerely believe that delaying *The Tonight Show* ... will seriously damage what I consider to be the greatest franchise in the history of broadcasting." Translation: O'Brien finally figured out that NBC will never quit Leno. And so, after sixteen years of hearing those words he'd come to dread — *stay tuned for Conan!* — it was time to quit NBC. In his letter, O'Brien said that "no one should waste a second feeling sorry for me," and after the events in Haiti later that week, no one did. Still, it took guts to walk away from *The Tonight Show,* and fans and creative types alike were energized by the boldness and virtuosity of his letter. "Ballsy," *Scrubs* creator Bill Lawrence told TV critics the day after the letter came out.

Meanwhile, the network continued its assault on O'Brien, blaming him for losing more of *The Tonight Show* audience (50 percent) in seven months than Leno had lost after taking over for Johnny (12 percent). Of course, in 1992 NBC had five Top 20 shows (versus zero today) and Leno's ratings back then didn't actually begin to rise until *ER, Friends* and, yes, *Seinfeld,* took off more than two years later. The people running NBC may be idiots, but they know good and well that after Leno retakes *The Tonight Show,* the ratings will bounce back. They almost have to, now that the millstone known as *The Jay Leno Show* has been cut. (When someone tells you Conan wasn't pulling his weight at 11:35, tell them this: The rating for *The Tonight Show with Conan* among adults ages 18-49, a key group for advertisers, declined by 20 percent compared to *The Tonight Show with Jay,* according to NBC. And the 18-49 demo rating for *The Jay Leno Show*? It was down *30 percent* from the abysmal number NBC was pulling at 10 p.m. a year ago.)

As historians look back on Late-Night War II, they'll see that Conan went to Fox and did just fine. And even though he never told another NBC joke again — his old employer made him sign a no-disparagement clause — he delivered the one parting shot that would endure for years afterward:

"Hosting *The Tonight Show* has been the fulfillment of a lifelong dream for me," he told his audience on one of his last NBC shows. "And I just want to say to the kids out there watching: You can do anything you want in life. Unless Jay Leno wants to do it, too."

The best and worsts of late night

Kansas City Star, October 20, 2009, updated in 2010 for *Tasteland*

Best show: The Late Late Show With Craig Ferguson on CBS. He hasn't learned to talk in an Indiana accent, but that's about the only thing the Scotsman has yet to accomplish since emerging as the dark-horse candidate for Craig Kilborn's job five years ago. Versatile, literate, spontaneous, a man who has seen the world, Ferguson is a latter-day Jack Paar, but built for the long haul. He has taken *Late Late Show* where it has never been — first place — so if you still think Jon Stewart is the front-runner for David Letterman's job, you don't know Scot.

Worst show: Last Call With Carson Daly. NBC has been screwing around with *Last Call* for years, and it just seems to get worse. Currently it's a low-budget, heavily edited interview show mostly shot at soundstages and hotels. Anyone could host it.

Best monologue: The Colbert Report. Stephen Colbert can take a single idea and carry it for five minutes — and all the while he's channeling that character of his.

Worst monologue: Letterman's. Actually, Jimmy Fallon's standup routine is probably weaker, but Dave's recital of the same topics, and sometimes even the same *jokes,* night after night is maddening. The Friday show is taped earlier in the week, and the jokes that night are so stale, he should just deliver them while wearing Paul Shaffer's Carnac headpiece.

Best one-on-one interviewer: Ferguson. Craig lets his life story — growing up near Glasgow, emigrating to L.A., getting sober, dealing with anger — inform and enlighten conversations. He shifts easily from laughter to intimacy with his guests and avoids scripted gags or other gimmicks.

Worst interviewer: Fallon. Generally, the only time his chats are even tolerable are when he's interacting with someone he worked with on *Saturday Night Live.* Good news for Jimmy: Conan wasn't any better with guests six months in.

Best ringleader: Chelsea Handler's three-comedian panels are the highlight of her nightly E! talk show *Chelsea Lately*. (I would enjoy her monologues more if I could follow her endless references to cable reality shows.) She knows not to talk over her guests' punchlines, and her deadpan look and razor-sharp comebacks are so impeccable, it's like watching the love child of Johnny Carson and Bonnie Hunt.

Best stunts: Before it went off the air, *The Tonight Show With Conan O'Brien* was doing the kind of big slapstick that Letterman was once famous for. Other stunts, like the host's fantastic "feud" with Newark Mayor Cory Booker and the portable drum set that rode Max Weinberg out of the studio, were inspired.

Best prerecorded bits: Jimmy Kimmel Live. Video gags are a staple of late-night comedy these days. *JKL* (which, despite the title, is itself prerecorded) does more video bits and gets more out of them, whether mocking local TV, using animation to make a news clip funnier, or bleeping random words so a clip sounds dirtier than it is.

The future of TV news is up in the air
Kansas City Star, February 7, 2010

Chances are you've never heard of Larry Doyle. I had no idea who he was until last week, when the news division at CBS let him go after forty years. Yes, CBS had another round of firings, and the loss of Doyle, the network's top war news producer, showed how deep these cuts really were. Dan Rather told *The New York Observer* that Doyle was "the soul of the place."

Everyone was told that this latest purge was a response to the devastating television advertising market of 2009. Network news layoffs are, indeed, often spun as cyclical, when in fact they are secular, part of the retrenching of a still-powerful but no longer influential media sector. Katie Couric can still get a lot of mileage from a gotcha, but there's no sense waiting for the next *Harvest of Shame* to come along. (Shame went out of style a long time ago at the networks.)

So what happens when there's a big, boring but hugely important story that affects 100 million Americans — say, airline safety? Well, we saw what happened last week, when the nightly newscasts all reported on the government's report into the Continental 3407 crash in Buffalo, which killed 50 people one year ago.

As CBS reporter Nancy Cordes told Couric's viewers last Tuesday, the report blamed the tragedy on "a series of easily avoidable mistakes" by the airplane's captain and first officer. She said concerns were also raised about the company that put these pilots in the cockpit: Colgan Air, a low-cost puddle jumper that partners with Continental and other major carriers.

And Cordes even mentioned that the problem might be systemic, requiring the Federal Aviation Administration to draft new regulations for regional airlines, which have been involved in every domestic plane fatality since 2002. But a two-minute news report is not a very large or sturdy container for ideas. Frankly, after Cordes had finished blaming the pilots, everything else seemed like *blah-blah-blah*.

The Colgan Air story soon faded from memory, pushed out by the media's relentless coverage of the Toyota recall — an important story to be sure, but one affecting a fraction of the people who take commuter flights. Both dramas involve a lot of behind-the-scenes with federal regulators, but a product recall means a hazard *could be sitting in your driveway*! That's an easy sell. And this recall came fully loaded with an us-versus-them sidebar. "As Toyota sales were falling last month, Ford's were up 24 percent," chirped Couric.

Here's the paradox of big, boring stories like airline safety: If you throw enough resources at one of them, you'll flesh out the details needed to turn it into a fairly spellbinding narrative. But if you do that, you won't make money. If you're smart with it, though, you might build your brand, maybe even your audience. Newspapers know this. CBS used to know this.

As it happens, the PBS newsmagazine *Frontline* chose the one-year anniversary of the Buffalo crash to air its investigation into Continental 3407. *Frontline's* report takes us back to the dawning of the deregulatory era thirty years ago, then walks us forward to the present day, methodically pointing out the steps by which the commuter business grew to 52 percent of all airline travel and, not coincidentally, allowed two inexperienced pilots into that Colgan cockpit. As someone who's studied the history of government oversight of media, I found *Frontline's* reporting an all-too-familiar case of overburdened regulators asking the industry to keep tabs on itself. The industry responded by building what one of *Frontline's* talking heads called a "firewall" between the major carriers and their regional partners.

A former Colgan pilot told *Frontline* he got promoted to captain with 500 hours of flight time — less than a third of what the majors require. Pilots are paid only when the cabin door closes, so they work sixteen-hour days for $21,000 salaries. There's no pay for cancelled flights, so they take chances with stormy weather. And when a plane goes down? Incredibly, the major airline that "incentivizes" this risky behavior is shielded from liability. As for the government, *Frontline* asked Mary Schiavo, the FAA's plain-speaking inspector general during the Clinton/Valujet years. "The FAA protects airlines," she said flatly.

Frontline's correspondent is Miles O'Brien, who was one of my favorite CNN anchors until he and the network's entire science, technology, and environmental team were fired in 2008. Between the PBS exposure and tie-ins with NPR, O'Brien's reporting will probably be seen and heard by more Americans than saw him on cable. PBS will also put the report online in perpetuity.

But *Frontline* is the exception. During a decade when the cost of gathering news plummeted, meaning that networks could do more with less, they have instead done less with less. *The New Yorker's* Ken Auletta recently documented how correspondents like NBC's Chuck Todd have become victims of the Internet news cycle. They are on camera all day, while enterprise suffers. And truth be told, a nonprofit venture like *Frontline* isn't immune to this trend. In 2009 it produced sixteen films that ate up seventeen hours of PBS prime time. Ten years earlier, *Frontline* produced seventeen films with twenty-two hours of in-depth reporting. Five fewer hours, and one less assignment, no doubt saved PBS stations a pile of pledge dollars.

Everywhere you look, TV news is saving money. And as Miles O'Brien, Larry Doyle and thousands of other journalists might say in response: At what cost?

I, CRITICUS: THE 100 BEST

(2005 illustration by Neil Nakahodo)

INTRODUCTION

Are these the 100 greatest television programs of all time? Not exactly. But they are the 100 best shows (actually more than 100) that I reviewed during my years on the television beat that you can now enjoy on your own.

This is not an obligatory list of "classic" shows that aired during those years (my apologies to fans of *Seinfeld*, *Friends*, *Curb Your Enthusiasm*, and *CSI*); nor a list of the news and information programs I rely on most (for the record: *60 Minutes*, *The Daily Show*, the *NewsHour*, *Countdown*, *Fox Report*, and *Fareed Zakaria GPS)*. You already know my late-night favorites, and they aren't anthologized, anyway (except for a couple of Conan DVDs and *The Daily Show*, which has its entire video archive online).

My point in making "The 100 Best" was to suggest a thousand hours or so of programs for your viewing pleasure, and make the list varied enough so that even devoted couch potatoes will find things they have overlooked. I've tried to identify strong individual seasons. (The online reference tool I use the most is epguides.com.) I've supplemented many of my picks with related recommendations, including programs I never reviewed for print. I hope you find my list useful.

The vast majority of titles below were found on Amazon or Netflix. Some are only available for purchase through eBay, or a proprietary site like iTunes or ShopPBS.org. Many shows are also airing in repeats somewhere in the vast tasteland (I use tivo.com to check local listings). Hard-to-find shows can often be located with file-sharing software, *or so I am told*. Finally, you can try video-on-demand Web sites, though it will be a while before most people can enjoy Hulu on their living room flat screens.

DRAMA SERIES

1. The Wire (entire series, five seasons)

What allows *The Wire*, in my opinion, to surpass *The Sopranos* in the pantheon of greatest American TV shows are its ambition — its voracious, audacious insistence on telling the whole story about a second-tier city, such as Baltimore, and how it is permitted to suffer and bleed while its leaders, their fixed on tonier, tourist-ready areas, declare that the city is "back" — and its anger, its unrestrained fury at the fact that, as far as the writers of *The Wire* are concerned, no one except them seems to give a damn. This anger is then converted into sprawling, demanding, self-righteous drama filmed with the realism of a documentary. Small wonder that its creator, David Simon, has been called to Congress and asked onto news programs to elaborate on everything from the American social-welfare system to the state of journalism. Personally, I thought Simon should have stopped while he was ahead — then again, *The Wire* has arguably contributed more to our understanding of our times than the combined wisdom of all the cable news pontificators.

Where to begin with *The Wire*? There is a seemingly endless parade of memorable working-class stiffs on both sides of the thin blue line, a cast of characters so long and variegated that it is hard to pick a favorite. You have McNulty (Dominic West), the obsessive cop whose preoccupation with busting the city's drug gangs overrules any imperative to clean up his wretched personal life; his on-again, off-again partner, Bunk (Wendell Pierce), who just has a way with words; the gang leader, Avon Barksdale (Wood Harris), whose marginalization as the series progresses shows the futility of putting away kingpins so long as the pipeline stays open; Barksdale's right hand, Stringer Bell (Idris Elba), a hustler who wears a green eyeshade and behaves like a legitimate businessman, an obvious suggestion to the viewer that businessmen behave like legitimate hustlers; the wild card, Omar Little (Michael K. Williams), a freelance thug beholden seemingly to no one; Snoop (Felicia Pearson), whose purchase of a nail gun in the opening of season four is as chilling a scene as any in the show's long litany of chilling scenes; Carcetti (Aidan Gillen), the reformer politician who's going to change everything and, of course, changes nothing; and on and on and on.

Then there are the storylines, new every season. Simon and co-producer Ed Burns had the entire series mapped out when they pitched *The Wire* to HBO. The show debuted in 2002 and would reboot every year, with new characters, backdrops and intrigues that would make it seem more like five miniseries with a returning core of regulars. Amazingly, despite a bumpy start in the ratings and almost no recognition of the show's existence from Emmy voters, HBO gave Simon and Burns the five seasons they had asked for, "to depict an American city at the millennium," as Simon put it, "and ask why it is that the richest, most powerful country in the world can't solve its fundamental problems when it comes to places like Baltimore. And there are a lot of places like Baltimore."

2. The Sopranos (Seasons 1 and 2)

So there was Tony Soprano, king of all he surveyed, in his case a two-bit mob franchise confined to a few townships in New Jersey. But at least Tony had the love of his good-hearted wife Carmela — and a mistress and some other women who were well compensated, in more than one sense of the word — and he also had two beautiful if vacant-eyed children, Meadow and Anthony Jr. (or A.J.).

Then one day Tony passed out, just like that, so he went to see Dr. Melfi, and they talked awkwardly about his "work" and even more awkwardly about his feelings, making no progress at all, even when it became obvious that Tony's mother Livia was trying to pull a reverse Oedipus and knock off her son. Livia's brother-in-law was the syndicate's figurehead, Uncle Junior, and she played him like a Strativarius, whispering in his ear things that were calculated to make him Tony's mortal enemy. But Tony had a loyal band of captains with names like Paulie, Silvio and Big Pussy, and the ensuing turf war would get very bloody until FBI agents, of all people, stepped in to break it up.

Meanwhile, nephew Christopher was thinking about becoming one of Tony's "made men," but he was also thinking about a screenwriting career, since he had heard that people close to the mob had made it big in Hollywood. He sold a script to Jon Favreau, and then he put out a rap album, and then he hustled the stock market — but each of these ventures ended more tragically than the previous one.

Back at home, Carmela was confessing to her parish priest the Faustian bargain she made by marrying a mobster. In gratitude for cleansing her soul, Carmela cooked food for the priest, food being a transparent symbol for sexual intimacy, until she saw other wives in the parish cooking for him and realized Father Phil was nothing more than a back-door daddy of casseroles. At least Tony had the decency to keep his affairs out of her sight.

Other memorable characters who drifted into the two best seasons of
The Sopranos (1999–2000) were Richie Aprile, who got out of prison and
not only began muscling in on Tony's turf but hooked up with Tony's
sister Janice, who herself was hell on wheels. There was Artie, a very
nice guy who owned Vesuvio, a restaurant favored by Tony's gang until it
mysteriously burned to the ground, setting in motion a peculiar series of
events. There was the associate named Furio, who came in from the old
country speaking little English but full of that can-do spirit that makes
America great. And, of course, there was the one-legged Russian girl who
used to do it with Tony and would, in the end, be the only person in the
world that gave a shit about Livia Soprano.

3. Mad Men (Seasons 1–3)

This pitch-perfect recreation of life on Madison Avenue in the early
1960s beautifully captured not just the clothing and furniture of the late
Eisenhower era, but its social mores and cultural conservatism. A s the
show found its stride, it did something even more remarkable: It dialed
down the social commentary and began to develop the stories of its
amazing ensemble of characters to a degree rarely seen on a television
drama. The show, which premiered in 2007, focused on the career and
personal life of Don Draper (Jon Hamm), an advertising executive at the
top of his game, an impeccably groomed Fifties man with a pretty wife
named Betty (January Jones), two children and inner demons that push
up his blood pressure and drive him to drink. Draper is a master at the
black art of consumer persuasion. Selling things comes easy, because
it lets him draw on his own reserves of desire and loneliness. He and
Betty don't communicate very well, and the long stretches of silence and
mundane chatter draw attention to the destructive forces lurking just
beneath the surface.

Over time, *Mad Men* familiarizes us with Don's coworkers at Sterling
Cooper: the co-founder Bert Cooper, whose office is a Japanese domicile
you remove your shoes before entering; Roger Sterling, the rakish son of
the other co-founder, whom we watch evolve from a carefree boor to a
man with something to prove; Joan Hathaway, the effortlessly efficient
office manager who would be CEO material in the non-glass-ceiling
age; Peggy Olson, who seizes the chance to make something of her life
besides toiling in Sterling Cooper's secretarial pool; Pete Campbell, the
company striver (and Peggy's secret tryst partner); the junior creatives
— Sal, Harry, Kinsey; and on and on. So deeply have these characters
insinuated themselves in viewers' psyches that, when Twitter began

to catch on, several Mad Men devotees began posting obsessively, in character, as @PeggyOlson, @_DonDraper and others. As I write this, *Mad Men* has just finished a brilliant third season filled with exploring the depths of these characters to such a degree that I would recommend starting from the beginning, to more fully appreciate what Matt Weiner and the other people behind the scenes at *Mad Men* have done.

4. House (Season 2)

He avoids medical consultations, long hours at the hospital and above all, seeing patients. "Treating illnesses is why we became doctors," says Dr. Greg House. "Treating patients is what makes most doctors miserable." Funny M.D.'s have been carriers of sudden TV-show death syndrome ever since Hawkeye Pierce left Korea. But Hugh Laurie defied all logic as the sarcastic, Vicodin-popping, cane-clutching healer in *House,* which signed on in 2004 as Fox's first procedural. He's forever locking horns with Dr. Cuddy, the hospital administrator (Lisa Edelstein), and his crack staff of junior doctors, led by the excellent Robert Sean Leonard, who must arm-twist him into taking on a new case every week. Patients on *House* always collapse in a heap, their bodies always betray them like out-of-control cars roaring toward the embankment, and Laurie always spends half the episode fighting with everyone around him before pulling the miracle cure out of his hat. The reason I picked Season 2 was that this all seemed fresh and exciting then, before the script writers got bored and veered off track into having House stage a *Survivor* competition for new doctors. The show was still having fun doing the simple things, like the opening scenes where victims presented symptoms in unexpected ways (one was filmed like a CBS crime show and depicted a woman being attacked — turns out, by her husband in a bedroom game). Or the clinic scenes where House would deliver verbal shock treatment to unsuspecting patients. Or the storylines that tested the viewer's loyalty to House, like the one by pitting him against a telegenic doctor who's using his illness to call attention to TB in Africa.

5. The Shield (Seasons 1, 4 and 5)

When people look back at the rise of basic cable in this decade, the arrival of *The Shield* in 2002 will be seen as a watershed. Brutal, funny, ingenious — and all from the mind of Shawn Ryan, who was an unproven screenwriter when he threw the pilot over the transom at FX. *The Shield* is one of the most intense shows ever to hit American TV, and unlike almost any that had a series run this long, its most elemental story arc remained over the course of seven seasons. (In fairness to an earlier era of serial television, *The Fugitive* produced 120 episodes in the 1960s while keeping its core chase scene going, compared with 88 episodes of *The Shield*.) You must begin with Season 1, not only because Michael Chiklis shocked the industry by winning the Emmy for Best Actor in a Drama Series — a first for basic cable —but because it sets up the storyline that will continue right through the series finale: Rogue L.A. strike-force cop Vic Mackey (Chiklis) tries to evade responsibility for a terrible thing he does in the opening scene of the first episode. Because Vic has a golden mouth (and, as you'll see, a seemingly endless supply of *deus ex machina* at his disposal), he manages time and again to escape his comeuppance. Then, skip ahead to the brilliant seasons featuring Oscar winners Glenn Close and Forest Whitaker in recurring roles. As good as these actors are, they never outshine the show's outstanding ensemble, including Jay Karnes, Walton Goggins and CCH Pounder.

> **If you liked this:** *Boomtown: Season One* presented the crime and its investigation from various points of view: the detectives, the perps, the prosecutors and the media. And it insisted on a nonlinear style that challenged the viewer to mentally assemble the pieces of the puzzle as the show unfolded. The low-rated show's unusual format was abandoned after season one. *Sons of Anarchy* earned some early comparisons to *The Sopranos* — it's about a biker gang that has run a small town in California, more or less peacefully, for decades — but stepped out on its own with a violent, intricate and ultimately heartbreaking second season.

6. Homicide: Life on the Street (Season 6)

I don't find too many readers who aren't aware of *Homicide's* brilliance, who don't know that many of the techniques we see in today's best cable dramas were first introduced on a low-rated NBC series starring Andre Braugher and adapted from a book by David Simon, who would go on to create *The Wire*. However, with the show now gone from cable, it's easy to forget how good it was. If you're going to rent one season on DVD, the 1996-97 collection is a good choice. One of three seasons that earned *Homicide* a Peabody Award, it's best known for the episode titled "The Subway," which took place on a train platform and guest-starred Vincent D'Onofrio as the doomed passenger.

If you liked this: From another era, the *Studio One Anthology* DVD collection captures some of the outstanding performances from the golden age of live network drama.

7. Lost (season 1)

A jet disintegrates at 40,000 feet ... and dozens survive. A crippled man leaps out of his wheelchair. Someone's dead dad is spotted wandering the island. Not for nothing were millions convinced that *Lost,* from its 2004 debut on ABC, was some sort of allegory for heaven or purgatory. Whatever it is — and as this book was going to press, the final season of *Lost* was just starting to air — the fact that such a sprawling, ambitious series even got on network TV was something of a miracle (though you could make the case that *Lost* greatly improved the chances of a show like *Lost* getting made today). Besides its unforgettable opening ten minutes, where we join the survivors dazedly wandering around the wreckage, *Lost* constantly tantalized viewers, revealing detail after detail about its characters and the weird time warp they seem to have landed in (like the fact the distress signal for their flight had been playing for sixteen years). *Lost* also had one of TV's most diverse casts, and used its Hawaii location and special effects marvelously to create a jungle island so grotesque, magical, and alluring that H.G. Wells would have felt right at home.

8. Friday Night Lights (Seasons 1 and 3)

This 2006 drama series about high school life in football-crazy Texas, was based on the true-life Buzz Bissinger book that also inspired a movie. Season one was a wonder — a documentary-style teen drama with engaging performances from Kyle Chandler as Coach Taylor, a winner who's tough but not cruel (unlike the real-life subject of Bissinger's book); Connie Britton as his loving wife Tami; and a cast of talented young actors playing the kids of Dillon High, who are engaged in life-and-death struggles over success, football, true love, and pride. It was engaging, full of great performances and grace notes ... and almost nobody watched. So, the producers ratcheted up the drama in season two, with unfortunate results: A guy wound up dead in the first episode and it just went downhill from there. And then a miracle: DirecTV, the satellite company, was looking for original content to offer its 18 million subscribers. It partnered with NBC on season three, sharing the rock-bottom production costs (*FNL* is filmed in and around Austin) in exchange for an exclusive fall window. That infusion of satellite money seemed to calm down the show. And, as we saw kids leave Dillon High and try to make it in the world, *FNL* the show seemed to veer closer to the somewhat desparate tone Bissinger struck while chronicling Texas football as both escapism and escape.

9. Life on Mars (UK)

Cop is hit by a car while investigating a murder. When he comes to, it's 1973. And that's just the kickoff to one of the best-executed conceits in fantasy television I've ever seen (though I should note that sci-fi is probably my least-favorite genre after crime procedural). Sam Tyler (John Simm) awakens in period clothes, gets in his period car and drives back to the dusty, smoke-filled station where nobody, period, has heard of solving crimes with DNA. In 2006 Sam is apparently hanging onto life by a respirator, but in '73 he's alive and well and solving crimes for a brutish inspector named Gene Hunt (Philip Glenister), who embodies the pre-*CSI* school. He considers Sam, with his fascination for examining corpses and adherence to procedure, a bit of a patsy. Forensics strikes him as theoretical rubbish, and is forever overruling Sam's explanations with hare-brained ones of his own, like the variation on the fart rule that declares whoever mentions a crime first is the one that did it. The culture clash between these two men is a source of ongoing amusement on the show, as are the messages that Sam occasionally receives from the world he left behind, usually sent over the phone or the television.

> **If you liked this:** *Ashes to Ashes,* the UK sequel set in 1981, stars Keeley Hawes as a female cop transported from the future and Glenister reprising his role as Hunt.

10. Burn Notice

This easy-sipping mojito of action, spy intrigue and laughably trivial family drama has been one of my favorites since it signed on cable's USA Network in 2007. In the show's fantastic pilot episode, spy Michael Western (Jeffrey Donovan) finds himself suddenly exiled from the intelligence agency that employed him — while he is still on assignment. After the ensuing bare-knuckle escape from a band of gun-toting thugs chasing him on motorbikes, he winds up in south Florida. And while he tries to unravel the enduring (and still unsolved) mystery of why he was given his "burn notice," he passes the time and stays on his toes by helping one hapless schlub after another out of danger. He's aided in his hourlong missions by his two associates, Sam (played by beloved character actor/raconteur Bruce Campbell) and Fiona (Gabrielle Anwar).

If you liked this: The 2009 series *White Collar,* also on USA, has not yet been released on DVD, but is appealing for many of the same reasons as *Burn Notice.*

11. Damages (Season 1)

This show began in 2007 like so many legal whodunits, but about half an hour into the first episode, it took off around the corner and viewers spent the rest of that season chasing its shadow. Glenn Close played Patty Hewes, the conniving, self-righteous head of a law firm devoted to defending the underdog, while Ted Danson played billionaire cokehead Art Frobisher, whose mismanagement just put thousands of employees out of work. But if Frobisher was textbook baddie, Patty, we soon discovered, was no saint herself, and we soon wondered if she really had the interests of her clients at heart. Her aggressive recruitment of a promising young lawyer, Ellen Parsons (Rose Byrne), just so Patty could get at Ellen's friend Katie (Anastasia Griffith), was pathological. The whole thing played out *Rashomon*-style (or *Seinfeld* wedding episode style, take your pick), beginning at the end and then piecing together the rest of the storyline like an upended jigsaw puzzle whose pieces we kept picking up, over and over, trying to figure out how they fit together, all in ways that intrigued rather than bewildered.

12. EZ Streets

CBS never did know what to do with this dark 1996 drama starring Ken Olin as a compromised cop and Joe Pantoliano in a pre-*Sopranos* role as a thug you couldn't help but like. (If the show hadn't driven the network to record ratings lows, I would even call this the breakout role for Joey Pants.) *EZ Streets* is a show about hard times and the hard choices made by people with few options left in life. It makes us see good in evil people and vice versa, and does so with high purpose. The conversations between the principals stand on their own as outstanding dialogue — even if you're not always sure what's going on. Bravo released episodes of *EZ Streets* under its "Brilliant but Cancelled" line of DVDs, but a full collection was never released.

13. Six Feet Under (Seasons 1 and 5)

Overshadowed by *The Sopranos* for most of its run, *Six Feet Under* began promisingly in 2001 with a fresh perspective on death told with the right amount of whimsy (as opposed to the, um, overkill of its Showtime counterpart, *Dead Like Me*), but without sacrificing the intensity we've come to expect of HBO dramas. It told the story of the Fisher family that ran a funeral home out of its own home, and while the pilot had its share of grabbers (the patriarch is violently killed and the show's leading couple consummates their relationship before it even begins), what really sold me on this show was the unfolding torment of David Fisher (Michael C. Hall), a nice young man and devout Episcopalian who hadn't told anybody in his family that he's gay. His struggles to fit in at his conservative old parish, where gay worshipers are expected to stay in the closet, while managing the family business and a tricky relationship with his LA cop boyfriend Keith (Mathew St. Patrick), pushes him quietly to the edge. *Six Feet Under* would have trouble sustaining this level of quality in the messy middle seasons. However, creator Alan Ball tied up the series nicely at the end, so I recommend Season 5 as well.

14. The Secret Life of the American Teenager

Though it started out in 2008 as a show about a pregnant band geek, *The Secret Life of the American Teenager* was actually more earnest and, surprisingly, more morally sophisticated than *Juno,* to which it was inevitably compared. Perhaps the most surprising part, given the saccharine quality of *7th Heaven,* the previous series from *Secret Life* creator Brenda Hampton, was its web of interesting relationships, adult as well as teenage, and its assertion that sex, while not unimportant, often is actually the least of everyone's problems. Though the dialogue was often TV-scripted and the story arcs were as obvious as any on the ABC Family channel, *Secret Life* acknowledged that teenagers have strong desires without cravenly serving them — and indeed, making clear time and again to its young audience that decisions triggered by desires will have consequences.

15. Law and Order (Season 7)

TV's longest-running drama debuted in 1990 and eventually faded into a pathetic shadow of what it once was, and a mindless zombie that plodded onward toward *Gunsmoke's* record of twenty seasons on television, under the remote-control guidance of its creator Dick Wolf.

But turn back the clock to season seven, when it won the Emmy for Best Drama, when Ben Bratt and Sam Waterston and, above all, Jerry Orbach were stars on the show, and you'll see a TV series as good as any that's ever been on. In its prime, *L&O* was unparalleled in its ability to frame legal and ethical dilemmas as addictive light entertainment. A highlight was *Corruption,* in which Lennie (Orbach) tries to keep Rey (Bratt) from investigating an old buddy of his and winds up getting hauled into court, with a most unexpected ending.

> **If you liked this:** Season 4 was pretty stellar, too. It was the first year for Van Buren (S. Epatha Merkerson), the show's most enduring female character, and Claire Kincaid (Jill Hennessy). It was also the last season for prosecutor Ben Stone (played by famous hothead Michael Moriarty). And Chris Noth was still on his first *Law & Order* tour of duty.

16. Eureka (Season 1)

This sweet, funny little whodunit is set in a top-secret village of quirky geniuses sequestered by the U.S. government. Jack Carter (Colin Ferguson), a U.S. marshal transporting a fugitive — as it turns out, his rebellious teen daughter Zoe (Jordan Hinson) — back to her mom, from whom he is separated. But they are sidetracked in Eureka and must have their truck serviced by Henry (Joe Morton), who (they find out) drives a tow truck when he's not rebuilding the wormhole machine from *Contact.* The dogcatcher (Matt Frewer) seems to be busy on some mad gadget in his spare time, though currently all it does is wreak havoc on cows. When Carter quickly solves a missing-person case, the superbrains in town take notice, and he's invited to stay. Estrogen is a welcome ingredient here, including the alluring Allison (Salli Richardson-Whitfield), a Defense Department official; and Barlowe (Debrah Farentino), a sexy shrink who also runs a bed-and-breakfast and knows secrets that you can't learn even with military clearance.

17. In Treatment (Season 2)

Based on a hit Israeli series, *In Treatment* is a series of mesmerizing dialogues between patients and their psychologist, Paul (Gabriel Byrne), whose own personal life is in shambles. An entirely new cast of patients in season two helped take the drama to another level. There's Mia, a patient he first saw twenty years ago and seems more screwed up than ever (Hope Davis); a chubby kid named Oliver (Aaron Shaw) caught between feuding parents; Walter (*Frasier's* John Mahoney), a CEO who wants to know why he's not sleeping; and the most compelling head case, a twenty-three-year-old student named April (Alison Pill, last seen in *Milk*), who's just been diagnosed with cancer. Each is in tremendous pain that they barely understand, let alone want to acknowledge. Paul probes each patient for deeper-seated problems, provides some relief for them, then probes deeper, exposing more pain, treating, repeating … and just when it's all getting to be a bit much, in walks Gina (Dianne Wiest), Paul's confidante, conscience and counselor, the pleasant, professional and candid antidote our neurotic Irish shrink needs on his weekly Amtrak trips to see his daughter. "Isn't it fun to be in therapy!" she exudes at one point. Well, it's fun to watch, anyway.

18. 24 (Season 5)

Part of a wave of innovative dramas that included *The Sopranos* and *CSI, 24* took two overdone TV genres — the family drama and the action thriller — and crashed them together, creating something new and riveting. I've written about *24* at length in the story that appears in the 2001 chapter. Since that time, it has become clear that *24's* success had very little to do with its initial gimmick: that all episodes would take place "in real time." Simply put, traffic doesn't move in L.A. the way it does on *24*. However, the show had so many tricks up its sleeve to propel the action forward, most viewers quickly forgave (and likely forgot) any continuity problems. Season 5 was the year *24* won an Emmy for best drama. It began tremendously, with the assassination of one of TV's most beloved U.S. presidents, David Palmer (Dennis Haysbert), and ended with Jack Bauer (Kiefer Sutherland) taking on Charles Logan (Gregory Itzin), perhaps the most diabolical POTUS ever.

19. The West Wing (Seasons 1–4)

I was less than kind to *The West Wing* during its run on NBC — partly, I know, because it cheesed me that its Emmy glow was so much brighter than that of *The Sopranos,* a vastly superior show in most respects. Things evened out in the end, and in hindsight, Aaron Sorkin's White House drama *was* remarkably nervy for network television. It also had more LOLs than most sitcoms of that era and above all, despite the pages and pages of dialogue Sorkin churned out in his four years as showrunner, it was rarely dull. Highlights for me included the touching holiday episode of Season 1; the three-episode arc bridging seasons 1 and 2 when gunmen tried to take out president Bartlet (Martin Sheen); the "can of whup-ass" episode (Season 2); the very McGarry episode from Season 3 where we learned dark secrets about presidential advisor Leo (John Spencer); and Sorkin's swansong at the end of Season 4.

> **If you liked this:** Little did we know it at the time, Sorkin's clever 1998 series *Sports Night* — featuring Josh Charles and Peter Krause as anchors on an ESPN-like broadcast, and Felicity Huffman as their producer — was setting the stage for something more ambitious.

20. Firefly

It's hard to imagine anyone this far into *Tasteland* who hasn't heard of Joss Whedon or *Firefly,* his all-too-brief attempt at a sci-fi Western that revolved around a band of twenty-sixth-century mercenaries living on the fringes of galactic civilization. Nathan Fillion starred as Captain Mal Reynolds, the leader of a motley crew that scrapes by while evading the totalitarian alliance that wants them dead or alive. The show's Ennio Morricone-inspired soundtrack set a nicely ironic retro tone, as did the old-fashioned train robbery in the first episode. But the desperadoes aboard the spaceship Serenity are an oddly upright bunch; there's even an ascetic, conscientious-objector man of the cloth. Each person in the ensemble is distinct and intriguing. This show was loaded with possibilities but, alas, the Fox network bailed too quickly, as is its wont. There is a happy ending: Whedon made *Serenity,* a satisfying and financially successful theatrical followup to *Firefly.*

21. Deadwood

And speaking of Westerns gunned down in their prime ... actually, I wasn't sure what I would think about *Deadwood* nearly four years after its cancellation — but it has aged well. HBO's Sam-Peckinpah-was-a-pussy Western was notable for being set at a whorehouse run by a sadist and having so many F-bombs that I hear the Navy made it required viewing to help recruits talk like sailors. It was so dirty, James Gandolfini turned to someone at a screening and said, "Who swears that much in real life?" But seriously, folks ... today I can appreciate, in a way I didn't at the time, what creator David Milch was trying to do. The Deadwood he created only bore superficial resemblances to the actual South Dakota boom town of the 1870s, but it was Milch's aim to show civilization emerging from the crude and cruel near-anarchy of the American frontier (the model being Chicago, which used prodigious energy to emerge from a swamp and become an industrial giant). Seen this way, the show's profanity is more than shtick; it's a symbol of chaos in the untamed West. Beyond its intellectual heft, *Deadwood* had Ian McShane as saloon-whore-keeper Al Swearengen. With his brogue and eyes of hate, he couldn't resist eating up every scene he was in.

22. Jericho

An apocalyptic serial drama for a 9/11 country, *Jericho* (2006) was the story of a small Kansas town whose petty dramas are violently swept away by an atomic cloud that appears on the horizon —but those dramas return as people take sides in a desperate attempt to survive nuclear holocaust and the lawlessness that follows. There are strong performances from Ashley Scott as Jake's onetime sweetheart and Lennie James as Mr. Hawkins, a newcomer to the western Kansas town of Jericho. I often complain about the lack of diversity on TV, but it was to *Jericho's* advantage that James was the only major black character. As we all learned after 9/11, news of an attack makes people suspicious of anyone who doesn't look and act just like themselves. The cagey and intelligent Hawkins will clearly be the surrogate for everyone who has served as a convenient scapegoat for an act of terror they had no hand in. He quickly forms a useful, though not entirely comfortable, alliance with Jake, the one native who seems to keep his head when everyone else is losing theirs. If I were you, I'd watch this entire series (29 episodes) right to the satisfying end — or ends. (There's an alternative finale on the DVD.)

23. The Guardian (Season 1)

Modestly successful for CBS for three seasons, *The Guardian* (2003) is now known as the series that put Simon Baker on the road to becoming TV's most popular smartass sleuth in *The Mentalist*. But this show was more interesting. Baker played Nick Fallin, a snotty young Pittsburgh lawyer who's busted for drugs and as part of his plea deal must volunteer 1,500 hours as a child advocate. On top of that, he must still put in time at the firm run by his old man (Dabney Coleman), who rides him hard. And then there are the mandatory surprise drug tests. But Nick rises to the occasion, though not in predictable CBS fashion. He was easily the softest-spoken hero on network television for many years, though there was no lack of drama between his competing girlfriends, battle with the bottle and often volatile clients.

24. NCIS (Seasons 3–6)

After *NCIS* signed on in 2003, it took me a while to warm up to this spinoff of another military procedural, *JAG*. Looks like I was not alone: *NCIS* has been on a midlife surge as I write this, and in its seventh season it not only overtook *CSI* in the ratings, but is the No. 1-rated scripted show on TV and has launched its own spinoff, *NCIS: Los Angeles*. In its early years, *NCIS* depended on a lot of counter-terrorist storylines, which I thought were cheap ploys for attention in the aftermath of 9/11 (as opposed to *24*, a show that was planned out *before* 9/11). When the drama shifted to character development, and the dynamics inside the agency, I thought the show picked up its game.

25. Playmakers

ESPN's dramatic series about the seamy side of professional football broke new ground for the all-sports channel. Unfortunately, it lasted only two seasons and then — after the NFL issued a few thinly-veiled threats — the show suddenly vanished. These exploits of a fictional NFL team depicted pro football as a mercenary enterprise where no one plays for the love of the game or betrays even the slightest fondness for it — a sharp contrast to the rest of ESPN programming. (Indeed, it is possible ESPN killed *Playmakers* because it was inconsistent with the company brand, not because the NFL was unhappy with it.) Making actors look like skilled athletes is an age-old problem for the movies and TV, but the realism level on *Playmakers* scored high. Emotional realism was there, too: in the second episode, one player replays tape of a game hit that paralyzed an opponent. As he scrolls through frame by frame, over and over, the viewer is caught up in the ambiguity of the player's split-second decision, which may have resulted in a dirty hit, or not.

26. Nothing Sacred

Probably the most underappreciated network show in my years on the beat was this 1997 drama set at an inner-city Catholic parish, where tart-tongued clergy and staff were confronted daily by moral dilemmas. If *Touched by an Angel* matched skeptical souls who had questions with heavenly beings who had answers, *Nothing Sacred* took people who are all answers and undermined them with people who are all questions ... and then, just because it could, the show often had everyone reverse roles. Unfortunately, the Catholic League, all one of him, used a fax machine and a conflict-driven news media to pummel advertisers with his outrage about the heretical views supposedly voiced on the show. The sponsors, who weren't that wild about the show's ratings in the first place, pulled their commercials — and intelligent treatments of religion have pretty much been a prime-time taboo ever since. Unfortunately, *Nothing Sacred* has never been anthologized on VHS or DVD, but I couldn't imagine it *not* on my "100 Best" list, so I am bending my rent-download rule a bit by including it here. If you visit TastelandBook.com, you will see links to episodes there. The video isn't high quality but the show itself is.

> **If you liked this:** *The Book of Daniel* stirred up a storm in 2006 for daring to show a married Episcopal priest (Aidan Quinn) struggling with his faith and his family. NBC pulled the plug after four episodes but all eight are on DVD. The documentary *Sister Helen* features a foul-mouthed nun who runs a home for recovering drug and alcohol addicts in the South Bronx, mostly by yelling at them. Despite her approach, the filmmakers eventually convince us we are watching a saint at work.

COMEDY/DRAMEDY

27. Everybody Loves Raymond (Season 7)

Even in the late 1990s, before it started collecting shelves' worth of Emmys and was still widely regarded as a poor replacement for *Seinfeld* in viewers' comedy diets — some said it was not even as good as *Friends* — I told anyone who would listen that *Everybody Loves Raymond* was the best-written show on television. Eventually, most critics would come around, in part because the show kept getting better and was great right to the end. (Compare with *Seinfeld* and *Friends*, which both petered out badly. Puerto Rican Day episode, anyone?) More remarkable is how little changed in the basic chemistry of the show over all those seasons. Always it came back to the tortured relationship between Ray and Robert (Brad Garrett), who despite his towering height, could never quite measure up to his brother; Frank (Peter Boyle), who was inseparable from his wife and family, no matter how hard he tried; Marie (Doris Roberts), a woman incapable of handing out a compliment unless it was lovingly wrapped in an insult first; and Debra (Patty Heaton), who must truly have loved Ray to put up with all of his idiotic male stunts — and his infernal in-laws — all those years.

I've chosen Season 7, in part because it introduces the last ensemble member, Robert's wife Amy (Monica Horan), but mainly because six years of mounting dysfunctionality seemed to crest here, with payoff after payoff: "The Shower," where Ray shows up to bail Debra out of jail for DUI and his first words are, "So. How was Amy's shower?"; "The Sigh," featuring some classic slapstick as Debra and Ray fight over the bathroom mirror; and the two-parter ending in Robert and Amy's wedding, a perfect occasion for emptying the writers' notebooks of zingers that couldn't be worked into any other episodes. Above all, Season 7 had my all-time favorite, "The Cult," where Robert starts attending a group that promises "the path to inner harmony." Debra and Marie beg the other two men to stage an intervention — with results that are surprising and touching and LOL all the way. The climax is an unbroken ten-minute sequence that begins in the kitchen, spills into the living room and then winds up in the kitchen again. It tests the audience's comfort level by taking the Barones into even more volatile territory than usual. The scene even has one of the show's few meta-references: "Nice try, Ray," says Robert, "but you're not *that* good an actor." Romano would, in fact, finally get his own Emmy Award at the end of Season 7.

> **If you liked this:** *M*A*S*H: The Complete Fourth Season* was my favorite season of the greatest sitcom of its era. *Frasier* has not aged well compared with its NBC peers *Seinfeld* and *Friends*, but its first five seasons (which predate my time on the beat) were golden. It's a rare show where the entire comedy tableau arrives perfectly intact out of the box, as *Frasier's* did.

28. 30 Rock

30 Rock bristled with newness the moment it signed on in 2006. Written by, produced by and starring a woman — Tina Fey, formerly head writer of *SNL* — *30 Rock* stormed to the front of the sitcom class, at a time when sitcoms were struggling to find new voices and a slice of the audience commensurate with the deep-dish days of the sitcom's heyday. Fey plays the head writer of *The Girlie Show,* a fictional sketch comedy program airing on what is essentially the NBC network in a parallel universe, a realm where a GE executive named Jack (wonderfully, archly played by Alec Baldwin), who knows nothing about television but lots about ovens, materializes one day as her boss. The supporting cast is strong (in particular, Jack McBray as a wide-eyed NBC page is a revelation) and after a few episodes *30 Rock* everyone was asking the same question: Why wasn't Fey this funny when she was writing for that other show? One of the only clinkers of that rookie season — where *30 Rock* began winning Best Comedy at the Emmys, a string that as of press time had not been broken — was an episode that was supposed to make fun of product placement. Unfortunately the cast went overboard making fun of a certain brand of bottled iced tea, which advertised during the show, and a lot of viewers weren't sure whether they were watching satire or the next wave in marketing. That minor quibble aside, however, it's hard to go wrong with *30 Rock*.

> **If you liked this:** *Police Squad!* introduced the world to Lt. Frank Drebin, the world's least competent supercop. This short-lived 1982 single-camera comedy, starring Leslie Nielsen, led to the hugely successful *Naked Gun* trilogy — and produced six of the funniest half-hours ever broadcast on an American network, if not actually watched by an audience. Even the commentaries on the *Complete Series* DVD are hilarious. When you see how much effort went into each episode (in once scene a kidnapper produces the victim's toaster, and a pair of waffles spring up right on cue), you'll understand when one of the directors comments, "If we were going to work this hard, we might as well make a feature."

29. Space Ghost Coast to Coast

This low-cost Cartoon Network production featured Space Ghost, a superhero on Saturday-morning TV from 1966-68 and again in 1981, plunked down in the middle of a campy late-night talk show, flanked by two former enemies. His bandleader was Zorak, a praying mantis who would just as soon eat Space Ghost's flesh as accompany him on keyboards; and his malevolent, or possibly just incompetent, producer was Moltar, a creature made of hot lava. The show's central shtick was Spacey's discordant banter with mostly B-list celebrities (Wynonna, the cast of *Gilligan's Island*), who had been interviewed on videotape. The clips were then superimposed on a cartoon TV screen perched next to Spacey's desk. He interviewed Lassie — no trainer, just the dog. He once told Michael Stipe, "I'm going to deliver a high-pitched message that only you can hear!" *SGC2C* served as proof-of-concept for an entire lineup of off-kilter TV shows that seemingly every teenage kid in America now stays up to watch (*see* my 2005 story, "Adult Swim: the edge of night").

30. Two and a Half Men

Possibly the raunchiest sitcom on the air right now is currently the LOL funniest on network TV. And like *Everybody Loves Raymond*, the formula works so well that nothing ever really changes — except, of course, for the child actor who went through puberty and shot up like a weed. Ninety-nine percent of the comedy comes from the interactions of just three characters: Charlie (Charlie Sheen), the fabulously wealthy jingle writer who is bored with his money and oceanfront house and frivolous sex; brother Alan (Jon Cryer), who moves in with his young son Jake (Angus T. Jones) after his wife kicks him out; and Charlie's sarcastic housekeeper Berta (Conchata Ferrell), who found her groove in the show by Season 2. Though Jake was a focus of earlier seasons, his role has diminished even as he has become much more than half a man. Since the show is hot in syndication right now, I'd recommend just setting a season pass and diving in.

31. 3rd Rock from the Sun (Season 6)

I always liked *3rd Rock*, every last predictable madcap moment of it. Every week the Solomons of outer space would try to mimic the ways of earthlings (collecting Beanie Babies, making whoopee). Every week, like sociologists on speed, they'd get hopelessly addicted to their newfound custom. Unlike a lot of sitcoms whose punchlines you can see coming down the street, the jokes on *3rd Rock* would often hit your blind side, or come rapid-fire, leaving you helpless. Like a metaphor for the aliens' own rootlessness, *3rd Rock* never found a home on NBC's schedule. The network moved its time slot seventeen times, which must be a record. That it lasted as long as it did was a testimony to the quality of the cast and the brilliant simplicity of the show's concept. I'm recommending the final season because it had a heckuva finale. Earthling Mary (Jane Curtin) finally suspects that Dick (John Lithgow) isn't who he's claimed to be all these years. For no good reason at all, other than the song is apt, Elvis Costello shows up to sing "Fly Me to the Moon."

32. King of the Hill (Seasons 2–3)

My favorite prime-time animated series of the past fifteen years, *King of the Hill* began simply enough, with Hank Hill, propane salesman; his wife Peggy, a not-very-fluent Spanish teacher who sounds like she got her training through Berlitz; their nerdy son, Bobby; and a block full of Bubbas that Mike Judge created mainly by looking around Texas, where he lived. *King of the Hill* arrived at a propitious moment in 1997, as imbecilic studio audiences and robotic joke-telling were killing the network sitcom. This slow-moving, cleverly-arranged comedy about the humiliations of daily life went where sitcoms feared to tread: storytelling with relatable characters. I'm still amazed that a show that used so few gimmicks and had so little action managed to churn out 250 episodes. I've watched dozens of them and don't think I've seen a bad one, but the second and third seasons — which saw the emergence of the Hank's trashy niece Luanne, his brief stint working at the Mega Lo Mart and the cliffhanger that began all those "Is Chuck Mangione dead?" rumors — are a great place to start.

> **If you liked this:** The first five seasons of *The Simpsons* would be on my list, had I been on the television beat then. Season 3 (1991-92) includes several classic episodes: in one, Homer nearly drives his pompous Christian neighbor Ned Flanders out of business, only to have a change of heart. In another, Homer is thrown into an asylum, where he is befriended by an obese inmate who is voiced either by Michael Jackson or someone who sounds a lot like him. Turn on the commentary track to hear *Simpsons* creator Matt Groening and longtime showrunner Al Jean discuss the sausage-making aspects of animation with admirable candor.

33. Buffy the Vampire Slayer (Season 6)

One reason television critics distrust the voters of the TV Academy is that they never nominated *Buffy the Vampire Slayer* for any Emmy Awards of consequence. And if any season of *Buffy* deserved a nod, this one was it. The highlight, indeed the most beloved hour of *Buffy* ever produced, is the magical, musical episode "Once More With Feeling." Some thought it might be a self-indulgent exercise by the show's creator, Joss Whedon, but "Once More With Feeling" is infused with beautiful ballads ("Under Your Spell"), elaborate show-stoppers ("Walk Through the Fire"), dialogues-set-to-music ("I've Got a Theory") and asides that raise the musical form to absurd heights ("They Got the Mustard Out!").

> **If you liked this:** Whedon's 2008 Internet sensation, *Dr. Horrible's Sing-Along Blog,* featured Neil Patrick Harris as a would-be villain whose efforts to seduce the fair Penny (Felicia Day) are foiled with

comical ease by the annoyingly perfect Captain Hammer (Nathan Fillion). It's now on DVD with many extras.

34. Slings & Arrows (Season 3)

Rarely has television woven high culture, graceful comedy, gut-busting gags, nimble dialogue and grown-up situations together so successfully as in this Canadian-produced dramedy. Each of the three seasons is framed around a Shakespeare play, beginning with *Hamlet,* which brings actor and director Geoffrey Tennant (Paul Gross) back to the New Burbage theater company where he trained. Season 2 finds Geoffrey still there, doing *Macbeth,* and then in the concluding season (and the series' high point), the drama both revolves around and mirrors *King Lear.* Charles Kingman (William Hutt), a lion of an actor who once schooled Geoffrey, reveals privately to his pupil that he hasn't long to live. In less talented hands this might turn mawkish, but I was captivated at how *Slings & Arrows* carefully balances the terror that Charles inflicts on everyone around him with his desperate state of affairs — not unlike that of the tragic king he's portraying. Readers without deep knowledge of the Bard need not be intimidated by *Slings & Arrows.* There's ample comic relief, as when Richard Smith-Jones (Mark McKinney), the company's underachieving general manager, sits in his new car telling himself how unfit he is to own such a fine status symbol ... only to realize he has pressed the on-board navigator by accident and confessed his inadequacy to a remote operator.

35. Andy Richter Controls the Universe

In between serving as Conan O'Brien's sidekick and his announcer, Andy Richter starred in this brilliant comedy as a daydreaming office drone whose wildly absurd fantasies made Walter Mitty (if anyone remembers him) seem repressed. *Universe* played to Richter's gifts as an improvisational performer and lovable straight man. He was aided by a talented and instantly likable ensemble, especially Paget Brewster as Andy's boss. In the third episode, which she steals, Brewster binges on all-night parties before paying the price in an instantly classic, pitch-perfect scene. *Andy Richter Controls The Universe* lasted nineteen episodes, six of which never aired on Fox.

If you liked this: *Andy Barker, P.I.* starred Richter as an accountant-turned-gumshoe. It lasted only six episodes on NBC — but four of them are brilliant. Fortunately, both series are now on DVD.

36. The Dana Carvey Show

Looking back at this 1996 series that was cancelled after just seven episodes (an unaired eighth episode is on the DVD), it is amazing how wrong everyone was about it— the critics who reviled it, the viewers and sponsors that ran away from it, the network that abandoned it and whose top executive later declared that sketch comedy was just too hit-and-miss to put on TV anymore. Some of the sketches are dated but a great many hold up, like "The Ambiguously Gay Duo" featuring the voices of two unknown comedians, Stephen Colbert and Steve Carell. That's right, *The Dana Carvey Show* was to that cartoon what *The Tracey Ullman Show* was to *The Simpsons*. Other still-hilarious bits: "The Gentle News," where Colbert holds a puppy up to the camera to take the edge off a commentary; a *Nightline* parody where Ted Koppel (Carvey) interviews Bob Dole (Robert Smigel) about his decision to name Strom Thurmond (Carvey again) as his running mate; NBC shooting contingency clips of Tom Brokaw (Carvey) announcing Gerald Ford's death so that he can "hang out in East Hampton all summer"; and much more.

37. Flight of the Conchords (2 seasons)

This deceptively simple, wonderfully sideways comedy stars New Zealanders Jemaine Clement and Bret McKenzie as two mumblecore musicians trying to make it in New York. The ensemble around them is surprisingly spare: their oddball part-time manager Murray (Rhys Darby), one highly untrustworthy friend Dave (Arj Barker) and Mel (Kristen Schaal), their No. 1 fan — in both the ordinal and Kathy Bates sense of that term. The show's core joke is that the Conchords are forced to be close, like brothers who can't stand each other. And yet anyone who comes between them is rejected like a transplant gone awry. It's a joke that should get old in a hurry, yet this conceit just kept paying dividends for *Flight of the Conchords*. Another ingredient in the show's winning recipe were the charming little ditties composed for each episode by McKenzie and Clement. Contrary to their alter egos, however, the real-life Conchords had no interest in making it in New York City. They balked at leaving New Zealand for more filming, and HBO shut down production after just two seasons.

38. Arrested Development (3 seasons)

Every now and then, a TV show adored by critics but ignored by the public is given a reprieve. *Arrested Development* got two, thanks to Fox executive Gail Berman, who renewed the show through three seasons despite lower-than-low ratings. This comedy about an over-the-hill real estate dynasty certainly packed a lot into twenty minutes of episode: madcap farce, satire (especially of soap-opera excesses), quick-witted banter, cutaway gags, rope-tight storylines and a dream team of comedic actors, led by Jason Bateman, Jeffrey Tambor, Jessica Walter and future geek hearthrob Michael Cera. *Arrested Development* won the Emmy for best comedy series in 2004, and some people will swear it is the greatest sitcom of the past decade. As a keep-it-simple guy, however, I often felt like the show was *too* complicated for its own good, too mediated by Ron Howard's constant narration, too dependent on wacky plot twists and scene editing. To be sure, I laughed a lot, and I am including it on this list — just not as high up as other comedies.

39. The Larry Sanders Show

The arc of *The Larry Sanders Show* almost perfectly overlapped the Leno-Letterman wars, from 1992 to 1998, and Garry Shandling's attempts to reflect the real-life backstage dramas in the alternate talk-show universe of his alter ego, Larry Sanders, was one of the more audacious efforts in television history, mainly because it worked so damned well. Shandling and his co-stars — Jeffrey Tambor as his fatuous sidekick, Hank, and Rip Torn in a memorable role as Larry's pitiless showrunner Arthur — formed an effective comedy triumvirate, even if over the years the abundance of topical jokes lose their sting. None of this diminished the pioneering role of *Larry Sanders* in ushering in a golden era of single-camera comedies. Because of a protracted legal battle between Shandling and his ex-manager Brad Grey (which, naturally, was worked into a *Larry Sanders* storyline), the DVD collection *Not Just the Best of the Larry Sanders Show,* with twenty-three episodes selected by Shandling, is probably the closest thing to a complete series set that fans of this pathbreaking sitcom will have.

> **If you liked this:** *Lateline,* another show-within-a-show comedy, starred Senator Al Franken (that still sounds so crazy!) as a nebbishy reporter on a show resembling Ted Koppel's *Nightline.* The "Shepoopi" episode was an instant classic: The *Lateline* team scraps a planned broadcast after word arrives of the death of actor Buddy Hackett.

40. Rescue Me (Seasons 1 and 5)

Denis Leary's tragicomedy about a FDNY firefighter, his shambles of a family life and the post-9/11 chaos raging inside his own head was a revelation when it arrived in 2004. Leary played Tommy Gavin, who was haunted by the loss of his buddies in the World Trade Center attacks. Gavin depended on his job saving lives and the insular, insult-driven culture of work to keep him sane, barely. The dialogue inside the firehouse was some of the saltiest, and funniest, on TV, and as a tradition-bound sexist with a big mouth, Gavin had a way of getting himself into some first-rate misadventures. Though some episodes pushed viewers' patience (a pill-popping monkey in Season 1 tried mine), Leary's long association with members of the Bravest allowed him to capture their humanity and see them as something other than one-dimensional rescue machines. *Rescue Me* seemed to lose its way for a while there, but I was impressed with Season 5 for re-examining 9/11 through the character of Franco, a firefighter fully immersed in the conspiracy theories surrounding the attack (interestingly, Franco's views echoed those of the actor who played him, Danny Sunjata).

If you liked this: Showtime's *Nurse Jackie* is an addictive little comedy starring Edie Falco as a pill-popping nurse and unfaithful wife that I would absolutely want bedside if I were ill again.

41. Mr. Show

When David Cross and Bob Odenkirk began doing their sketch comedy series for HBO in 1995, it had been a quarter-century since *Monty Python's Flying Circus*, the series that was the obvious touchstone for *Mr. Show*. For almost that length of time there had also been HBO and thus, a place on cable where people could drop F-bombs. I mention this because *Mr. Show* managed to be a very original and funny show anyway — and still is. One of the enjoyable aspects of writing this book has been pulling the DVDs off the shelf and sampling the old product to make sure it still holds up. I picked an episode that began with the entire audience transfixed by a low-speed chase on their little three-inch TV sets (today it would be their iPhones), segued to an O.J.-inspired chase of the Popemobile, segued to a Pope expert (who was not a Catholic) who ran something called the Pope Hall of Fame at the Pro Football Hall of Fame, segued to a guy suffering from I.D.S. (Imminent Death Syndrome), segued to a performance artist who was having trouble defecating on the flag ... and that was just the first fifteen minutes.

I laughed like an idiot the whole time. Cross and Odenkirk did DVD commentaries for all thirty episodes.

If you liked this: *The Kumars at No. 42*, a daffy British import about a family that hosts a talk show in their back yard, featured four improvisational comics as the Kumars, interacting brilliantly with their celebrity guests.

42. Saturday Night Live (Season 1)

I have tried to limit the scope of the "100 Best" list to programs that aired during my time on the beat — for a very good reason. Generally speaking, I did not write published reviews of shows that aired before the mid-1990s. I made an exception, though, when the DVD set of *NBC Saturday Night's* 1975-76 season was released. What a game-changer that was. Every week, it seemed, *SNL* was playing on the perilous edge of American comedy. Can you imagine a "Mr. Mike" today, doing impressions of celebrities with long needles jammed in their eye sockets, or writing a "Claudine Longet Invitational" where skiers were hit with stray bullets fired by the French singer (played by Laraine Newman)? In a season where Dan Aykroyd, John Belushi, and Chevy Chase all became major TV stars, *SNL* also had the deepest bench in its history, even though only four people were on it (Gilda Radner, Jane Curtin, Garrett Morris, and Newman). There were so many great moments, and Chevy Chase was involved with many of them: playing a hapless President Ford, wandering around in a ridiculous "land shark" outfit, reading the fake news on "Weekend Update" — the franchise that has endured, more or less unchanged, for thirty-five seasons of *SNL*. If I'd had the kind of year Chevy had, I'd have left for Hollywood, too.

If you liked this: *SNL* creator Lorne Michaels authorized a series of documentaries to chronicle the behind-the-scenes drama at the show, of which *Live From New York: SNL The First Five Years* (2005) is the most engaging.

43. Wonderfalls

Here's another show that Fox killed off before most of America had ever heard of it. This funny and enchanting series featured a young woman named Jaye Tyler (Caroline Dhavernas) who keeps getting divine messages from unlikely places — and I know this sounds a lot like *Joan of Arcadia*, except on *Wonderfalls* the Almighty doesn't even bother impersonating a human. Here the messages are coming from a talking bass wall plaque, a wax souvenir from Niagara Falls, a wind-up penguin ... basically any inanimate object in earshot might start talking to Jaye. Happy to be an underachiever, Jaye learns that she might actually be able to change the world — if only she'll start listening to that wind-up penguin on the shelf. Though it only aired four times on Fox, the *Wonderfalls* DVD features all thirteen episodes produced.

44. Daria

This unjustly overlooked MTV animated sitcom from 1997 told of the daily humiliations and tribulations of sixteen-year-old Daria Morgendorffer. Her unsparing commentary (voiced by one of the writers on the show, Tracy Grandstaff) came from a place deep in her old soul — the place that was quietly tormented by her cutesie little sister, Quinn, and her two high-powered, well-meaning, but parentally inept parents. "I don't have low self-esteem," she said, "I have low esteem for everyone else." With support from her equally catty friend Jane Lane, Daria faced challenges that never confronted a female character in an American cartoon, like the terrors of dating and the reassessment of familial ties (she grows to appreciate Quinn). Though she stayed true to form, and the show never became maudlin, it was clear that the Daria who went off to college two years later was a different person than the one in the show's pilot. *Daria* was spun off from *Beavis And Butt-Head* but otherwise unconnected with that show, having its own animation style and sensibility.

45. The Drew Carey Show (Seasons 2 and 3)

Before this sitcom collapsed, it was terrific farce and the most unpredictable prime-time comedy on the air in the late 1990s. No one did a musical number better than Drew and the gang. Why it didn't get nominated for Emmys during seasons two and three (1997–98) is beyond me, especially since the likes of *Mad About You* and *3rd Rock from the Sun* were. Carey, Kathy Kinney and Craig Ferguson may have been the most unlikely comedy triumvirate in the history of American television. All of them were well in their thirties; Kinney was a former secretary with little acting experience, while Ferguson, a Scotsman with a thick brogue, had barely landed in the U.S. when he got the part. It's funny to think that both Carey and Ferguson now host daily TV shows on CBS just down the hall from each other.

46. The Newsroom

Canadian Ken Finkleman's CBC series *The Newsroom* was ahead of its time — *The Office* before *The Office,* but with a pinpoint-accurate satire of TV news rolled in. Finkleman played George Findlay (Finkleman), a fatuous executive producer overseeing a highly dysfunctional group led by self-absorbed anchor Jim Walcott (Peter Keleghan). Thirteen episodes aired in 1996 and the CBC spent years pleading with Finkleman to make more; he finally relented in 2003. Portions of the third season (2004) were done mockumentary-style, a la *The Office.*

> **If you liked this:** His 1998 followup *More Tears* featured the same characters as *The Newsroom,* but in a darker, more devastating critique of the way the news is made; alas, it appears only Canadian TV buffs own copies of it.

47. Becker (Seasons 1–4)

You never heard much about *Becker* during its run on CBS. To be sure, it was overshadowed by a far superior show, *Everybody Loves Raymond.* Still, many weeks I laughed a whole lot harder while watching *Becker* than, say, *Friends.* Ted Danson — in the first of several great post-*Cheers* roles — played a grumpy doc at a clinic in the South Bronx, surrounded by equally jaded foils in Margaret (Hattie Winston), the overworked clinic nurse; Jake (Alex Desert), the blind newsstand owner; and Reggie (Terry Farrell), the sweet-and-sour proprietor of Becker's usual coffee shop. Stick to the seasons before Reggie leaves.

> **If you liked this:** Then you'll love the even more jaded 1980s sitcom *Night Court.*

HBO MOVIES/MINIS

This was originally the "Movies/Miniseries" section but when my list was complete, I noticed every single entry was from the same source. Not for nothing does HBO dominate the Emmys every year.

48. Iron-Jawed Angels *and* The Gathering Storm *and* The Girl in the Cafe

Here's an idea for a rainy weekend: rent these three HBO Films titles. *The Gathering Storm* stars Albert Finney as Winston Churchill in a charming and very personal portrait of the British leader between the two world wars, when his power and influence were at low ebb. *The Girl in the Cafe* is a captivating little romance set at the G8 summit in Iceland, starring Bill Nighy as a British bureaucrat and Kelly Macdonald as the smart young thing he falls for at a diner. Both were honored with Emmys for best movie and best writing. Less heralded, but arguably the best of the bunch, is *Iron-Jawed Angels,* in which director Katja von Garnier turns a semi-fictional period piece about women's suffrage into something relevant and righteous. Hilary Swank, as the suffragist Alice Paul, puts out more acting ferocity in her hunger-strike scenes than anything she did in *Million Dollar Baby.*

> **If you liked this:** Make it a week of movie nights with *Longford,* in which Jim Broadbent plays the real-life British Lord in an odd and mutually destructive relationship with a woman implicated in a string of notorious child murders (Samantha Morton); *Mrs. Harris,* with Annette Bening as the woman who was driven to the unthinkable in her relationship to the *Scarsdale Diet* doctor, Hy Tarnower (Ben Kingsley); *Bernard and Doris,* an absorbing little curiosity about the heiress Doris Duke (Susan Sarandon) and her assistant Bernard Lafferty (Ralph Fiennes); and *Path to War,* John Frankenheimer's final directorial effort in 2002, with Alec Baldwin as Robert McNamara during the Vietnam years.

49. American Splendor

I got to know Harvey Pekar, the crusty Clevelander whose daily dramas became a cult favorite comic called *American Splendor,* after his book *Our Cancer Year* was published. Pekar's specialty in his comics were stories like "Short Changed" (Harvey almost gets charged too much for grapes) and "Lost And Found" (Harvey keeps forgetting where he left his book) are carefully retold in all their real-life uneventfulness. But *Our Cancer Year* was different. He went through hell being treated for lymphoma in the early 1990s and he and his wife, Joyce Brabner, told their story with brute honesty and great insight. Harvey, you may recall, was on *Late Night With David Letterman* several times, where he and the host never failed to mix it up. Since Harvey's real life blended into his comic life, and also had a media component in the grouchy character he played on Letterman's show, the directors of this ultra-clever HBO film decided to weave three different genres together: documentary (Harvey and Joyce being inteviewed), docudrama (Paul Giamatti and Hope Davis playing Harvey and Joyce in reenactments) and cartoon (animated

dramas ripped from the comic books). It was superb moviemaking —
even hard-to-please Harvey liked it immediately — and it's essential
viewing for any fan of the Letterman that used to be.

50. Generation Kill

The producers of *The Wire* did a splendid job adapting Evan Wright's
book *Generation Kill* into a seven-part miniseries about young Marines
under fire in Iraq. For two months Wright rode with a platoon of the
elite, 364-member First Reconnaissance division as it pushed its way
through some of the most hostile resistance American forces would see
during the forty-day invasion. The drama centers on the dozen or so
men around Wright, extreme Marines whose brutal training regimen
included running for miles in the desert with a 150–pound pack, then
jumping into the water for a few miles' swim — still carrying the pack.
They are eternally bulking up and beating up on each other, even playing
psy-ops mind games on each other in a never-ending effort to remain
tough and ready for anything. With solid performances from Jake
Gyllenhaal and others (including Rudy Reyes, the Kansas City-born
Recon who plays himself in the movie), and Simon's and co-producer Ed
Burns's attention to detail (listen, for example, to the radio chatter in
the background), *Generation Kill* immerses you in the world of the men
who delivered Iraq to America, whether we were ready for it or not.

> **If you liked this:** *Over There* was a 2005 FX series from Steven
> Bochco that depicted combat at its most depersonalized and
> nihilistic. After low ratings forced FX to pull the plug, a veteran
> posted to TV Barn that the show "made me feel like I was still
> with my army buddies."

51. John Adams

Paul Giamatti (him again!) certainly makes John Adams seem like
the last guy you'd expect to be starting a political dynasty, as he does in
this much-honored HBO miniseries. *John Adams* does what television
history is supposed to do: it strips the sepia tone off the portraits of
epochal events and restores humanity to their actors. Forget about the
fancy clothes and British-sounding accents. Here is a man surrendering
uneasily to the march of time. There is nothing inexorable about
history when you're in the middle of it, and with Giamatti we instantly
realize there is nothing inevitable about the rise of Adams. However,
without the casting of Laura Linney as Abigail Adams, I suspect all of

John's brooding would've been hard to take. Yes, Linney is easy on the eyes, but she lets us know that Abigail was John's equal in every way: unfathomably strong and intelligent and passionate in that inner-directed way that people were in post-Puritan New England. The Adams dynasty began as a partnership between two people who were co-equals in every way — except under the law, as Abigail pointedly observed from time to time.

REALITY

52. Frontier House

The greatest single season of this genre, at least in this country, was this rueful meditation on American materialism brilliantly disguised as a reality show. *Frontier House* was a follow-up to *The 1900 House*, a PBS-BBC collaboration in which all the participants agreed to play roles in the highly stratified social environment of a British manor as it would've existed one century earlier. The premise of *Frontier House* was to see how three modern-day families would adapt to the harsh conditions of 1880s homestead life in Montana. And despite the very different context, what emerged was stratification again, this time in the form of class warfare between two of the participating families, the spoiled rotten Clunes and the struggling Glenns. This went far beyond the harmless feuding on *Survivor* — the Glenns' marriage actually fell apart before our eyes. In the series' concluding hour, we hear a regretful Mark Glenn telling the camera he wishes he were still in Montana with his wife and stepkids, still enjoying the simple life, forever removed from the cares of the world.

> **If you liked this:** The sequel, *Manor House*, was set in a Scottish mansion where participants — all pulled from the British middle class — were assigned different places in the caste system of Scottish society circa 1912. The lord of the estate quickly grows out of touch with the hardships of his underlings, while his ever-watchful butler brilliantly dissects the disparity for the cameras. In the 1973 classic *An American Family*, Pat and Bill Loud divorced and their son Lance came out as gay while filmmakers Alan and Susan Raymond captured it all on camera. That twelve-hour series is not available for home video, but two followups from the Raymonds are: *An American Family Revisited* (1983) and *Lance Loud! A Death in an American Family* (2003).

53. Survivor (Season 1)

One thing I've learned about reality shows is you never get a second chance to make the first season. After it airs, everyone starts figuring out how to play it; and if it's a huge hit, like *Survivor* was right out of the gate, then nothing is ever the same again. These days, my interest in *Survivor* is piqued only when a local person gets picked for it (two Kansas City area residents have won *Survivor* and another finished as runner-up). But the *Survivor* watchers I know generally agree that the show never had quite the cast of characters as it did for Season 1, when nobody even knew what a reality-competition show was. There was Rudy Boesch, the crusty ex-Navy SEAL for whom honor means something even in a game of skulduggery; Susan Hawk, a truck driver whose sense of outrage at other people's shenanigans was exceeded only by her hypocrisy; and of course, Richard Hatch, the corporate consultant widely acknowledged as the king of *Survivor's* palace politics and quite possibly network TV's first nude lead. As young neurologist Sean Kenniff said when casting his vote, "Richard is an out-and-out scoundrel. But I like him." Other types would be easier to replicate — a lot of *Survivors* had at least one contestant like Kelly Wiglesworth, a cute young river guide whose physical acumen made up for her lack of strategic savvy. But there was only one Richard, one Rudy, one Susan and one Season 1.

54. The Osbournes (Season 1)

As further proof of my first-season principle, it's worth checking out the wonderfully unpretentious debut in 2002 of *The Osbournes*, a series at heavy-metal rocker Ozzy Osbourne's bizarre household. Though the show would launch an entire subgenre of reality TV set in celebrities' homes, any chance that these shows would have a smidgen of authenticity were, alas, hopelessly compromised by the huge success of *The Osbournes* Season 1. Osbourne either had no idea what MTV as planning to do with the video of his everyday humiliations, or he just didn't care, and this not only gave *The Osbournes* a jaw-dropping realism, it humanized the man once demonized for biting the head off a bird. Ironically, it turned his less interesting family members — wife Sharon, son Jack, and daughter Kelly — into two-dimensional media cartoons, people famous for being famous. Despite the heavily bleeped audio, there's actually a sweetness to *The Osbournes*, like when the kids go out and Dad admonishes them, "Don't get drunk or stoned tonight," or when Ozzy struggles in vain to work the bleepin' remote control on his bleepity-bleep new big screen, an epic battle ending with the cry that became, more or less, the show's catchphrase: *Sharrrrron!*

> **If you liked this:** On the docuseries *Airline,* the skies are friendly — it's the airport that's treacherous. This popular cable series featured aggressive customers, overwhelmed employees and unpredictable delays at various gates of Southwest Airlines.

55. Mythbusters

Who knew that two unassuming pyrogeeks doing experiments based on rumors people spread on the Internet would prove to be endlessly entertaining? This amazingly long-lasting reality series began with what turned out to be a very typical episode: In an effort to get to the bottom of one urban legend, special-effects experts Jamie Hyneman and Adam Savage tried to blow up a service station — safely, of course! — by operating a gas pump and a cell phone at the same time. My favorite episode was No. 100, when several tricks seen on the TV series *MacGyver* were put to the test. Turns out you really *can* pick a lock using the filament inside a light bulb ... if you have an hour to spare.

56. The Joe Schmo Show (season 1)

In the 1998 movie *The Truman Show,* Jim Carrey played an ordinary person who had no idea his entire life was being broadcast on TV or that his entire sphere of reality, from his family to his job to his neighborhood, was a put-on. That was the premise for this delicious reality spoof in which a real-life Everyman named Matt Kennedy Gould was cast for what he thought was a competition show called *Lap of Luxury.* In fact, he was in a house full of improv comics in the roles of clichéd reality characters (the grizzled ex-Marine, the idiot, the schemer). Unbeknownst to Gould, the actors huddled with the show's producers every day to plan how they would steer him into ever more outrageous situations. Like Truman, young Matt seemed clueless to their shenanigans, but that didn't mean he couldn't unintentionally derail the show — and often did. A likable galoot, Gould was honest and honorable, and while that added much to the appeal of *Joe Schmo,* his refusal to indulge the producers' worst stereotypes about reality contestants caused them no end of frustration (which I found just as entertaining to watch). *Joe Schmo* was yet another instance of a reality series catching lightning in a camera, and its magic was not replicated when the producers tried a second season with a different mark.

HOLIDAY

57. A Charlie Brown Christmas

Robert Smigel once wrote a cartoon short for *Saturday Night Live* in which Jesus comes to Earth and goes crazy watching all the televangelizers taking His name in vain. In the end, though, our Lord sheds a tear of joy ... when he happens on a broadcast of *A Charlie Brown Christmas*. Smigel later said that he added this scene thinking it would get a laugh out of the audience, but everyone cheered instead. Such is the power of the first and best of all the *Peanuts* specials. And for that we have not only Charles Schulz to thank, but a man named Lee Mendelson, a TV producer who had exactly one network credit to his name in 1965 when he sold CBS on a holiday show from Schulz. Actually, it was Coca-Cola that pressed for the half-hour special — and even then, CBS executives almost overruled the sponsor when they saw the finished product. They were appalled that Mendelson had cast child actors in the roles of the characters instead of adults, then put grown-up dialogue in their mouths. The overt religiosity of Linus reading the Gospel —that was strange to network suits, too. And what, they demanded to know, was the deal with the *Peanuts* gang? Did they *like* Charlie Brown, or despise him? The soundtrack, too, was unlike anything ever heard on an animated program. Mendelson was a jazz buff and had commissioned pianist Vince Guaraldi to compose such works as *Linus and Lucy,* an energetic piano solo that would herald every *Peanuts* special to come. The melancholic "Christmastime Is Here," with its chorus of young singers straining for the high notes, served as the perfect counterpoint; both songs have since become jazz standards. CBS didn't get it, but America did. ABC bought the rights to *A Charlie Brown Christmas* a few years ago and restored it to its original running length. It now airs annually as a one-hour special.

58. Knowing Me, Knowing Yule

One of Great Britain's best-kept secrets has been broadcaster Alan Partridge, the insufferable, boorish alter ego of comedian Steve Coogan and inept host of his own dreadful daytime chat show, *Knowing Me, Knowing You* (an Abba song turned catchphrase that Alan insisted on using while greeting each guest). After six of these episodes, *Knowing Me* went out in a Yule-log blaze of glory with this hysterical Christmas special-in-a-Christmas special, a cliché-filled programme that goes off the rails early on and plummets hopelessly into the abyss. Alan is upbraided on his own show by an evangelical bellringer, scrutinized by a top BBC executive and tormented by a paralyzed golfer — a toxic brew that builds until the calamitous final minute of the broadcast. It's a high point for the Alan Partridge Project and a career low point for poor Alan, who resurfaces on a later BBC series as a late-night radio host, exiled to the nether regions of the UK.

59. A Colbert Christmas: The Greatest Gift of All!

What *can't* Stephen Colbert do? He can play a mostly-improvised satirical character day in and day out for years. He can knock the White House Correspondents Dinner on its ass. And, as this instant classic from 2008 proves, he can sing and dance his way through a holiday special. While Stephen sits in his "cabin" in the woods, he is visited by a steady stream of guests bearing musical treats — insanely great songs written by David Javerbaum (*The Daily Show)* and Adam Schlesinger (Fountains of Wayne). Toby Keith sings "War on Christmas," a pitch-perfect parody of Bill O'Reilly's message set to country music; followed by Willie Nelson, who sings the praises of that groovy herb "more powerful than frankincense or myrrh"; John Legend, paying raunchy tribute to nutmeg; Feist (who plays an angel); Jon Stewart, who shows why he is not usually called upon to sing on television; and Elvis Costello, who duets with Stephen on what is arguably the decade's best new Christmas song, "There Are Much Worse Things to Believe In."

60. Hallmark Hall of Fame: A Christmas Memory

As the hometown critic for the *Hallmark Hall of Fame,* I have reviewed more than my share of these holiday productions, most of which are forgettable. That is not true of this adaptation of Truman Capote's autobiographical short story, in which he recounts making fruitcakes and exchanging gifts with his elderly cousin Sooky when he was a boy. Eric Lloyd (from the *Santa Clause* films) plays young Truman/Buddy and Patty Duke is Sooky. While it is not without the usual Hallmarkian touches, it captures the bittersweet tone of the original story, too.

> **If you liked this:** Other worthy *Hallmark Hall of Fames* you can find mostly by resale are *My Name Is Bill W.,* featuring James Woods in an Emmy-winning role as the founder of Alcoholics Anonymous, as well as adaptations of August Wilson's *The Piano Lesson,* John Grisham's *A Painted House,* Kent Haruf's *Plainsong,* and the superb *Old Man,* based on a Faulkner short story about a convict (Arliss

Howard) who rescues a pregnant woman (Jeanne Tripplehorn) during the great 1927 flood.

DOCUMENTARY

I have devoted a full two-fifths of the "100 Best" list to documentaries because they are a wonderful antidote to same-old-same-old TV. Nick Fraser, who curates the BBC's outstanding *Storyville* and co-produced *Man on Wire* (No. 86 on the "100 Best"), once said that young people are flocking to documentaries "because there's been a reaction against the platitudes and stereotypes of television." I've stuffed as many titles in here as I can — 76 of them, if you include all the secondary picks — and frankly, the list would be even longer if not for the fact that so many outstanding documentaries are unavailable for rental or download.

Slice of Life

61. Devil's Playground

In this stellar 2002 documentary, Lucy Walker spent months filming Amish teenagers getting drunk and high on a rite tolerated by a number of Amish communities known as *rumspringa.* The idea is that they get this rebellion out of their systems and then return to the fold to live out their lives as good adult Amish. According to Walker, more than 85 percent of teens who undertake *rumspringa* eventually return to the church. This is understandable, since as *Devil's Playground* makes clear, Amish teens define the outside world as a den of instant gratification: beer, casual sex, cable TV and Nintendo. That is exactly how their elders see it, and with constant supervision over their young lives, this loathing of non-Amish society is seared on their unconscious. It's why so few Amish ever think to pursue an education beyond the eighth grade — which would be the truly radical step — instead of wasting their few months of freedom in a Lotus land of self-indulgent behavior that no sane teenager would want to continue indefinitely.

> **If you liked this:** *One Punk Under God,* a six-part Sundance Channel series, followed Jay Bakker — the heavily tattooed son of the famously downfallen televangelists Jim and Tammy— as he started a church in a bar. Prepare to have your stereotypes of orthodox Christians shaken.

62. Belfast, Maine

Fred Wiseman has been called the master of observational documentary, and this 248-minute feature from 1997 is as good as it gets. *Belfast, Maine,* Wiseman told me in an interview, came about because "I thought it was a beautiful little town and I thought there was enough material there to make a movie." Over the course of the film we see a cook making doughnuts, a painter dabbing oils on a canvas, assembly-line workers at a food-processing plant, social workers assisting the infirm, women arranging flowers, citizens speaking up at town hall, a choir rehearsing, and so on. Wiseman's gift is that he deems all these activities worthy of documenting and has the vision to make them fascinating to watch — even for four hours. Check with your public library to see if they have any Wiseman films; DVDs, which are sold exclusively from his zipporah.com website, are not cheap.

> **If you liked this:** In *Public Housing* (1999), filmed in the Ida B. Wells project in Chicago, Wiseman captures heartbreaking scenes so empathetically that after a while the walls break down and you start to imagine yourself in the shoes of the residents. *Law And Order* (1969) has some amazing footage of Kansas City cops on their rounds. And of course *Cops*, Fox's longest-running show, is an oft-underestimated gem of observational documentary.

63. First Person

Errol Morris, the celebrated director of *The Thin Blue Line, Fog of War,* and *Fast, Cheap and Out of Control,* made this television series for Bravo (Season 1) and IFC (Season 2). It featured interviews with strange and intriguing people, who talked directly into the camera — though they could see Morris at all times, thanks to a special invention of his to facilitate this called the Interrotron. These interviews were augmented with moody, slo-mo imagery. It was *First Person* that introduced me to Temple Grandin, the autistic designer of slaughterhouses known for her "stairway to heaven." Other subjects include a man who went to high school four times and also competed on *Who Wants to Be a Millionaire*; a woman who cleans up crime scenes; and the airline pilot who pulled off a miracle crash landing ... almost. Morris' ability to find the whimsy in each of these accounts without denigrating his subjects is a magic act that he never tires of performing and I never tire of watching.

64. The Wild Parrots of Telegraph Hill

It begins as a charming urban tale of a documentary filmmaker (Judy Irving) happening upon an aficionado of exotic birds (Mark Bittner) that gather in a certain leafy section of San Francisco. But then, rather improbably, it develops into a daily drama revolving around the birds — with names like Mingus, Connor, Picasso, Sophie, Olive, Pushkin, Tupelo, and each with a very distinct personality — and you can feel yourself, and Irving, being drawn into this picayune world. And then something extraordinary happens as Irving follows her passion to its logical conclusion. You'll never look at birds the same way again.

65. Greensburg

Greensburg, Kansas, a community of 1,300 in the wind-swept, high-elevation western half of the state, was wiped out by a massive tornado. So powerful was the storm that meteorologists had only seen its kind once before — and the town it destroyed was never rebuilt. Greensburg decided to rebuild, and furthermore, it resolved to do so as a sustainable community, with renewable energy and some of the most energy-efficient public buildings ever put up. To this day almost no one in Greensburg claims to be an "environmentalist," but its commitment to becoming a community again is a great story out of rural America. (And by the way, they prefer to use the word "stewardship" when talking about going green.) This Discovery-produced docu-series follows the lives of a handful of Greensburg families as they rebuild their lives and their town. If you can't visit Greensburg, which I highly recommend you do, then this is the next best thing.

66. High School Confidential

High school is a favorite topic for documentary studies: Fred Wiseman, Alan and Susan Raymond and R.J. Cutler have all made them. I would put Sharon Liese's first-time effort up there with any of these masters. Like many anxious mothers, Liese fretted about what lay ahead for her eighth-grade daughter Justine when she entered high school in suburban Kansas City. Unlike those other moms, Liese coped by interviewing Justine's classmates on camera ... for four years. The result was this absorbing tour of the what confronts today's teenage girls: drugs, pregnancy, ambition, self-loathing, issues with parents, and the desire to be free versus the yearning to belong. If you can forgive *High School Confidential* for being edited to meet the imperatives of the cable channel that co-produced this, you'll be rewarded by seeing these girls evolve and change over four tumultuous years of secondary education. (This series is available only on iTunes.)

67. **Frontline: Country Boys**

A reader confessed to me recently, "I still think of those kids sometimes. I wonder what happened to them?" Those kids, Chris Johnson and Cody Perkins, were subjects of David Sutherland's three-year documentary project that aired as a 2006 PBS miniseries. The two boys lived in eastern Kentucky, with few options for their future ... but they do have some options, and on this Sutherland hangs an six-hour miniseries. As a storyteller, Sutherland insinuates his subjects so deeply into our empathies that I suspect many viewers found themselves responding to Cody and Chris like the nurturing parents that neither boy had. Both boys have dreams, but it's clear that between the abundant social problems that ravage rural Appalachia — alcohol, drugs, teenage pregnancy, joblessness — and the region's pervasive poverty, those dreams could vanish at any moment.

> **If you liked this:** Sutherland's earlier PBS miniseries, *The Farmer's Wife*, followed a couple trying unsuccessfully to live off the land, and trying (also unsuccessfully) to cope with the consequences.

68. **My Flesh and Blood**

Susan Tom adopted eleven special-needs children and took them into her home. This is the kind of heartwarming story you've likely seen on TV before, except that this is not that story. Susan Tom is unemployed and single and she seems like she'd be kind of difficult to be around all day. She doesn't seem like the best person to be filling her house with incredibly high-maintenance children. And this, I suppose, is the wrinkle that makes Jennifer Chaiken's first feature documentary so compelling. At no point during the film are you likely to think, "Now *there's* a saint." Then again, you'd probably need to be a tough cookie yourself to deal with Joe, who is fifteen, has both cystic fibrosis *and* bipolar disorder, and is relentlessly hostile to everyone, including Susan. A couple of times, though, his guard comes crashing down, and he reveals himself as a vulnerable child who knows that life has dealt him a losing hand. Most of the other kids seem well-adjusted, with friends and activities at school that don't seem affected very much by their birth defects or gruesome skin problems. Indeed, living together has given the Tom household its own sense of normalcy, which is what you want every kid to have.

69. A League of Ordinary Gentlemen

The glory days of the Professional Bowlers Association, or PBA, are long past. But as we learn in this entertaining film, that didn't stop a group of determined investors from trying to revive the PBA and market it to America as a kind of extreme sport for squares. Televised bowling became popular because it faced limited competition, airing on Saturday afternoons on one of a handful of channels available to viewers in the 1970s. Skilled, unassuming, workmanlike players dominated the PBA back then, like the great Earl Anthony, who won more titles than anyone in PBA history, usually while wearing polyester pants. *A League of Ordinary Gentlemen* introduces us to Walter Ray Williams Jr., the league's reluctant legend, who tied (and later broke) Anthony's mark of forty-one tournament wins; and his main rival Pete Weber, the fist-pumping, crotch-chopping competitor who reacts to every strike like he just sunk a birdie putt at Pebble Beach. Weber's antics provoke grumbling from other bowlers, but the reality is that he, not Williams, is the marketable face of today's PBA.

70. Hopkins (2008)

In 2000, ABC News producer Terence Wrong made *Hopkins 24/7*, a six-part docuseries based on months of filming by his crew at Johns Hopkins Medical Center in Baltimore. In 2005 he went back to Hopkins again, but the new series, *Hopkins*, put more emphasis on the personalities involved in making life-and-death decisions and what drove them into this most demanding of medical assignments. We meet third-year medical student Sneha Dehai, who describes with great relish her first day on the job, when she got to drain an abcess from a patient's head. Later, she counsels a first-year student that "you don't stop what you're doing just because the patient screams in pain" — and then she laughs. We get to know a triage wizard, Dr. Michael Londner, who advises his students at this inner-city teaching hospital: "Any monkey can be taught to put a stitch in. But not any monkey can be taught when to put a stitch in and when not to." *Hopkins* won a Peabody Award and is must viewing for anyone thinking about a career in medicine. (This DVD is sold only at ABCNews.com.)

If you liked this: *Hopkins 24/7* (also at ABCNews.com) was more in the vein of 1990s docuseries like *Trauma: Life in the ER*.

Justice

71. The Staircase

I never believed in the clean, compartmentalized justice system
that so-called "realistic" TV crime shows had conjured up — where
prosecutors wore white hats and practiced ethical law while their
counterparts on defense performed shifty legal maneuvers on behalf
of their obviously guilty clients. Eight riveting hours of *The Staircase*
demolished this house of cards. This real-life thriller from two French
filmmakers tells the story of crime novelist Michael Peterson, who
was accused in 2001 of killing his wife by pushing her down the stairs
of their mansion. Viewing the case through the eyes of the defense,
Jean-Xavier de Lestrade and Denis Poncet show a morally upright legal
team undercutting the prosecution's case at every turn, exposing its
flimsy construction and, thus, calling into question the motives of the
DA's office. At the same time, *The Staircase's* unblinking eye shows the
defense's case slowly coming apart. Peterson is revealed as an unsavory
fellow with dark secrets in his past, each revelation more damning
than the one before. By refusing to take sides, *The Staircase* produces
a relentless tug of war between the competing stories — one pulling
for conviction, the other for exoneration — leaving many viewers both
exhausted and unsure if the jury has reached the right verdict.

> **If you liked this:** From the same directors, *Murder on a Sunday
> Morning* focuses on the tactics of detectives in a Jacksonville case
> as they are uncovered by a charming public defender.

72. Roman Polanski: Wanted and Desired

This is the well-researched polemic that put the controversial director
back in the news in 2009. Filmmaker Marina Zenovich doesn't dispute
the particulars about the liberties Polanski took with a thirteen-year-old
girl in the 1970s. However, Zenovich shows persuasively that the judge
presiding over Polanski's case was determined not to give him a fair
shake and was himself a megalomaniac with Cecil B. de Mille tendencies.
Less persuasively, she tries to explain how the accused might not be a
pervert after all, but a man whose relationship to pleasure was forever
altered by two horrifying events: the Holocaust, which claimed his
parents, and the Manson murders, which claimed his wife and unborn
baby while he was off making a movie. Still, you don't have to agree
with every point Zenovich makes to appreciate *Wanted and Desired* as a

long-overdue corrective to a story whose broad outlines were formed by sensational media accounts.

If you liked this: *Guerrilla: The Taking of Patty Hearst* uses rare first-person interviews and vintage news footage to fully immerse you in another strange criminal case of the 1970s.

73. Capturing the Friedmans

Andrew Jarecki was shooting a documentary about birthday clowns in New York City when he came upon David Friedman, aka "Silly Billy," one of Manhattan's most in-demand entertainers of kids. Friedman's father Arnold and brother Jesse had been charged years earlier with molesting a bunch of neighborhood kids in the basement of their Long Island house. The media had a field day while the Friedman family, five of them, disintegrated. David Friedman captured it on camera as it happened, and let Jarecki use the video in *Capturing the Friedmans*. The film would be riveting enough if it had stopped there. But Jarecki, channeling Errol Morris, probed further. Through interviews with alleged victims and his own research, he smashes the case against Jesse Friedman to smithereens. Since the film's release, Jarecki has insisted he doesn't really know if either Friedman was guilty, a little guilty or what. I think he's being coy — this is crusading documentary-making of a high order, and it's hard to imagine a fair-minded observer coming away from *Capturing the Friedmans* believing that the system worked.

If you liked this: Errol Morris's *The Thin Blue Line* is probably the best-known example of a crusading filmmaker getting a conviction reversed. It may also be the most influential crime documentary ever, as Morris's re-creations inspired a generation of filmmakers and cable TV producers.

74. Frontline: When Kids Get Life

Ofra Bikel, an Israeli national living in the U.S. since 1977, has been exploring the American criminal justice system for PBS *Frontline* since 1991, when her explosive *Innocence Lost* undermined the prosecution's case in the Little Rascals daycare center sexual abuse case in North Carolina. Bikel made two follow-ups to *Innocence Lost*; just before the final one aired in 1997, all seven defendants were released from prison. Unfortunately, due to rights issues, your only hope of seeing those programs is if your local library bought the videotape when it was on sale. Instead, I'm recommending this outstanding effort, viewable in full at the pbs.org/frontline site, that explores why the United States is the only country in the world that routinely sentences minors to life in prison without parole. Her reporting on Andy Medina, an accomplice to a carjacking at age fifteen, is especially galling. Based on spurious anonymous charges that he was not allowed to appeal, Medina was transferred to the Colorado Supermax facility after serving one year in a regular prison. Medina was treated worse than a terrorist — no counsel and no appeal.

If you liked this: The pbs.org/frontline site offers scores of *Frontline* episodes at full length, includ Bikel's *The Hugo Chavez Show, The Unexpected Candidate, Close to Home,* and *The O.J. Verdict.* See if your library has any of the *Innocence Lost* series or her heartbreaking *Requiem for Frank Lee Smith,* which exonerated a man convicted of murder — *after* he was put to death.

75. Dear Zachary

When filmmaker Kurt Kuenne learned his childhood friend Andrew Bagby had been slain — and that the accused killer was his girlfriend, now on the lam in Canada and pregnant with the couple's child Zachary — he decided to chronicle his friend's life so Zachary would know who his dad was. And that's just the opening to a remarkable exploration of how we can touch so many lives, for good or evil.

If you liked this: *Talhotblond,* about a cyberaffair that ended in murder, is another labyrinthine crime narrative with a stunner at the end.

History

76. The National Parks: America's Best Idea

I'm not entirely sure I agree with the sentiment in the film's title (which was first uttered by Wallace Stegner), but this is certainly Ken Burns' best documentary, in my estimation, since *The Shakers* in 1985. Look, I enjoyed *The Civil War* as much as anyone, but wars, and the sporting events Burns is also fond of chronicling, are ready-to-wear dramas you can pull off the rack. Not so our humble, picturesque national park system. The usual Burnsian story hooks are mostly missing here, like racial conflict and tragic death. Instead the filmmaker is left to create drama out of staggeringly gorgeous high-definition landscape shots, tales of bureaucratic infighting and some rather theoretical environmental history — all of which Burns, and his longtime collaborator Dayton Duncan, manage to make incredibly fascinating. The result is a remarkably powerful film that holds your attention for nearly twelve hours and reminds you that there are some things that only we the people, collectively through our government, can get done.

If you liked this: Ric Burns has made films every bit as good as his more celebrated brother, notably *The Donner Party* (1992) and the eight-part *New York: A Documentary Film* (1999–2003).

77. Shays' Rebellion *and* Freedom Summer

These are two episodes from *10 Days That Unexpectedly Changed America,* an outstanding series that aired in 2006 with one-hour films from leading directors commissioned by the History Channel. In *Shays' Rebellion,* about the 1787 farmers' uprising that led to the drafting of the Bill of Rights, director R.J. Cutler used the vibrant, abstracted images of renowned animator Bill Plympton to depict the anger of alienated Revolutionary War veterans. *Freedom Summer,* from Marco Williams, is a reinterpretation of the Mississippi murders that helped convince President Johnson of the need for civil rights legislation, with rare video and fresh reminders of what a different time that was — like the fact that while fishing the streams for the bodies of three civil-rights workers, law enforcement discovered (and failed to publicize) the corpses of nine other activists, all black, including a headless torso wearing a Congress of Racial Equality T-shirt.

If you liked this: There really isn't a bad film in the *10 Days That Unexpectedly Changed America* catalog. When you get done with those, Williams's PBS documentary *Two Towns of Jasper* is a searing look at how white and black residents of a small Texas town interpreted the same grisly hate crime.

78. Lindbergh's Great Race: Are There Any Mechanics Here?

I saw this on the History Channel in 1997, not long after *The Star* hired me, and was so impressed I figured all documentaries from this upstart cable channel would be as good. Ha! History rented this film from its director, Cameron Richardson. It is devoted to Charles Lindbergh's transatlantic flight — and only the flight, in fascinating detail. Richardson includes rare footage that chronicles every moment of the fateful weeks leading up to the crossing of the Atlantic. The result is unlike any other Lindbergh documentary. It only aired a couple of times on History, then was replaced with something cheaper that the channel produced in-house. *Lindbergh's Great Race* is only available in VHS from resale sites.

> **If you liked this:** *Miracle in Stairway B* (sold at History.com) is the account of the men of Ladder Co. 6 who somehow survived the collapse of the World Trade Center.

79. Chicago 10

Chicago 10 is about the famous Chicago 7 trial, as the media called it (as the title suggests, "Chicago 7" leaves out Bobby Seale, the Black Panther who was removed and tried separately after he mouthed off in court, as well as the group's two lawyers, who were put in jail for contempt of court). Brett Morgen's unapologetically political send-up of the kangaroo trial that followed the melee outside the 1968 Democratic National Convention uses animation, news footage, court transcripts, and rock 'n' roll to bring to life one of those moments that seemed frozen in history. At its heart, *Chicago 10* is a nostalgic film, made by a guy too young to remember 1968. Morgen romanticizes an era when people regularly channeled their outrage into outrageous acts. Say what you want about the yippies, but they had an uncanny sense of theater and of tactics and masterfully goaded the Establishment (Chicago Division) into showing the world its ugly side.

80. Black Magic

Based on Kansas City author Milton Katz's biography of hoops pioneer John McLendon, *Black Magic* (ESPN, 2008) tells the story of African-American schools that were excluded from college basketball's mainstream for decades. Left alone, they developed a style of play based on flashy offense and menacing defense that would prove hugely influential once the sport integrated. It is impossible these days to think about baseball without remembering its ugly segregationist past. Thanks to *Black Magic*, it will be hard to think about basketball as well without recalling its period of separation — but also, the happy ending that racial integration produced, as the game reached new heights of excitement, creativity and popularity.

81. The Capitol

C-SPAN, the cable network with gavel-to-gavel coverage of both houses of Congress, was granted rare access to rooms inside the U.S. Capitol building that are not offered on the public tours. Knowledgeable guides recounted the lore of such places as the Board of Education Room, where former House Speaker Sam Rayburn would take recalcitrant members to educate them on the merits of voting his way and where Vice President Harry Truman first learned of his promotion. The high-definition camera moves at a leisurely pace, showing us floor and ceiling.

> **If you liked this:** *The White House*, filmed two years later, offered the same members-only tour of 1600 Pennsylvania, some of it led by then-First Lady Laura Bush just weeks before she and her husband vacated. *The Supreme Court* did the same for the third branch of government, but was more notable for its unprecedented interviews with all eleven living justices.

Of Local Interest

82. Be Good, Smile Pretty

The only Kansas City-produced program to win a National Emmy for documentary was this 2003 film made by Tracy Tragos to chronicle her quest to uncover the identity of her father, Donald Droz, who died on a swift boat in Vietnam when she was three months old. After her mother remarried, talk of Droz was kept to a minimum in the Tragos home. But a reopened wound can hurt just as greviously thirty years later as when it was fresh, as we discover when Tracy turns on the camera and points it at her mother. That begins an odyssey for biographical detail that takes Tragos to Rich Hill, Mo., in search of family and friends of her father; to a meeting with Sen. John Kerry, who was commanding one of the other swift boats in the Mekong Delta when Droz was killed; and finally to Vietnam, to visit the place of sorrow itself. First-rate storytelling from a first-time filmmaker in collaboration with station KCPT.

If you liked this: *Regret to Inform* (1998), chronicles a widow's odyssey to Vietnam two decades after her husband died there.

83. Bad Blood

This is the best television account I've seen of the tug of war between pro-slavery and anti-slavery forces in Kansas in the 1850s. It is now a widely accepted fact among historians that the casualties of "Bleeding Kansas" were the first of the American Civil War. KCPT producers Angee Simmons and Pam Reichart present an account of that time that is both more balanced and more complicated than the popular accounts handed down over the years. More voice is given to the ordinary people, the vast majority of settlers who came neither for slavery nor abolition but for cheap land and opportunity. And we see not just battle re-enactments in *Bad Blood* but political re-enactments, as actors in period clothing sit in the interview seat and, like subjects in an 1858 documentary, complain of the "blackest of all evils, human slavery," or the "scum and filth of the Northern cities" coming to pollute Kansas, or (in the case of one settler's wife) protesting that they "were just comin' to Kansas for the land, not the cause."

84. Rare Visions and Roadside Revelations

This thoroughly entertaining half-hour local production is not just for viewers in Kansas City, but anyone who appreciates the wonderfully loopy world of untrained folk artists. Over the course of more than a decade, Kansas City Public Television's Don Mayberger, Mike Murphy and Randy Mason toured the entire country in a minivan, meeting ordinary folks who just one day picked up a paintbrush, or a blowtorch, and began expressing themselves using whatever materials they found close at hand. The result was artwork that was colorful, whimsical and, it turns out, sustainable. If you're into folk art (which the KCPT guys clearly are), you may even be familiar with some of the characters featured on the program. But it's the show's writing and playful transitions — always respectful, never full of itself — that make *Rare Visions* sparkle.

If you liked this: *Off the Charts: The Song-Poem Story* (2003), takes you deep within the subculture of song-poems, a little-known industry in which amateur bards pay to have their poems set to music. If you're curious to hear what "Non-Violent Tae Kwon Do Troopers" sounds like set to music, don't miss this movie.

Arts and Sciences

85. Planet Earth

This BBC nature spectacular, shot entirely in HD, is sort of an
unending can-you-top-this compendium of spectacular nature shots
that were not possible until recent technological innovations, like a long-
lens helicopter camera that can capture a hunt from high up enough not
to alarm the animals. Each hour explores a realm of nature: mountains
in hour two, oceans in hour three, and so on. Thanks to HD cameras
that can capture video in near darkness, we see such weird sea critters
as the vampire squid that can evade predators by shining bright lights in
their eyes. Of course, some of the most impressive footage came about
through good old human stubbornness, like the cameraman who staked
out a polar bear mama and her two cubs for five weeks in the 30-below
tundra of Norway. Be sure you seek out the British version of *Planet
Earth* featuring the original narrator, Sir David Attenborough.

> **If you liked this:** It's easy to be blasé about nature photography in
> an era of hand-held HD camcorders, but Sir David's breakthrough
> nature series from the 1980s, *Life on Earth,* still takes my breath
> away.

86. Man on Wire

The winner of the 2008 Academy Award for documentary film (and a
co-production of Discovery and BBC) relives the breathtaking tightrope
walk of Philippe Petit between the two World Trade Center towers in
August 1974. Petit's forty-five-minute stunt was years in the making, as
we learn in this thrilling reconstruction that uses old home videos and
interviews with Petit and many of his co-conspirators. The destruction
of the buildings on 9/11 revived interest in Petit's derring-do and, as it
turns out, there was a dramatic story behind his feat. Part engineering
feat, part cloak-and-dagger, *Man on Wire* shows Petit's walk as a reckless
gambit and a thing of unprecedented beauty. Somehow Team Petit was
able to string 450 pounds of heavy-gauge wire across the Twin Towers in
the dead of night and secure it with guy wires (engineers later marveled
at their handiwork). Thanks to someone's decision to film much of
the planning of "le Coup" in 1974, *Man on Wire* is able to reconstruct
that narrative with a minimal number of re-enacted scenes, and we see
the many sides of Petit: visionary, imp, shrewd operator, free spirit,
manipulator, daredevil — and artist.

87. The Kid Stays in the Picture

This dreamy profile of Robert Evans, the man who rescued Paramount Pictures in the 1960s and made it a legendary studio, won a technical Oscar for its use of still photographs that makes them appear to be in motion. Evans became an actor by the luckiest of breaks, then aspired to become a Hollywood titan. Under his control, Paramount ran off a string of hits that may be unparalleled in the movie business, from *Rosemary's Baby* and *True Grit* to *The Godfather*. Along the way Evans bought a palace in Beverly Hills, a Shangri-La that is examined in loving detail throughout the film. He wooed Ali MacGraw away from another man and — in an even more impressive bit of persuasion — starred in a film short he produced in order to convince Paramount's owner, Gulf & Western, not to shutter the studio. At other times life was a nightmare: MacGraw left him for Steve McQueen, and Evans was busted for cocaine possession. Through it all Evans survived to create a dazzling embroidery of his life. He narrates *The Kid Stays in the Picture* in his coarse, rumbly voice; it adds to the film's distinctive character, but you might want to turn the captions on.

88. Mr. Warmth: The Don Rickles Project

At 81, the foremost insult comic of his or any other generation was still packing them in at casinos across the country. He looks like a lizard in a tuxedo — hairless, with large folds of neck skin, he prowls the stage slowly, his eyes darting around constantly, looking for prey. Rickles is an equal-opportunity kidder from an equal-opportunity era. When he says he means no harm, you believe him. You can ask his victims. Among the numerous supporters seen in the film are Sidney Poitier and Bob Newhart, two of the nicest people in show business. But here's the amazing thing about the documentary. *Mr. Warmth*, directed by John Landis, isn't a nostalgic walk through old videotape, where now-dead entertainers laugh entirely too hard at Rickles' hockey-puck routine. I know I've laughed harder at a film than I did watching *Mr. Warmth*, but I can't remember when.

If you liked this: There are numerous Johnny Carson anthologies out there, but the only one worth your time is *The Best of Carson, Volume 1*. Of course, it includes the classic broken-cigarette-box incident with Rickles.

Political/Current

89. The Awful Truth *and* TV Nation

Between *Roger and Me* and *Bowling for Columbine*, Michael Moore
— the greatest left-wing provocateur of our generation — spent a
decade largely working in television. Of these efforts only *The Awful
Truth*, which aired two seasons on Bravo, has been anthologized on
DVD. That's a shame, because *TV Nation*, which spent a summer on
NBC and then a summer on Fox (and can be found on VHS), was every
bit as good. There is an undercurrent of rage running through both
shows, an anger that is directed not only at political outrages but the
way in which media have been used to prop up exploitative and corrupt
activities. What network reporter would have the nerve to ask a bunch
of politicians grandstanding in front of a Ten Commandments plaque to
name the Eighth Commandment? *The Awful Truth* features such classic
bits as Moore entering a ficus tree in a congressional primary against
an incumbent who, until then, was running unopposed; and holding
a funeral in front of an HMO's headquarters for a patient who hadn't
yet died. The patient had been refused life-saving treatment, which the
HMO finally approved after the cameras showed up.

90. King Corn

I keep recommending this movie and lending out my copy to friends.
It's about two buddies who rent an acre in Iowa and use it to grow
America's most abundant and troubling food stuff. Corn is in everything
from our gas tank to our hamburger to our soda pop and the question
you come away from this movie asking is, why? Though derivative in
nature — author Michael Pollan first exposed the monolithic nature
of American industrial agriculture in his book *The Omnivore's Dilemma*
and has subsequently appeared in another documentary, *Food Inc.* —
there's something endearing about a couple of dudes just following their
curiosity. Among other things, this leads filmmakers Ian Cheney and
Curt Ellis (and the off-camera director, Aaron Wolf) to brew their own
high fructose corn syrup and track down Earl Butz, the architect of our
current food policy, in an old folks' home. While *Food Inc.* is preachy,
King Corn's nonjudgmental, gee-whiz approach has broader appeal.

91. Frontline: Poisoned Waters

"If we don't start to care about the bodies of water we know and love, we're not going to have them," warns Pulitzer Prize-winning reporter Hedrick Smith. It's hard to pick just a few gems from *Frontline's* embarrassment of riches, but everyone needs to see Smith's 2009 report about the steep decline of our country's biggest bodies of water. Drawing on interviews with scientists, fishermen, bureaucrats, chicken farmers, whale watchers and other people who rely on and care deeply about America's waterways, Smith tells a fascinating and disturbing story. One of television's best storytellers on serious subjects, Smith knows how to make the water crisis riveting without bogging down viewers in technical mumbo-jumbo or leaving his audience with the burden of knowing there is so much wrong and so little they can do about it.

If you liked this: Smith's *Spying on the Homefront* (2007) explores the troubling implications of being able to monitor everyone, everywhere.

92. Blue Vinyl

Judith Helfand and Dan Gold's wonderful 2002 film opens with a seemingly innocuous event. One day in 1996 Helfand's parents decide to have new siding put on their modest Long Island, N.Y., home. They choose vinyl, the "versatile plastic" used in everything from medical supplies and bathroom pipes to shrink wrap. Helfand, a sweeter Jewish version of Michael Moore, marches out to learn the truth about PVC, with Gold, her sharp-eyed cinematographer, right behind. Though much of the film has a whimsical air to it — their attempt to interview an official of the Vinyl Institute on-camera devolves into "we're filming you filming us filming you" high jinks — *Blue Vinyl* presents the dilemma of polyvinyl chloride (or PVC) in all its troubling complexity. Yes, vinyl is a cheap, durable building material that is toxic as hell at *both* ends of its life cycle, its creation and destruction. On the other hand, it has allowed thousands of families to live in homes they can afford. Helfand acknowledges this by filming a Habitat for Humanity house-raising, funded by the Vinyl Institute. Yet the ultimate message of *Blue Vinyl* is clear: Nothing is cheap. Somewhere, somehow, somebody else is paying for our low-cost, high-consumption way of life.

93. Trouble the Water

The cream of the Katrina documentary crop. Kimberly Roberts was in her attic with her family, riding out the fury unleashed by Hurricane Katrina in New Orleans' Lower Ninth, when she picked up the used camcorder she'd recently bought on a street corner and took some of the most harrowing storm video you'll ever see. *Trouble the Water* follows the couple on their odyssey out of New Orleans and eventually, like most of those who fled, their exodus back. For all the roadblocks, insults and setbacks they encounter, their unbreakable spirit leaves you feeling remarkably upbeat about the human condition. Rare among documentaries, *Trouble the Water* actually had me shedding more tears the *second* time I watched, because by then Kim and Scott felt like friends. They seemed like people who wanted to make a difference in the world — and this only heightened my sadness and anger when I saw how they were treated by their government.

> **If you liked this:** Spike Lee's Katrina documentary, *When the Levees Broke,* is worth it just for the irresistible harangues of one pissed-off survivor named Phyllis Montana LaBlanc. In a similar vein to *Trouble the Water* is *Hoop Dreams,* considered by many to be one of the greatest achievements in documentary film. I never formally reviewed the film, which was widely in movie theaters before it was screened on PBS, so it's not eligible for my "100 Best." But *Hoop Dreams* is essential viewing. Over several years it tracks the odysseys of Chicago inner-city basketball prodigies Arthur Agee and William Gates as they make decisions about school, career, and life with conspicuously little adult guidance. It is a rare film, both heartbreaking and uplifting.

94. Section 60: Arlington National Cemetery

This beautiful little short is more of a meditation than a documentary. It was filmed entirely at the burial area in Arlington National Cemetery reserved for the fallen in Operation Iraqi Freedom and the Afghanistan conflict. I was particularly moved by the parents of Humayan Khan, a Muslim-American killed in Iraq in 2004. Mr. Khan explains that the family moved to America twenty-five years earlier "because of the opportunity for freedom." And then Mrs. Khan, her grief still raw, expresses her freedom of religion through her tears: "God bless us all. Everyone here."

If you liked this: *Off to War* follows reservists from the Arkansas National Guard, and the families they leave back home, during a tumultuous tour of duty in Iraq. *Kansas to Kandahar* (available at ShopPBS.org) followed two hundred Army reservists from Kansas who shipped off to Afghanistan in the fall of 2005 and returned without a single loss —remarkable considering their job was to make precision helicopter landings in the jagged mountainous regions, usually under heavy fire from Taliban and Al-Qaeda.

95. Bus 174

Filmmaker Jose Padilha explores the troubling subtext behind the hijacking of a city bus in downtown Rio de Janeiro in 2000 by a homeless man. Padilha was among tens of millions of Brazilians riveted to their TV sets as the incident was broadcast live — and from just a few feet away, as cameras were allowed to hover around the bus during the hours-long standoff and carry the hostage-taker's wild behavior. In the aftermath of the Bus 174 incident, Padilha noticed something about the press coverage: Hardly anyone was talking about the young man, identified as Sandro do Nascimento. He soon learned that as a street kid, Sandro had been one of those targeted by off-duty policemen in a notorious 1993 massacre, and later was thrown into one of the city's infamous prisons. Padilha takes a camera and a survivor into some of these holding pens, which would not be suitable for keeping livestock. His provocative conclusion: All Brazilians were, to a degree, responsible for causing Sandro's behavior in the bus.

If you liked this: *Frontline: The Hugo Chavez Show* (viewable at pbs.org/frontline) is an odd and disturbing film about the Venezuelan president, who conducts his weekly cabinet meetings on live TV. *Terror in Mumbai* uses intercepted cell phone calls and surveillance video to put you right in the middle of the 2008 terrorist attacks that paralyzed India's largest city.

96. Enron: The Smartest Guys in the Room

An almost pitch-perfect distillation of millions of words of journalism written about the collapse of one of the greatest corporate fictions in history. Enron was a company built on bluster and hype and investors on Wall Street who, seemingly, would believe anything. Director Alex Gibney collared key insiders and outsiders who spilled the beans and explained, in ways almost any sensible adult will understand, how a $65 billion company could just keel over and die in less than a month's time. There's so much outrage to this story — and it's conveyed here with a kinetic intensity rarely seen in this genre — but at its core, the story is a tragedy, with thousands betrayed, bankrupted and kicked to the curb. Gibney confers all this with the mesmerizing quality of a dream, a weirdly beautiful high-definition nightmare of greed and self-deception.

If you liked this: Another great study in media manipulation is *Frontline: The Merchants of Cool* (viewable at pbs.org/frontline), a still-relevant 2002 program that went behind the scenes at MTV to show how it uses market research to figure out what teens think is cool — and then sell them more of it through cheap programming.

97. Control Room

Control Room is a stereotype-busting film about the al-Jazeera media empire that built its brand on presenting the most unvarnished view of Muslim resentments of the West. By focusing on a U.S. military spokesman named Josh Rushing and his friendship with al-Jazeera reporter Hassan Ibrahim, *Control Room* offers a look at one of the world's most vilified news organizations in a way that will appeal to many Westerners' sense of fairness. It's an impression further reinforced when you learn that Rushing later went to work for al-Jazeera's English-language channel.

If you liked this: Two other important films to come out of the 9/11 attacks were *Beneath the Veil*, Saira Shah's eye-opening exposé on the treatment of women in Afghan society; and *Frontline: The Man Who Knew* (viewable at pbs.org/frontline), about colorful counter-terrorism agent John O'Neill, whose dire warnings about Al-Qaeda were understood only after he died in the World Trade Center attacks.

98. The New Americans

Immigration has long been a popular focus of American documentary makers. *The New Americans* is a sprawling work covering several families, countries of origin, and years. Produced by two-thirds of the brain trust behind the classic *Hoop Dreams*, this seven-hour miniseries follows two families of Nigerian political refugees, two Dominican baseball players, a Palestinian who marries an Arab-American and a Mexican family that

moves to the meatpacking capital of Kansas. It makes the argument of
many films in this subgenre: that America can often be as hostile a place
to its new arrivals as the place they left behind.

> **If you liked this:** *Harvest of Shame* (from the *Edward R. Murrow
> Collection)* was the classic 1965 CBS report on the plight of
> migrant farm workers. *The Betrayal (Nerakhoon)*, filmed over the
> course of seventeen years, is a haunting chronicle of a family's
> attempts to adapt to America after fleeing Laos. *Lost Boys of Sudan*
> shows teenage refugees from a war-wracked nation slowly getting
> used to the strange folkways of a white, Christian land. *Balseros* is
> much like *New Americans* but focuses on Cuban refugees. *Daughter
> From Danang* is an emotional account of the reunion between
> a Vietnamese woman and the daughter she sent to the United
> States in the 1970s as part of Operation Babylift.

99. 30 Days (Season 1 and 3)

Super Size Me guinea pig Morgan Spurlock narrated and/or took part
in a dozen social experiments. By examining race, class and sexuality
through monthlong filmed immersions, Spurlock gave us a slice of
life that most of us wouldn't touch — he even talked his girlfriend
into moving with him, in the dead of winter, to Columbus, Ohio, to
experience the minimum-wage lifestyle. But *30 Days* transcended
voyeuristic entertainment and became the empathy machine that
all good documentaries should be. The show's third season is worth
watching (Spurlock goes to work in the coal mines), but I prefer season
one which featured one episode with a mom trying to binge-drink
like her daughter and another where a rather paranoid Bible-believing
Christian tried living with Muslims.

100. This Film Is Not Yet Rated

This feature from the Independent Film Channel was not only
entertaining and damning, it struck a blow for cash-strapped
documentary makers everywhere. Director Kirby Dick's critique of the
Motion Picture Association of America's ratings system used dozens of
clips from Hollywood films to demonstrate the capriciousness of the
MPAA. He used the clips without permission, citing the newly-expanded
interpretation of the fair use provision, which allows copyrighted
works to be freely used for the purposes of commentary. Legal scholars
backed him up, and *This Film Is Not Yet Rated* aired without incident,

a breakthrough that should embolden cultural critics in an era when anyone can post video to the Web. Besides pointing out the hypocrisy of MPAA ratings, the film exposed the names of the formerly secret membership of MPAA's ratings board. Dick controversially hired a private investigator to smoke them out. Be sure you watch the DVD extras, featuring Dick's telephone run-ins with the MPAA.

GONE BUT NOT FORGOTTEN

Many terrific TV shows and documentaries are not on this list because — so far as I can tell — they cannot be rented or bought or legally downloaded. If you or someone you know has some pull at the studios that produced these great shows, or if you are looking for some grant money to spend on a worthy documentary cause, then please do your part to help get all these programs onto the Web, Amazon, or Netflix, where they belong. Thank you.

An American Family
American High
Amish in the City
Any Day Now
China Beach
Ed
Frank's Place
Frontline: Requiem for Frank Lee Smith
Gulag
I'll Fly Away
Judging Amy
Keeping Time: Milt Hinton
The Knights of Prosperity
L.A. Law
Life After War
Make 'Em Dance: The Hackberry Ramblers
Nothing Sacred
100 Centre Street
Playhouse 90
Queer Eye for the Straight Guy
Recycle
Strip Search

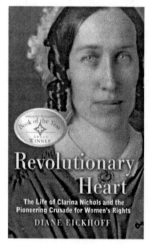

LaVergne, TN USA
11 August 2010
192940LV00004B/3/P